RICHARD SENNETT

Building and Dwelling

Ethics for the City

PENGUIN BOOKS

PENGUIN BOOKS

UK | USA | Canada | Ireland | Australia
India | New Zealand | South Africa

Penguin Books is part of the Penguin Random House group of companies
whose addresses can be found at global.penguinrandomhouse.com.

First published by Allen Lane 2018
Published in Penguin Books 2019
002

Copyright © Richard Sennett, 2018

The moral right of the author has been asserted

Set in 9.35/12.4 pt Sabon LT Std
Typeset by Jouve (UK), Milton Keynes
Printed and bound in Great Britain by Clays Ltd, Elcograf S.p.A.

A CIP catalogue record for this book is available from the British Library

ISBN: 978-0-141-02211-6

For Ricky and Mika Burdett

Contents

List of Illustrations

Every effort has been made to contact copyright holders. The publishers will be pleased to make good in future editions any errors or omissions brought to their attention.

Acknowledgements

A few years ago the Grim Reaper paid me an exploratory visit in the guise of a stroke (tobacco). Those who cared for me during this time were the physician Rom Naidoo and the physiotherapist Jayne Wedge; my stepson Hilary Koob-Sassen served as exercise drill-sergeant; my walkers were Dominic Parczuk, Ian Bostridge and Lucasta Miller. At a particularly depressing moment, Wolf Lepenies explained why medical stats should not rule one's outlook on life.

As people do after a serious illness, I reckoned what has really mattered to me. In looking back, I've taken particular satisfaction in the urban studies programme Richard Burdett and I created at the London School of Economics fifteen years ago. The project Ricky and I launched seeks to connect how cities are built to how people live in them – which is the theme of this book, and the reason it is dedicated to Ricky and to his wife Mika.

John Lindsay, for whom I first worked as a young man, had a vision of New York as open to all; he held steadfast to this belief in the midst of racial violence and ethnic tensions, in a city sharply divided economically and decaying physically. The fact that he could not solve these problems does not make his vision wrong; in *Building and Dwelling*, I try to understand how it could be carried forward – how cities in our time might open up.

For helpful discussions in creating this book I'd like to thank the late Janet Abu-Lughod, the late Stuart Hall, Ash Amin, Kwame Anthony Appiah, Homi Bhabha, John Bingham-Hall, Craig Calhoun, Daniel Cohen, Diane Davis, Mitchell Duneier, Richard Foley, David Harvey, Eric Klinenberg, John Jungclaussen, Adam Kaasa, Monika Krause, Rahul Mehrotra, Carles Muro, Henk Ovink, Anne-Marie

Slaughter, and most of all my partner of thirty years, Saskia Sassen: critic, *bonne vivante*, playmate. It's thanks to her that I first began to understand the ethical dimensions of city life. Günter Gassner helped me explore the built environment, as did my students at Harvard University's Graduate School of Design and MIT's Department of Urban Studies and Planning.

Finally, I want to thank those who have worked on producing the book, especially two editors, Alexander Star and Stuart Proffitt, who have been the most careful of readers; one agent, the ever-vigilant and ever-caring Cullen Stanley; and one former assistant, now my colleague and friend, Dominick Bagnato, who has kept me afloat throughout.

I

Introduction: Crooked,
Open, Modest

I. CROOKED

In early Christianity 'city' stood for two cities: the City of God and
the City of Man. St Augustine used the city as a metaphor for God's
design of faith, but the ancient reader of St Augustine who wandered
the alleys, markets and forums of Rome would get no hint of how
God worked as a city planner. Even as this Christian metaphor
waned, the idea persisted that 'city' meant two different things – one
a physical place, the other a mentality compiled from perceptions,
behaviours and beliefs. The French language first came to sort out
this distinction by using two different words: *ville* and *cité*.[1]

Initially these named big and small: *ville* referred to the overall city,
whereas *cité* designated a particular place. Some time in the sixteenth
century the *cité* came to mean the character of life in a neighbourhood, the feelings people harboured about neighbours and strangers
and attachments to place. This old distinction has faded today, at
least in France; a *cité* now most often refers to those grim locales
which warehouse the poor on the outskirts of towns. The older usage
is worth reviving, though, because it describes a basic distinction: the
built environment is one thing, how people dwell in it another. Today,
in New York, traffic jams at the poorly designed tunnels belong to the
ville, whereas the rat race driving many New Yorkers to the tunnels
at dawn belongs to the *cité*.

As well as describing the *cité*'s anthropology, '*cité*' can refer a
kind of consciousness. Proust assembles from his characters' perceptions of the various shops, flats, streets and palaces in which they
dwell a picture of Paris as a whole, creating a sort of collective

place-consciousness. This contrasts to Balzac, who tells you what's really up in town no matter what his characters think. *Cité*-consciousness can also represent how people want to live collectively, as during Paris's nineteenth-century unheavals when those in revolt couched their aspirations more generally than specific demands about lower taxes or bread prices; they argued for a new *cité*, that is, a new political mentality. Indeed, the *cité* stands next to *citoyenneté*, the French word for citizenship.

The English phrase 'built environment' doesn't do justice to the idea of the *ville*, if that word 'environment' is taken to be the snail's shell covering the living urban body within. Buildings are seldom isolated facts. Urban forms have their own inner dynamics, as in how buildings relate to one another, or to open spaces, or to infrastructure below ground, or to nature. In the making of the Eiffel Tower, for instance, planning documents in the 1880s canvassed places in eastern Paris far away from the Eiffel Tower before it was built, seeking to assess its urban-wide effects. Moreover, the financing of the Eiffel Tower could not alone explain its design; the same, huge amount of money could have been spent on another kind of monument, such as a triumphal church, which was the monument Eiffel's conservative colleagues preferred. Once chosen, though, the tower's form involved choices rather than being dictated by circumstances: straight rather than curving struts would have been much cheaper, but efficiency alone did not rule Eiffel's vision. Which is true more largely: the built environment is more than a reflection of economics or politics; beyond these conditions, the forms of the built environment are the product of the maker's will.

It might seem that *cité* and *ville* should fit together seamlessly: how people want to live should be expressed in how cities are built. But just here lies a great problem. Experience in a city, as in the bedroom or on the battlefield, is rarely seamless, it is much more often full of contradictions and jagged edges.

In an essay on cosmopolitan life, Immanuel Kant observed in 1784 that 'out of the crooked timber of humanity, no straight thing was ever made'. A city is crooked because it is diverse, full of migrants speaking dozens of languages; because its inequalities are so glaring, svelte ladies lunching a few blocks away from exhausted transport cleaners; because of its stresses, as in concentrating too many young graduates chasing too few jobs ... Can the physical *ville* straighten out such difficulties? Will plans to pedestrianize a street do anything about the housing crisis? Will the use of sodium borosilicate glass in buildings make people more tolerant of immigrants? The city seems crooked in that asymmetry afflicts its *cité* and its *ville*.[2]

It is sometimes right that there be a mis-fit between the builder's own values and those of the public. This mis-fit ought to occur if people reject living with neighbours unlike themselves. Many Europeans find Muslim migrants indigestible; big chunks of Anglo-America feel Mexican migrants should be deported; and from Jerusalem to Mumbai those who pray to different gods find it difficult to live in the same place. One result of this social recoil appears in the gated communities which are today, throughout the world, the most popular form of new residential development. The urbanist should go against the will of the people, refusing to build gated communities; prejudice should be denied in the name of justice. But there's no straightforward way to translate justice into physical form – as I discovered early on in a planning job.

At the beginning of the 1960s, a new school was proposed for a working-class area in Boston. Would it be racially integrated, or segregated as were most working-class parts of the city in those days? If integrated, we planners would have to provide large parking and holding spaces for buses to bring black children to and from school. The white parents resisted integration covertly by claiming the community needed more green space, not bus parking lots. Planners ought to serve the community rather than impose an alien set of values. What right did people like me – Harvard-educated, armed with sheaths of statistics on segregation and impeccably executed blueprints – have to tell the bus drivers, cleaners and industrial workers of South Boston how to live? I am glad to say my bosses stood their ground; they did not succumb to class guilt. Still, the jaggedness between lived and built cannot be resolved simply by the planner displaying ethical uprightness. In our case, this only made things worse, our virtue-signalling breeding more anger among the white public.

This is the ethical problem in cities today. Should urbanism represent society as it is, or seek to change it? If Kant is right, *ville* and *cité* can never fit together seamlessly. What, then, is to be done?

II. OPEN

I thought I had found one answer to this when I taught planning at MIT twenty years ago. The Media Lab was near my office, and for my generation it shone as an epicentre of innovation in new digital technology, translating innovative ideas into practical results. Founded by Nicholas Negroponte in 1985, these projects included a super-cheap computer for poor kids, medical prostheses like the robotic knee, and 'digital town centres' to plug people living in remote areas into the doings of cities. The emphasis on built objects made the Media Lab a craftsman's paradise; this glorious operation entailed much furious debate, the diving down into technological rabbit-holes, and a vast amount of waste.

Its rumpled researchers – who never seemed to sleep – explained the difference between a 'Microsoft-level' project and an 'MIT-level' project as follows: the Microsoft project packages existing knowledge, while MIT unpackages it. A favourite pastime in the Lab was tricking Microsoft programs into failing or aborting. Whether fair or not, Media Lab researchers, being on the whole an adventurous lot, tended to snoot normal science as mundane and instead look for the cutting edge; according to their lights, Microsoft thinks 'closed', the Media Lab thinks 'open' – 'open' enables innovation.

In a general way, researchers work within a well-worn orbit when performing an experiment to prove or disprove a hypothesis; the original proposition governs procedures and observations; the denouement of the experiment lies in judging whether the hypothesis is correct or incorrect. In another way of experimenting, researchers will take seriously unforeseen turns of data, which may cause them to jump tracks and think 'outside the box'. They will ponder contradictions and ambiguities, stewing in these difficulties for a while rather than immediately trying to solve them or sweep them aside. The first kind of experiment is closed in the sense it answers a fixed question: yes or no. Researchers in the second kind of experiment work more openly in that they ask questions which can't be answered in that way.

In a more sober spirit than the Media Lab, the Harvard physician Jerome Groopman has explained the open procedure in clinical trials of new drugs. In an 'adaptive clinical trial', the terms of the trial change as the experiment unfolds. This is not following one's nose wherever it leads. Since experimental drugs can be dangerous, the researcher has to exercise great caution in the course of charting unknown realms – but the experimenter in an adaptive clinical trial is more interested in making sense of things that are surprising or intriguing than in confirming what might have been predictable in advance.[3]

Of course adventure in a lab can't be divorced from the plodding and plugging grind of sifting in a yes-or-no fashion. Francis Crick, who uncovered the double helix structure of DNA, remarked that its discovery came from studying small 'anomalies' in routine lab work. The researcher needs orientation, and fixed procedure provides it; only then can the self-critical work begin of exploring the odd result, the curious outcome. The challenge is to engage with these possibilities.[4]

'Open' implies a system for fitting together the odd, the curious, the possible. The mathematician Melanie Mitchell has pithily summarized an open system as one 'in which large networks of components with no central control and simple rules of operation give rise to complex collective behavior, sophisticated information processing, and adaptation via learning or evolution'. This means that complexity comes into being in the course of evolution; it emerges through the feedback and sifting of information rather than existing as in a *telos* preordained and programmed at the outset.[5]

So, too, the open-systems idea of how these parts interact. 'Linear equations', the mathematician Steven Strogatz remarks, 'can be broken into pieces. Each piece can be analyzed separately and solved, and finally all the separate answers can be recombined . . . In a linear system, the whole is exactly equal to the sum of the parts.' Whereas the parts in a non-linear, open system can't be broken up this way; 'the whole system has to be examined all at once, as a coherent entity.' His idea is easy to grasp if you think of chemicals interacting to form a compound: it becomes a new substance of its own.[6]

Such views had a solid grounding at MIT. The Media Lab was built on the intellectual foundations of the Electronic Systems Laboratory, which Norbert Wiener, arguably the greatest systems analyst of the twentieth century, founded at MIT in the 1940s. Wiener stood on the cusp of an era in which large amounts of information could be digested by machines; he explored different ways to organize the digestive process. He was particularly intrigued by electronic feedback which is complex, ambiguous or contradictory in character rather than straightforward. If what he called a 'learning machine' could speak, it would say 'I didn't expect that X, Y or Z to happen. Now I'll need to figure out why, and how to re-tool.' This epitomizes an open-ended environment, though one inhabited by semi-conductors rather than people.[7]

How would the open-laboratory ethos relate to a city? The architect Robert Venturi once declared 'I like complexity and contradiction in architecture . . . I am for richness of meaning rather than clarity of meaning.' Though attacking much modern architecture for its stripped-down, functionalist buildings, his words cut deeper. His is the Media Lab transposed to a city – the city is a complex place, which means it is full of contradictions and ambiguities. Complexity enriches experience; clarity thins it.[8]

My friend William Mitchell, an architect who eventually took over the Media Lab, made the bridge between system and city. A *bon vivant* who frequented the nightlife hotspots of Cambridge, Massachusetts (such as they were in those days), he declared 'the keyboard is my café'. His *City of Bits* was the first book about smart cities; published in 1996, and so before the era of hand-helds, Web 2.0 interactive programs, and nano-technology, Mitchell's book wanted to welcome whatever the future might hold. He imagined that the smart city would be a complex place: information-sharing which would give citizens ever more choices and so ever greater freedom; the physical buildings, streets, schools and offices of the *ville* would be made of components which could continually be changed and so could evolve, just as does the flow of information. The smart city would become ever more complex in form, its *cité* ever richer in meanings.[9]

In one way this technological fantasy was nothing new. Aristotle wrote in the *Politics* that 'a city is composed of different kinds of men; similar people cannot bring a city into existence'. People are stronger together than apart; thus in wartime, Athens sheltered a diverse range of tribes who fled the countryside; it also took in exiles who then remained in the city. Though their status was ever un-resolved and ambiguous, these refugees brought new ways of thinking and new crafts to the city. Aristotle drew attention to the fact that trade is more vigorous in a dense city than in a thinly populated village, and in this he was hardly alone; almost all ancient writers on the city noted that diverse, complex economies were more profitable than economic monocultures. Aristotle was also thinking about the virtues of complexity in politics; in a diverse milieu, men (in Aristotle's time, only men) are obliged to understand different points of view in order to govern the city. In all, Aristotle calls the drawing of different people together a *synoikismos*, a putting together like 'synthesis' and 'synergy' – the city is, like Strogatz's equations, a whole greater than the sum of its parts.[10]

'Open' figures as a key word in modern politics. In 1945, the Austrian refugee philosopher Karl Popper published *The Open Society and its Enemies*. He asked a philosopher's question about how Europe had fallen into totalitarianism: was there something in Western thought which had invited people to scupper rational and fact-based debate among different groups in favour of seductive myths of 'we are one' and 'us against them' spun by dictators? The book's theme doesn't date, though *The Open Society and its Enemies* is in a way misnamed, because Popper analysed a long line of illiberal political thought rather than happenings in everyday society. Still, the book had an enormous impact on people engaged in those activities – particularly on his colleagues at the London School of Economics who were at the time devising the British welfare state, hoping to devise a plan which would keep its bureaucracy loose and open, rather than rigid and closed. Popper's student, the financier George Soros, later devoted vast sums of money to building up institutions like universities in civil society which reflected Popper's liberal values.

It might seem that the liberal values of an open society suit any city that contains many different sorts of peoples; mutual toleration will allow them to live together. Again, an open society should be more equal and more democratic than most today, with wealth and power spread through the entire social body rather than hoarded at the top. But there's nothing especially urban about this aspiration; farmers and people in small towns deserve the same justice. In thinking about urban ethics, we want to know what makes ethics urban.

For instance, freedom has a particular value in the city. The German adage *Stadtluft macht frei* ('city air makes you free') derives from the late Middle Ages; this saying promised that citizens could be freed from a fixed, inherited position in the economic and social pecking order, freed from serving just one master. It didn't mean citizens were isolated individuals; there might be obligations to a guild, to neighbourhood groups, to the Church, but these could shift during the course of a lifetime. In the *Autobiography* of Benvenuto Cellini, the goldsmith describes shape-shifting in his twenties, once his apprenticeship was done. He availed himself of differences in the laws and mores in the Italian cities where he worked; these allowed him to adopt different personas to suit different patrons; he undertook a variety of jobs – metalworking, versifying, soldiering – as they appeared. His life was more open than it would have been if he had remained in a village, because the city set him free from a single, fixed self to become what he wanted to be.

At MIT, I had occasion to see *Stadtluft macht frei* take form among a group of young architects from Shanghai. Their home city epitomizes the urban explosion occurring throughout the developing world today, a place expanding economically at a headlong rate, drawing young people from all over China into its orbit. Although my band of Shanghainese went home to their villages or small towns each New Year, in the city they left their local outlooks and habits far behind. Some of the young male architects came out as gay; young female architects delayed or refused to have a child – both sexes causing grief to those at home. When I introduced my charges to *Stadtluft macht frei*, they translated the phrase into Mandarin as 'wearing different hats'. The superficial words convey a deep truth, that when life is open, it becomes multi-layered. As it became for Cellini.

MIT made me think that all these strands of 'open' might address the conundrum of relating *cité* and *ville*. Rather than try to straighten out this relation, an open city would work with its complexities, making, as it were, a complex molecule of experience. The role of the planner and architect would be both to encourage complexity and to create an interactive, synergetic *ville* greater than the sum of its parts, within which pockets of order would orient people. Ethically, an open city would of course tolerate differences and promote equality, but would more specifically free people from the straitjacket of the fixed and the familiar, creating a terrain in which they could experiment and expand their experience.

Idealistic? Of course. Idealism of an American sort, framed by the pragmatist school of philosophy whose key concept was that all experience should be experimental. The worthies of pragmatism – Charles Sanders Peirce, William James, John Dewey – would, I suspect, have felt quite at home in the Media Lab. Those same worthies resisted equating 'pragmatic' and 'practical', because the hard-faced, practical men who dominated the country's values in the late nineteenth and early twentieth centuries scorned the ambiguous or the contradictory, and celebrated efficiency.

Within my small corner of the pragmatist frame, though, it was not so easy to dismiss these hard-faced values. Most urban projects cost a fortune. *Stadtluft macht frei* doesn't tell the urban planner how wide the streets should be. A planner has to be accountable to people who may not appreciate being obliged to live in a caprice, or in an experiment which has proved an interesting failure. Both Dewey and James were not naive in this regard; they recognized that pragmatism had to figure out how to move from experiment to practice. If you are unpacking an established practice, the deconstruction doesn't tell you what to do next. James even suspected that the open, experimental mindset – so critical of the world as it is, so minded that things could be different – betrays in fact a fear of commitment; in his words, the eternal experimenter suffers from 'dread of the irrevocable, which often engenders a type of character incapable of prompt and vigorous resolve'. Free of that neurosis, the maker follows a crooked path from the possible to the doable.[11]

The pragmatist problem of how to crystallize an open practice came home to Mitchell in a particular way. A few years after *The City of Bits* appeared, Mitchell, along with the architect Frank Gehry, sponsored a project seeking to design a high-tech, self-drive automobile which would be a pleasure to ride in, rather than serve just as a mechanical container; they wanted to achieve an elusive goal Mitchell called the 'aesthetics of motion'. Pressed by me to define this phrase, he answered, 'I don't know yet' – which was a Media Lab sort of answer. Dropping in on the project from time to time, I noticed that its personnel seemed to change quite often; asked why lab assistants left so frequently, one manager explained to me that many people didn't understand their roles. 'I don't know yet' furnishes no directions to others; the project manager remarked laconically (we were in Mitchell's presence) that the frustration level in this open experiment was 'abnormal'. The two geniuses in search of the undefinable did not, moreover, seek to enlighten their staff; they expected those below to grasp intuitively the inspiration and then carry it out. Thus the open, cutting-edge experiment teetered on the edge of dysfunctional.

Mitchell died of cancer in 2010 and so did not live to see his vision play out, but even in the last years of his life, the tech-world was in transition. It was moving from an open to a closed condition. Yochai Benkler writes, 'what typified the first quarter century of the Internet was an integrated system of open systems . . . resisting the application of power from any centralized authority' whereas today 'we are shifting to an Internet that facilitates the accumulation of power by a relatively small set of influential state and non-state actors'. Facebook, Google, Amazon, Intel, Apple: these names embody the problem Benkler sees now: the closed era of the internet consists of a small number of monopolies, producing the machines and the programs engaged in mass mining of information. Once acquired, monopoly programming becomes ever more personalized and more controlling.[12]

Though Karl Popper died long before the digital age began, his ghost might well have declared, 'I knew it.' Popper abhorred economic monopolies just as he feared totalitarian states. Both make the same seductive promise: life can be made simpler, clearer, more user-friendly, as we would now say about technology, for example, if only people would submit to a regime which does the organizing. You will know what you are about, because the rules of your experience will be laid out for you. What you gain in clarity, however, you will lose in freedom. Your experience will become clear and closed. Long before Popper, the great Swiss historian Jacob Burckhardt framed the same threat by warning that modern life would be ruled by 'brutal simplifiers', which to him meant the seductive simplicities of nationalism. For both Popper and Burckhardt, those catchphrases of open experience – 'complex', 'ambiguous', 'uncertain' – imply resistance to an oppressive regime of power.[13]

The cities we live in today are closed in ways that mirror what has happened in the tech realm. In the immense urban explosion today in the Global South – in China, India, Brazil, Mexico, the countries of central Africa – large finance and construction firms are standardizing the *ville*; as a plane lands you may not be able to tell Beijing apart from New York. North as well as South, the growth of cities has not produced much experiment in form. The office park, the school campus, the residential tower set in a bit of green are not forms friendly to experiment, because all are self-contained rather than open to outside influences and interactions

My experience in Boston, however, cautions against seeing closure as simply Big Power squashing the People. Fear of others or an inability to cope with complexity are aspects of the *cité* which also close in lives. Judgements that the *cité* has 'failed' to open up are thus Janus-faced, as I also discovered in Boston: one side of the coin shows angry populist prejudice, but on the other face can appear the self-satisfied smile, the virtue-signalling, of an elite. The closed *cité* is therefore a problem of values as well as political economy.

III. MODEST

The word 'make' is so common that people usually don't think much about it. Our ancestors were not so blasé; the Greeks were full of wonder at the power to create even the most ordinary things. Pandora's box included not just exotic elixirs but also knives, carpets and pots; the human contribution to existence was to create something where before there was nothing. The Greeks possessed a depth of wonder which has diminished in our more jaded age. They wondered at the sheer fact that things exist at all – that a potter could keep a pot from cracking, or that the colours in which their statues were painted were so vibrant, whereas we wonder only at things which are new, like a pot shape or a colour never seen before.

This celebration of making entered a new domain in the Renaissance. *Stadtluft macht frei* applied the word 'make' to the self. In his *Oration on the Dignity of Man*, the Renaissance philosopher Giovanni Pico della Mirandola declared 'man is an animal of diverse, multiform and destructible nature'; in this pliant condition 'it is given to him to have that which he chooses and to be that which he wills'. This is not immodest boasting, but rather as Montaigne argued at the end of the Renaissance that people construct their lives by distinctive tastes, beliefs or encounters. Waging war against your own father is an experience particular to you; courage in waging war, of any sort, appears or is absent in everyone. Montaigne's essays convey a distinctive contrast between personality, as something which is of a person's own making, and character, which is constituted by beliefs and behaviours common to everyone. Still, that man could be his/her own maker was for Pico more than a matter of personality; it contracted God's power over man's fate; Pico, an intensely religious believer, spent his own life trying to reconcile the two.[14, 15]

Eighteenth-century philosophers sought to relieve this tension by focusing on one aspect of making: the impulse to do good-quality work. This maker's virtue had from the medieval era on been taken as acceptable in the sight of God, good work a sign of service and commitment to something objective which lay beyond personal selfishness. Now the philosophers asserted in worldly terms that people fulfil themselves when as workers they seek to do good-quality work. *Homo faber* appeared in this guise to readers of Denis Diderot's *Encyclopédie*, written from 1751 to 1771, volume after volume of which illustrated how to work well whether one is a cook, a farmer or a king. The *Encyclopédie*'s emphasis on practical work done well challenged Kant's image of crooked human timber, since the able worker is a cooperative being, straightening out his relations to others in the shared effort to create things that are well made.

In modern times, belief in *Homo faber* has dimmed. Industrialism darkened the picture of the skill-proud labourer, as machines took over his or her crafts, and factory conditions demeaned the social setting of work. During the last century, both Nazism and state communism turned Man as Maker into an obscene ideological weapon; *Arbeit macht Frei* ('Work is freedom') was written over the entrance to concentration camps. Today, while these totalitarian horrors have gone, new forms of short-term, episodic labour, plus the advance of robotic labour, have denied to large numbers of people pride in themselves as workers.

To understand *Homo faber*'s role in the city, we have to conceive of the dignity of labour differently. Rather than espousing a worldview, *Homo faber* in the city acquires honour by practising in a way whose terms are modest: the small house renovation done as cheaply as possible, or planting a street with young trees, or simply providing cheap benches where elderly people can sit safely outside. This ethic of making modestly implies in turn a certain relationship to the *cité*.

As a young urbanist, I was persuaded to the ethics of modest making by reading a book by Bernard Rudofsky written in the 1960s, *Architecture Without Architects*. Removed from the hot issues in those far-off days of postmodernism and theory, Rudofsky documented how the materials, shapes and siting of the built environment have arisen from the practices of everyday life. Away from its main square, Siena exemplifies Rudofsky's view. Its windows, doors and decor covering basically similar building volumes have accumulated in unpredictable ways over the course of centuries, and the accumulation still continues. A walk down a Sienese street – plate-glass shopfronts next to medieval wooden doorways, next to a McDonald's, next to a convent – gives you a strong sense of a process unfolding in this place, which imbues it with a complex and particular character. More, these variations have been made largely by the people who lived here, creating and adapting buildings in time; the glass-front of McDonald's had to negotiate their signage with a neighbourhood association, and now looks a comfortable fit.

Rudofsky argued that the making of places had no need of self-conscious artiness, citing as examples elegantly shaped elliptical granaries in the Central African bush, or finely detailed towers in Iran built to attract pigeons whose droppings accumulated and so transformed the towers into fertilizer plants. Which is what he meant by architecture without architects: the primacy of the *cité*; making derived from dwelling. The care with which the granaries, towers and white-washed streets are tended show that people have taken ownership of these places. When we say about a neighbourhood that we feel at home there, I think we are asserting this kind of agency – the physical environment seems to emanate from how we dwell and who we are.[16]

Rudofsky appealed even to seasoned urbanists like Gordon Cullen, who thought more technically about how the lessons of experience should guide physical form. For instance, Cullen studied how changes in building at 'grade level' (the ground plane) appeared in cities built next to seas or rivers; below-grade spaces gradually emerge to accommodate loading and unloading, as in the quays of Paris, or above-grade in the raised squares of Agde built up to avoid flooding, the height calibrated by year-after-year experience. In both cases, use gradually established a precise visual scale. The professional should follow that scale bred of experience, rather than arbitrarily elevating spaces or gouging them out just because the grading looks good on paper.[17]

Rudofsky and Cullen caution the maker against arbitrary innovation for another reason too. Every innovation suffers by definition from a mismatch between the ways people currently do things and the ways they might do them. Open-ended in time means the way an object will evolve, how its use will change; the process cannot often be predicted in advance. Take the scalpel used in surgery, which came into being in the sixteenth century when an advance in metallurgy meant that knives were made with a sharper and more durable edge. It then took doctors nearly eighty years to figure out how to use these sharp knives medically – how, for instance, to hold the knife delicately rather than wielding it too forcefully, like a blunt sword. The knife-blade and handle slimmed down erratically during those eighty years, different versions of blade-handles appearing each decade, some of these versions adapted into tools for new practices for butchering animals and, thankfully, passing out of the domain of human surgery. In craftwork, it's common for a tool, or a material, to appear before people know what to do with it, discovering its various uses only through trial-and-error experiment. Time reverses the mantra that form should follow function; instead, function follows form – and often follows slowly.[18]

In the same way, people need time to learn the built environment.

Common sense speaks of people knowing 'intuitively' how to move around or make sense of a building or place, but arbitrarily innovative buildings can disrupt just these taken-for-granted habits. This issue arises in school designs which incorporate advances in online learning. A traditional schoolroom consists of rows of seats staring up at a master in front, whereas the new is a more informal clustering of work-stations. Like the tempered-steel knife, teachers don't know immediately how to relate their own bodily presence to these work-stations – for instance, where to stand to command everyone's attention – it takes time to learn the new building. Likewise, if our plans for racial integration had succeeded, people would have had to learn how to adapt the hard surfaces accommodating the school's buses as playgrounds when the buses were absent.

Jane Jacobs combined all these views. The great writer-warrior did not dispute the worth of urban design itself, but asserted that urban forms emerged slowly and incrementally, following the lessons of use and experience. Her bête noire *Homo faber*, Robert Moses, the New York City planner and power-broker, built in exactly the opposite way: big, fast and arbitrarily. As will emerge in these pages, I dwelt in Jane Jacob's shadow as a young man. Gradually, I have emerged from it.

In part this was because the scene of my own practical activity shifted. As a planner, I have always had a modest practice; indeed, looking back, I regret not grasping the pragmatist nettle by practising more and teaching less. My practice in America was locally based and oriented to strengthening community. In middle age, I began consulting at the UN, first for UNESCO, then for the UN Development Programme, lately for UN-Habitat. In the Global South, cities were growing so fast and so big that large-scale design was required; slow, cautious and local provided an inadequate guide for how to provide mass housing, schools or transport. How, on a larger scale, could urbanism be practised in a modest spirit? I didn't abandon the ethical outlook that shaped me, but it needed to be reinterpreted.

Another change in outlook has been personal. Several years ago I suffered a serious stroke. In recovering from it, I began to understand buildings and spatial relations differently from the way I had before. I now had to make an effort to be in complex spaces, faced with the problem of staying upright and walking straight, and also with the neurological short-circuit that in crowds disorients those affected by strokes. Curiously, the physical effort required to make my own way expanded my sense of the environment rather than localized it to where I put my foot next or who is immediately in front of me; I became attuned on a broader scale to the ambiguous or complex spaces through which I navigated; I became Venturi's sort of urbanite.

Both changes have prompted me to explore how *Homo faber* can play a more vigorous role in the city. A more vigorous urbanism has also to be a visceral urbanism, since place and space come alive in the body. As I'll try to show in these pages, proactive urbanism can combine with ethical modesty. Modest does not mean cringing subservience; the urbanist should be a partner to the urbanite, not a servant – both critical of how people live and self-critical about what he or she builds. If this relation between *cité* and *ville* can be forged, then the city can open.

There is an argument to be made against this view. Part of the maker's self-respect resides in his or her sheer will. All the great city-makers have taken a deep pride in what they do independent of, indeed against the grain of, the desires of others; the phrases 'not possible', 'unheard of', 'an ego trip', 'so out of context' etc. are all red flags, inspiring even more assertion. A maker who approaches his or her labours in a spirit of modesty, as Gordon Cullen or Jane Jacobs want, will certainly reduce the tension between making and dwelling. Yet he or she may avoid taking risks. If the immodest, assertive, creative will is full of fire, can a more sensitive, cooperative, self-critical urbanism become as energetic?

Plan of the book This book is the last of three exploring *Homo faber*'s place in society. The first volume studied craftsmanship, particularly the relationship between head and hand it involves. The second studied the cooperation good work entails. This book puts *Homo faber* in the city. The first part of this study looks at how urbanism – the professional practice of city-making – has evolved. City-makers in the nineteenth century tried to connect the lived and the built; these tissues were fragile and tore easily. In the twentieth century, *cité* and *ville* turned away from each other in the ways that urbanists thought about and went about city-making. Urbanism became, internally, a gated community.[19]

The book then explores how three big issues are affected by this fault line between the lived and the built. I start with the huge expansion of cities in the Global South, in which the unresolved conflicts of the Global North have reappeared. Socially, cities today are traumatized sociologically by Aristotle's proposition that a *cité* should be composed of different sorts of people. Mitchell's smart city has evolved humanly, now either a nightmare or a place of promise, as technology can either close or open the *cité*.

In the third part, I present what a city could be like, were it more open. An open *cité* requires those who live in it to develop the skills to manage complexity. In the *ville*, five open forms can make urban places complex in a good way. I've then tried to show how urbanists might collaborate with urbanites in using these open forms.

The final part of the book takes up the essential crookedness of the city. Underlying its social, technological and architectural fissures, the work of time disrupts the relations between lived and built – which is a practical rather than poetic proposition. The turbulence and uncertainties of climate change illuminate ruptures which occur in any city as it evolves. This turbulence takes me back at the end of this book to the issue which first dogged me in Boston – can ethics shape the design of the city?

PART ONE

The Two Cities

2

Unstable Foundations

I. THE BIRTH OF URBANISM — AN ENGINEER'S STORY

In 1859, The Spanish architect Ildefons Cerdà first brought the words 'urbanism' and 'urbanist' into print. Why so new? People have lived in cities for thousands of years. The words appeared because the conditions of modern life demanded a distinctive understanding of cities.[1]

Early in the eighteenth century a huge migration began in Europe to big cities, mainly of young, poor people, and principally to London and Paris. Once they arrived, they found work to be in short supply, with only about 60 per cent of London's urban poor in 1720 being employed full-time. In America, many immigrants passed through New York and Philadelphia on their way to the frontier, whereas in Britain and France these unemployed masses remained, like clotted blood. By the onset of the French Revolution, there was a widely felt need for reform, and some proposals targeted these material conditions, as in proposals to tear down jerry-built slums. But the economic crisis was not on the minds of the people Cerdà called 'urbanists'. Public-health issues moved them to think the city afresh, diseases which afflicted rich and poor alike.

Plague had always been a danger in cities – the Black Death wiped out a third of Europe in the late Middle Ages. As early modern cities became bigger and denser – and so more shit-and-urine filled – they became fertile gardens to feed rats and rat-borne disease. If an infant managed to survive its birth (a real achievement in that era of primitive obstetrics), it could look forward to death by dysentery brought on by filthy water. Population growth also meant more houses; more houses meant more chimneys polluting the air, the foetid air nurturing tuberculosis.

The first urbanists who sought vigorously to address these conditions were engineers rather than doctors. Civil engineering is not generally considered a glamorous pursuit, but engineers became heroic figures in Cerdà's generation because they dealt with public-health issues in the city more proactively than doctors, who had no real ideas about how to prevent tuberculosis or the causes of plague.

Among citizens as among medical experts, the cultural practices surrounding cholera were rooted deeply in ignorance. The disease was wrongly thought to be airborne rather than water-borne; thus, during an epidemic in 1832, many Parisians sought to defend against a plague sweeping the city by covering their mouths with white handkerchiefs when talking to others – the white colour seemed particularly important as a shield. The Palais-Royal, a former market-cum-whorehouse, was converted into a hospital where sick people were lined up in narrow rows under the glass roof; the crowding of sick bodies ensured that they could re-infect one another if by chance someone showed signs of recovery, but both doctors and patients clung to the conviction that sunlight streaming down on the dying had disinfectant powers, a desperate legacy of the old belief in God's healing light.[2]

Civil engineers became the craftsmen of the modern city, seeking to improve the quality of urban life through experimenting technically. Plague-infested streets prompted a rethink among the engineers about the manufacture of materials used for construction. Smooth stone paving for streets, necessary to clean up horse droppings effectively, were first laid around London's eighteenth-century Bloomsbury squares, but came into wider use only when machines could – from around 1800 – produce sliced stone on an industrial scale. Civil engineers created a market for machined stone. Their thought was that, if the streets are physically easier to clean, people will become more minded to clean them, not throwing garbage out the windows of houses, for example (previously a standard practice). Indeed, the engineers assumed that if the infrastructure was changed, more rational public-health practices would follow – the *ville* can alter the *cité*.

Similarly, inventions like the *pissoir*, first contrived in 1843 in Paris, marked a real advance in public health. The multiple-user *pissoir* (called the 'Alexandrine'), appearing in the 1880s, was health technology particularly suited for a crowded street. Again, the idea was that providing the mechanism for a healthy practice will induce a change in attitudes: up to 1843 men exposed their cocks without shame in order to pee in public, and they peed like dogs on the sides of buildings as much as in the street; after the arrival of the *pissoir*, urine could be channelled below ground. The values of the *cité* correspondingly shifted; it gradually began to seem shameful to relieve yourself in view of strangers. More positively, a knock-on effect of removing shit and urine from the street was that it made the outdoors more usable as social space; the huge outdoor café fronting a boulevard was the sanitary engineer's gift to urban civilization.[3]

The engineering of healthy cities had been foreshadowed by a fundamental discovery about the human body made three centuries before the urbanist engineers set to work. In 1628, William Harvey's *De motu cordis* explained how the human heart causes blood to circulate mechanically through arteries and veins, whereas earlier medicine had thought blood circulated as it heated up. A century later, Harvey's discovery about the circulatory system became a model for urban planning; the French urbanist Christian Patte used the imagery of arteries and veins to invent the system of one-way streets we know today. Enlightenment planners imagined that if motion through the city became blocked at any major point, the collective body would be prone to a crisis of circulation like that an individual body suffers during a heart attack. The one-way streets prompted by the circulatory model could be realized fairly easily in small cities with relatively light traffic; in big cities like Paris, whose people and traffic swelled relentlessly through the nineteenth century, free-flowing traffic became more challenging to plan, requiring more systemic interventions in the city fabric than simply posting one-way signs.

Still, the engineering of public health beneath and above ground was a great accomplishment of the nineteenth century. By 1892, in a new preface to the book he had written a half-century earlier about the miseries of the working classes of Manchester, Friedrich Engels remarked that 'the repeated visitations of cholera, typhus, smallpox, and other epidemics have shown the British bourgeois the urgent necessity of sanitation in his towns and cities . . . the most crying abuses . . . have either disappeared or have been made less conspicuous.' A Victorian story of progress, certainly, but many consequences of engineering the city were often accidental and unintentional: the engineers did not set out to create boulevard cafés.[4]

Much nineteenth-century infrastructure-building was open in the way of the Media Lab in its heyday. Engineers guessed, and discovered by accident, not knowing in advance the knock-on effects of their technical inventions. The engineers working for Joseph Bazalgette, for instance, when building London's sewers in the 1850s to 1860s, invented such technology as solid-waste screens in the course of fitting sections of piping together, experimenting with several different filter designs, rather than knowing right away which size to use. Bazalgette was certain about what to do overall: the realm of the sewer – the realm of *Les Misérables* – had to be made into a network of pipes mirroring the streets above. But still, he was friendly to uncertainty. Bazalgette often built the sewers with pipes larger in diameter than seemed to be needed, saying that planning could not predict future needs.[5]

This experimental process required the engineer-urbanist to develop new visual tools. Before the time of Cerdà and Bazalgette, artistic conventions of drawing and artistic imagery had provided the ways for conceiving what the city should look like; in Donald Olsen's phrase, 'the city was conceived as a work of art'. Even military engineers, thinking through how best to design a city which could be protected when under siege, resorted to decorous artistic standards; in a star-shaped design for the city of Palmanova in Italy, for instance, its military planners imposed on a rough, irregular terrain the image of the city on a flat field, with pleasing gardens within, nice embellishments of walls and the like. Drawing in section and plan is a classic technique perfectly suited for rendering a single building distinctly, by making a vertical slice and a horizontal footprint; the messy compound of forms along a dense, disordered street requires a different means of representation.

We can visualize that complexity now thanks to the montage

capabilities of computer-assisted design, but our forebears could only see it in the mind's eye. Nor could classical representations show how gas lights, which first appeared on London's streets in 1807, variously affected their night-time look, nor could architects graphically depict the speed at which traffic flowed. The infrastructures the engineers were building below ground were invisible. Traditional representations didn't provide the techniques the engineer-urbanist needed.

For all these reasons, they were not practising an exact science. They did not apply established principles to particular cases, there were no general policies that dictated best practices; rather, the engineers foreshadowed Jerome Groopman's description of the 'adaptive clinical trial' by learning as they went along. One of the truly admirable aspects of Bazalgette's character is that he exuded Victorian confidence without claiming that he knew exactly what he was doing, believing only that he would get it right in the end. This is more largely true of civil engineers in the city at that time; their technical knowledge was open-ended.

It produced, however, something like the difficulty Mitchell encountered in trying to translate his own ideas so that others could understand them. Renaissance urban architects like Palladio were mindful of how their work could best be seen. Viewing his church of San Giorgio across the water from Venice's Piazza San Marco, one sees how it's been placed and sized, how the work was an insertion into the fabric of the city, yet somehow absorbed by it: Palladio makes a clear demonstration of complexity. A different intervention ruled engineers; their work was not so tangibly evident to others. The public might feel the consequences, as in a street which does not smell, without being able to imagine from that evidence how the sewers were laid beneath. Ambiguity characterizes such complexity. The making of a sewage system involved a lot of hard research into the materials in which pipes were laid, but the decision about whether to use 6- or 9-foot pipes Bazalgette could not really explain to others – because he could not explain it to himself. The obscurity is akin to Bill Mitchell not being able to explain the 'aesthetics of motion' in such a way that his studio assistants knew what to do the next morning.

Ambiguous complexity connected the engineer-urbanists of the *ville* to writers chronicling the *cité*.

II. THE *CITÉ* – HARD TO READ

The difficulty of reading the *cité* became evident to the young Friedrich Engels when, in the early 1840s, he travelled to Manchester to document the miseries of the poor. It was an odd voyage for this young man of twenty-four to be making. Engels, the son of a wealthy German merchant, was a debonair flitter about town, and when in the country an ardent fox-hunter; though awed by Karl Marx, the young Engels was the more adventurous spirit. There was a long tradition of writing about scenes of daily life among the 'lower orders' both in Britain and France, but radical reformers tended to write at armchair length. To find out about the poor who worked in Manchester's factories, Engels actually went there, walking the streets, poking his nose into brothels, hanging out in taverns, and even attending nonconformist churches (though he had a visceral loathing of them).

The historian E. P. Thompson observed that grimy, oppressive Manchester inspired Engels to create a language of class, inventing words and categories for the poor which had not existed before; in writing up Manchester he coined the words 'proletariat' and, below it, the 'lumpenproletariat'. *The Condition of the Working-Class in England in 1844* was not, however, simply horror-story reportage; the young fox-hunter turned anthropologist began to notice aspects of the city which did not entirely fit with the new language of class, such as the way children played in the streets, or the speed at which women walked them, or the pleasures people snatched in taverns.

His sensitive urban antennae linked Engels to certain novelists of his time, in particular to Balzac and to Stendhal (pseudonym of Marie-Henri Beyle). It's true that the peptic novelists and the budding communist had different cities in their sights. Rather than an industrial centre like Manchester, or, closer to home, Lyons, where France's fabrics and glass were made, Paris composted glittery luxury, financial and governmental corruption, massive bureaucracies and mass misery. This thick urbanity needed innovative novelistic techniques to convey it – just as the engineer-urbanists needed new visual techniques.

To evoke a city which was hard to read, novels like Balzac's *Lost Illusions* or Stendhal's *The Red and the Black* start with a seemingly simple storyline: a provincial young man comes to the big city, full of hope; the city then either disappoints his desires or renders them self-destructive. The novelists then fine-tune this simple narrative in two ways. First, they play on the ambition of their young heroes, who are hard-driven by the adage *Stadtluft macht frei*. In Balzac's *Père Goriot*, the young Rastignac shakes his fist at Paris – declaring 'À nous deux, maintenant!' ('It's between you and me now, you bastard') – only to find, like Lucien Chardon in *Lost Illusions*, that there are many other egos shaking their fists too. Like balloons, the ambitious young protagonists deflate. Stendhal shapes a second way the city can break youth's spirit. The young, provincial, father-abused Julien Sorel in *The Red and the Black* is more than a monster of ambition; escaping to the city, Julien discovers new, urgent sexual desire in himself. There are no moral stop signs in Paris; without external prohibitions, Sorel cannot handle himself, and in the end his excess of desire proves fatal; he too deflates.

The nineteenth-century urban novelists revelled – I don't think the word is too strong – in the ways a city can crush the hopes of the young. There are what can only be described as exquisite passages in Balzac when he describes the humiliations or indifference to which his rutting young are subject. In Flaubert, a quickening of sentence rhythms and ever-more colourful imagery appears – the novelist is thrilled! – as he leads his young men in *Sentimental Education* into disaster territory. The novelists created aesthetic pleasure in the process of crushing their characters.

Less perversely, lesser coming-of-age novels share with these masterpieces that problem in the *cité* which is also a problem for their readers: the fulfilment you seek will come from people you do not yet know. You must master strangers who are difficult to read because they are shrouded.

The era of these novels was an age in which urban dwellers no longer felt at ease speaking spontaneously to strangers in the street. Today, we don't usually do so either, so it's hard to imagine it was not always thus. But in mid-eighteenth-century Paris or London a stranger felt no hesitation in coming up to you in the street, interrogating you, and gripping your arm (man to man) to hold your attention. Similarly, in a coffee house, when you bought your cup of coffee, you sat down at a long table, expecting to spend quality time discussing matters of the day with perfect strangers. Stendhal's Paris marked a turning point when people on the street, or at a café, assumed that they had a right to be left alone, nursing a drink and their own thoughts. In public, people came to want to be protected by silence, shielded from the intrusion of strangers, which is still true: in the modern city, strangers relate to one another more visually than verbally.

The nineteenth century was an age of black clothing – not in the fashionable Japanese red-black used as a colour highlight, but a mass of dull grey-black, the urban crowd a sea of black-draped and black-hatted men. It was also the first age of ready-to-wear, of clothes cut by machines in standardized patterns. Black and ready-to-wear combined to make an anonymous uniform, shielding individuals from notice, from standing out – the fashion equivalent of the man left alone with his drink and thoughts in the café. Again there was a contrast to eighteenth-century Paris and London, whose streets were full of colours; people's dress in the *ancien régime* city marked not just their place in the social hierarchy, but more particularly the professions or the trades they pursued (butchers wore striped red-and-white scarves; pharmacists sported rosemary in their lapels). Now, the sea of uniformity meant it was harder to read a stranger just by looking at his or her dress.

Both his fictional protagonists and the purchasers of Balzac's novels sought to read this shrouded public realm in a particular way. They tried to deduce the character of a stranger by sifting through small revealing details of dress. For instance, people thought buttons which actually unbuttoned on a coat sleeve indicated that the wearer was a 'gentleman', even though his coat was cut almost exactly the same as those worn by tradesmen and was the same shade of black. Throughout the novels which compose Balzac's *La Comédie humaine*, the author invites us to deduce the history of a family by analysing the stains on a carpet or the presence of cat fur on a cushion; the reader works from the minutiae of environment inwards to the character of its inhabitants. More broadly, the outsider needs to understand what Balzac calls the 'physiognomy' of streets, their surface appearances, how and why they are connected – these surface physical phenomena containing clues about the lives of strangers behind the street's doors.

Like a craftsman focusing on getting small things right, only the precise analysis of details will make the *cité* comprehensible to the urban dweller. The big picture is big, black and homogeneous; the mental space of complexity consists of analysing small bits of reality. Learning to 'read' the city in this way promises to make the newcomer street-smart. Yet few of these novels were stories of triumph. The city's anarchic economy, its political instability, its swelling territory, all made the 'science of the *cité*', as Balzac called it, a science all too frequently misleading. You might have read the buttons on the stranger's sleeve wrongly, for instance; he is in fact a high-class crook who can afford a good tailor, and he is swindling you.

The ethical compass of the urban novelists transcended any simple contrast between village virtue and urban vice. Rather, they sought to convey how human character changes its structure in the modern city. Compare two wicked Parisians, Balzac's Vautrin and the villainous Marquise de Merteuil in *Les Liaisons dangereuses*, written by Laclos in the previous century. Madame de Merteuil belongs wholly to one environment, the aristocratic salon, whereas Vautrin – thief, police chief, seducer of both women and boys – is more chameleon, harder to place; he appears, disappears and reappears; he is continually self-transforming. Madame de Merteuil certainly has many strands in her makeup, but Vautrin is complex in a different way: nothing in him is settled and complete. You could spin out the same contrast between Pushkin and Dostoevsky as between Laclos and Balzac: Pushkin's evocations of court life are wonderfully rounded and polished, while Dostoevsky's of Moscow are purposely jagged descriptions of morphing human beings.

The unsettled character of urban life produced perhaps the most resonant definition of modernity itself. This appeared in *The Communist Manifesto*, written by Friedrich Engels and Karl Marx in 1848, a year of revolutionary upheaval across Europe: 'All fixed, fast-frozen relations, with their train of ancient and venerable prejudices and opinions, are swept away, all new-formed ones become antiquated before they can ossify. All that is solid melts into air . . .' Their declaration paired with Charles Baudelaire's evocation a few years later, in 'The Painter of Modern Life', that modernity consists of the 'the transient, the fleeting, the contingent'. The idea of modernity they evoke is summed up now in the philosopher Zygmunt Bauman's phrase, 'liquid modernity'. Liquid modernity appeared in the urban novelists' way of writing, whereby character becomes unfixed, evoked by a language focused on details and fragments.[6, 7, 8]

The phrase can seem just a cliché – modern life as the enemy of tradition – unless we reckon a tension it contains. Baudelaire recognized that something was amiss in framing modern art as purely fleeting and liquid; art also aims at permanence, indeed, the artist must 'distil the eternal from the transitory'. The laboratory echoes this, in the play between routine and discovery; so, too, in everyday life we want to balance change and stability. All city-makers have a particular experience of this tension just because of the brute fact that buildings are weighty things; if not eternal, buildings are going to be in place a long time. How can they be reconciled to the swift changes of modern life, to its liquid, dissolving flow of old economic, social or religious forms? How can one relate a solid *ville* to a liquid *cité*?

1848 marks the year in which a wave of revolution swept Europe from small German towns to big French cities. Hereditary privilege trembled – but it did not collapse. Nor were labour conditions much touched by the revolutions; the emancipation of workers that Marx and Engels trumpeted in *The Communist Manifesto*, written the same year, was a hope extinguished in a few months. In retrospect, we can see that this watershed year elevated the importance of civil society in general, and the city in particular. A great generation of urbanists appeared in the 1850s who sought to make the *ville* respond to the *cité*. They sought to resolve the *cité*'s ambiguities – but in contrasting ways.

III. THE *VILLE*

In this generation, three figures stand out. They were Cerdà himself, who devised a planning fabric for Barcelona; Baron Haussmann, who remade Paris as a network serving a mobile city; and Frederick

Law Olmsted, who, in laying out Central Park in New York, derived certain principles of relating built form to the natural environment. So far as I know, the three urbanists had little contact with one another, perhaps because their visions were so different.

Like the engineers, these three were visionaries masquerading as practical men of affairs. Unlike the engineers, they had no specialized training. Napoleon III is supposed to have written down the initial 'vision statement' for the new Paris on the back of an envelope (probably not true but believable). Baron Haussmann's method of 'urban analysis' was to oblige his surveyors to shimmy up tall poles to gain a bird's-eye perspective on streets, drawing what they saw while somehow managing not to fall off, then comparing notes once back on the ground. Olmsted began life as a journalist and reinvented himself almost by the stroke of a magic wand as a landscape architect; in making Central Park, he knew little more about plants than its users. Cerdà was indeed a professional architect, but he entered city planning as a vocation as a by-product of his politics in 1848.[9]

A network Paris in the first half of the nineteenth century was hell to move through; twisted, irregular streets had been imprinted on the city by a thousand years of history; a carriage journey in Paris before 1850 from the Champs de Mars to the Jardin des Plantes could take two hours, slower than on foot. Baron Haussmann straightened out the city in two decades. He joined its parts through a system of traffic, laying out three networks – *réseaux* – of boulevards which spanned the city north to south and east to west. This straightening was full of political implication.

Three revolutions – of 1789–94, 1830 and 1848 – had preceded Haussmann's appointment by Napoleon III as chief planner in the 1850s. Insurgents in the two last revolts appropriated the twisted streets by barricading them, impeding access by soldiers or police. Building a barricade was then fairly simple. Light objects like chairs and boxes were laid across a road, on top of which were stacked up heavier chests and tables, topped by a carriage or other truly weighty object. When a cannonball hit the barricade, these weighty objects would cause the structure to sink down rather than fly apart; access thus would remain blocked.

In straightening the streets, Haussmann made them harder to barricade. As in the currently named Boulevard de Sébastopol, he asked engineers to calculate widths and straight-runs so that during insurrections horse-drawn cannon could rumble down the boulevard two abreast, firing over and behind the houses lining opposite sides of the street. This embodied a change in the relation of civil engineering to military engineering. Traditionally the emphasis had been to fortify a city around its perimeter. Medieval city walls were thus built as thick as possible to resist enemy incursion. Renaissance walls, as in Vincenzo Scamozzi's proposals for Palmanova, were more carefully designed, in order to keep cannonballs firing over the wall from hitting any significant target within; still, the planners focused on guarding the perimeter and its gates. Haussmann's potential enemy, by contrast, was already inside the gates.

But reducing his plans to the servicing of a police state would not explain much about their particular character. Once the city had been made safe from revolution, he intended the *réseaux* – big boulevards into which feeder streets poured – to serve more positive social purposes. Centre-city parks, principally the Tuileries, were now opened up to Parisians throughout the city; he elaborated the Bois de Boulogne near new bourgeois districts at the western edge of the city, and the Bois des Buttes-Chaumont and the Bois de Vincennes for workers living to the north-east and south-east of the centre.

Once the boulevards were in place, Haussmann lined them with housing that catered to the new middle classes of Paris; these citizens were unlikely to throw their possessions out of the window to make barricades. The Haussmannian dwelling was mixed in a way which had existed in the past, but was executed irregularly. A courtyard might contain shops and workshops which serviced the local *quartier*; then, in an abrupt break, the rich would occupy the next level up – so far, this was an old pattern. Haussmann sorted out the further upper storeys systematically so that as one climbed the stairs, one encountered respectable but less wealthy tenants, with the servants hidden up in the garrets. Despite the seductive image of *La Bohème* concocted by the popular novelist Henri Murger, artists were seldom housed in the garrets; they mostly inhabited shacks in peripheral spaces like Montmartre. So, too, the huge mass of labourers in the city were hidden away behind the boulevard houses, in untouched, festering quarters. The economic ecology of the new city resembled soiled underwear beneath a ball gown.

Still, by many accounts Haussmann was a genuinely popular figure throughout France, even among some members of the working classes. Wildly improvident, he took to heart the adage 'make no little plans', borrowing vast sums on promises he knew he could not keep; bankrupting Paris after fifteen years of development, he was brought down in 1869 by accountants who caught up with him. Quite quickly the big cafés on the new boulevards produced a happy counter to what Haussmann initially planned; they became popular rather than exclusive places for all Paris.[10]

The crowds who invaded Haussmann's boulevard cafés constituted no sort of threatening mass such as the bourgeoisie once had feared. Instead of the big common tables of the old inns and rotisseries, by 1900 most café space consisted of small, circular tables fit for one or two persons, or, on the occasion of social dinners, tables to seat three or four. As noted earlier, one aspect of modern urban life was the veil of silence cast over public places, protecting individuals from strangers. The small café table was the furniture of this protection; only people you knew would sit at your table. ('Une table a vous seul ou vos intimes,' as the Café de la Paix advertised its new furniture.) This solitude in the mass was paralleled in the forms of public transport: the trams and the free-moving omnibuses which Haussmann promoted along the *réseaux* boulevards echoed a diverse, tightly packed mass in which people kept to themselves, silent in motion, whereas in the post-carriages of the *ancien régime* passengers behaved in the carriages as they did in the taverns, chatting away the entire journey.[11]

Haussmann's Paris met with widespread popular approval not simply because the *réseaux* made it function better than before. The boulevards acquired a spectacle quality which drew people to them, even if as spectators they occupied, as it were, solitary seats. As later with the construction of the Eiffel Tower, design of the *ville* was more than utilitarian; indeed, display displaced the ethical reckoning of life on the street.

Haussmann's architects loaded the exterior of the boulevard

buildings with elaborate ornaments framing windows and marking out the different levels of a building, in contrast to the ways in which opulence was constructed in the eighteenth century: then, elaborate ornament was concealed within the interior of a structure, while the exterior was blank, if not forbidding. Napoleonic building in the right bank quarters which attracted Balzac mediated between inner and exterior display, the carved lintels and door-frames hinting at the wealth within, but with Haussmann, the exterior face of the building became a theatrical event of its own.

The networked city was a theatre of the vertical surface, a combination which coalesced in a new kind of commerce: the giant department store located on the grand boulevard. This commerce in part relied on a building form newly created: the plate glass window. Until the late Middle Ages a building material so expensive that it rarely figured in construction, glass gradually came into more widespread use with small panes that could be easily poured. Large sheets of plate glass were first produced on an industrial scale in the 1840s in France and Holland, made possible by the invention of heavy hotrollers for the molten glass; the cooled sheets were then encased in iron frames which held them more rigidly than traditional wood casements.

Inserted into the ground-floor level of a building, framed on the back and sides like a stage set, large plate-glass windows created the DNA of the department store, displaying the goods on offer inside. The transport *réseaux* enabled people from all over Paris to come to its new department stores in the city centre, the big windows enticing crowds of people who stopped and stared at them. This commercial theatre did not display fifty examples of a cooking pot for sale inside; it displayed only one or two, mixing the prosaic item with perhaps a precious porcelain plate from China, a chest of tea from the British colonies or a giant parmesan cheese from Italy. The idea was to entice by intriguing and surprising, the pot given an allure by association with other, unexpected things, lifting it out of the realm of sheer utility. It was this mix-up of associations which Marx called 'commodity fetishism'; the large-paned window in a department store served as the tangible locus of commodity fetishism. The theatre of things weakened sober reckoning of their worth.

The department store contrasted in this theatrical display to the arcade. An arcade in form is a glass-roofed passage cut into the fabric of big streets, faced on its insides by small shops. After the Napoleonic Wars, Paris began to develop elaborate networks of these weather-proof commercial blood vessels. The arcade shops were mostly speciality stores whose windows were filled with choice items of stock, inviting the lust of ownership rather than the disoriented stimulation of commercial theatre. The walls and paths between buildings have been straightened out gradually over time, making them now seem like *réseaux*, or internal boulevards, but this is a retrospective illusion. Originally, many arcades involved bridging existing buildings with the iron-framed glass plates. The large-scale, fast public transport in the *réseaux* fed the department store; the interior arcade was fed by pedestrians. It was slower-growing and small in scale. Haussmann disliked the arcades precisely because they were cobbled together rather than planned in advance. In his view, a modern network should be coherent and clear – even though the transport network connected people to a large, complex and often disorienting city.

This contrast between department store and arcade defines Haussmann's most potent legacy.

Place and space As a general proposition, people move through a space and dwell in a place. The Haussmannian city privileged space over place. Its transport networks connected people spatially, but diminished their experience of place. What made the difference between space and place was the speed at which people could navigate the city. Human physiology grounds the distinction between the two. The faster you move, the less aware you are of the particularities of the environment; if, by driving 60 kilometres an hour, your attention is distracted by an enticing shop window or sexy pedestrian, you are going to crash. Increasing speed orients the body forward: you need to stare straight ahead, and edit your peripheral vision so that you take account only of what impedes you or allows you to hurtle. People, when walking, take in far more liminal visual information than when moving forward fast in an automobile or bus; one esti-mate is that the brain is processing 50–55 per cent more at-the-side visual information on foot than in a car.[12]

Movement as such isn't a problem. In walking about, most of us have pleasurable reactions similar to those of Edgar Degas, who wrote to his friend Henri Rouart, 'It's not bad in the city . . . You have to keep on looking at everything, small boats and bigger ones, people moving about restlessly on the water and on land too. The movement of things and people distracts and even consoles . . .' These are the pleasures of the *flâneur*; moving about provides the sort of first-person information which taught Engels in Manchester. Parisians began to sense the problem of sheer speed in travelling on the horse-drawn trams which moved faster than individual carriages, or on steam-driven railroads which serviced the suburbs. 'Where in the [Boulevard now named Sébastopol] are we?' remarked one guide-book to the city in the 1880s; 'it goes by so fast and it all looks the same.' This is the inception of the problem of motor traffic in later times, which dissolves environmental awareness, with places losing their character as one speeds through space.[13]

A new anxiety equally seems to have afflicted Parisians: they weren't moving as fast as they wanted; reports of widespread road-rage surfaced in Paris during the late 1870s and early 1880s. In times when slow urban movement was the norm, there was much less anxiety about blockage; in the twisted streets of old cities traffic jams were accepted as just a fact of life. Now, traffic jams signalled that something had gone wrong – the city wasn't working. A physical change in the environment prompted a visceral response, the feeling of blockage escalating from anxiety to anger. Like not being physically touched in public, the desire to move freely – and not be stuck in traffic – is a sensation we take for granted as natural – but it's a historical construction of our sensibilities. We become deeply anxious – whereas our pre-modern ancestors were more relaxed; they took slow movement through a city for granted – as they did what we would now call 'slow food' – without feeling the city had 'ground to a halt'.

Haussmann's emphasis on moving through a network of boule-vards freely and easily put mobility at the heart of defining a 'good city'. The emphasis on free flow became the guide for big-city plan-ners in the twentieth century such as Robert Moses, the builder of New York's highway network, to whom it seemed self-evident that mobility should be the prime concern of city planning. So too in today's urban growth spurt, as in Beijing, planners in Haussmann's shadow pour vast sums into highways. The experience of street-speed defines a certain version of modernity: fast is free, slow is unfree. Moving around wherever you want, whenever you want, as fast as you can: the formula diminishes the sense of dwelling in a place, knowing it viscerally; you are just passing through. Haussmann's legacy in this is perverse: the networked *ville* has diminished the *cité*.

Fabric Ildefons Cerdà was a more people-oriented urbanist, though coming from a technical background. Barcelona in his time harboured a strong professional class inspired by Enlightenment ideas of rational progress, in contrast to the Habsburg-Spanish darkness which lay outside the borders of Catalunya. Like other port cities rimming the Mediterranean, it was a cosmopolitan mixture of ethnicities and religions. Cerdà melded these elements into a kind of cooperative socialism which flourished in parts of Western Europe in the mid-nineteenth century, one which aimed, recalling the old Aristotelian model, at integration of groups in the city rather than provoking class conflict of the sort which had failed in 1848.

The Barcelona Cerdà knew as a youth was as unhealthy a city as Paris during the plague years of the 1830s. Quarantine of the sick had failed in big cities before the 1850s; mid-century it was now evident that plague could be tackled only by promoting sanitation in the entire populace. Thus, as the modern Barcelona urbanist Joan Busquets observes, 'This idea of a hygienic, functional city was, according to Cerdà, to produce conditions of equality between all the residents who used it.' This – to us – self-evident proposition did not figure in Haussmann's selective development of Paris, nor did engineers like Bazalgette in London think of sanitation as a tool to combat inequality.[14]

As an urbanist, Cerdà is now remembered as the designer of the Cerdian grid, and to measure his achievement something should be said in general about city 'fabric', that is, plans which aim to knit together the city into one whole. To understand his own plans, we need to unpack this allusion.

Fabric, texture, grain, knot: these four words, derived from weaving, describe the character of plans, both at the large scale and at particular points and places in the plan. 'Fabric' means the warp and woof in a design, the pattern form created by tying buildings, streets and open spaces to one another. 'Grain' could be thought of as the intricacy of the pattern, the width of streets, the relation of interiors to exteriors, the skyline heights likened to the thickness and colours of threads. 'Texture' is sometimes used interchangeably with 'grain', but it more particularly refers to the mixture of uses and the relation of formal to informal activities in a plan. 'Knots' is my own coinage for places in the plan. In weaving, a knot can tie together the threads in a fabric, but nubbly or big knots can also ruffle the fabric's smooth surface, creating a tactile emphasis. So too in a city, knots are made of everything from a vest-pocket park to a centrally placed statue or fountain – anything that has a distinct character in itself.

Urban fabric comes in three forms. The first is the orthogonal grid, like that which shaped ancient Roman cities. When the Romans founded a new city, they established the principal right-angled road-crossing at its centre (the *decumanus* and the *cardo*), locating the main institutions of the new city here; they then subdivided each quadrant of the city in the same orthogonal way, creating more local centres by crossing main streets, and then again smaller neighbourhoods with crossings at right angles. This was meant to be the plan for Roman new grids from London to Jerusalem. Outside the West, the Mayans and then the Aztecs used the same design. The orthogonal grid would have made sense to any culture which knew how to spin cloth.[15]

The second kind of fabric emerges when courtyards are joined together, creating a cellular city. Again this form is known throughout the world, and seemingly from the beginnings of urban times. Basically, buildings are built within a wall; inner courtyards are the focus of development, rather than the streets outside. Cellular fabric tends to much variation in the process of being spun; the cells of Beijing's Nanluoguxiang district or Sana'a's Arabic old town compose a mottled tapestry of courtyards of varying size and shape within the walls. Most courtyards house families, but can also contain more public places – souks and bazaars, and churches, mosques and synagogues – which exist as secret realms rather than being nakedly exposed.

The third kind of fabric is the additive grid. This was Cerdà's plan for Barcelona. In it, there is a system of repeating, equal-sized blocks without the central orienting axis that there is in the Roman, orthogonal form. Cerdà imagined that his blocks could be extended across the Barcelona plain, wrapping around its old city, opening it up at its edges. His idea to add block after block began to be realized in the 1860s in the new Eixample neighbourhood, stretching along the Mediterranean coast. Rather than monotonous repetition, there are focal points in the overall plan Cerdà made for Barcelona in 1859 – green spaces distributed throughout the city rather than concentrated in one place, like pearls sewn into an otherwise even fabric.[16]

Today, the rapid growth of urban population favours the creation of additive grids in cities flooded by mass migration, as in Mexico City, because it can provide housing fast. A cellular grid is more slowly spun; an orthogonal on the Roman model demands a level of overall planning control missing in many barrios and other informal settlements. In terms of built form, the skyscraper is a vertical additive grid, each floor repeating the ones below and above. Today, eighteen to thirty-four storeys is the norm for housing in Chinese cities built from scratch, forty to sixty storeys the commercial norm for construction in both Global North and South; it will soon be more cost-effective to build much higher. Within the envelope of the vertical grid, as internal support posts become ever fewer, the service stack, that is, the floor's toilets and elevators, becomes the node of each storey.

Each of these grid forms defines a particular space of power, or of resistance to power. The divisible grid enacted Roman domination, political power radiating out from the centre and reproducing itself in each subdivided space. The cellular grid has often served powerless inhabitants as a secretive space, difficult for the authorities to penetrate – as it did for Christians in ancient Jerusalem, or for Shanghai residents in Mao's early reign. The additive grid has in the modern era served as a tool of capitalist power. Lewis Mumford asserted, in plans like that for New York in 1811, which envisioned endless, regular blocks above Greenwich Village, that it 'treated the individual lot and the block, the street and the avenue, as abstract units for buying and selling, without respect for historic uses, for topographic conditions or for social needs'.[17]

Two of these forms are hospitable to social life in the *cité*, court-yard fabric obviously so by conducting so many activities out in the open in a shared space. The Roman-style grid has also focused social life by concentrating activities at the intersections of streets. The problem is the additive grid. How do you make it sociable? How, in fabric terms, do you make it nubbly?

This is the question Cerdà sought to solve in Barcelona. His grid scheme went ahead in 1860, after a proposal by the architect Antoni Rovira i Trias foundered, a plan which would have expanded the city slowly, in waves of concentric circles radiating out from its medieval centre. The Cerdà scheme, though initially consisting of just thirty-two blocks, was far more grandiose, the planner seeking to incorporate the immense amounts of empty land which lay outside the legal boundaries of the city. 'He hoped', the urbanists Eric Firley and Caroline Stahl note, 'that this virtually unlimited supply would keep land values low, therefore allowing him to provide affordable accommodation for the poor.'[18]

Cerdà envisioned mixed housing on what has come to be called the 'Dutch model', in which the apartments made for different social classes coexist in the same building without being visibly distinguished: ringing the bell for apartment 4-C, you have no idea how rich are the people within; there would be no 'poor doors' of the sort which typifies schemes for mixed housing today in New York – the rich entering by the front, the poorer residents by the side or back. In his own time, Cerdà's intention for housing sharply contrasted to the Haussmannian building, where the higher you climb, the poorer you know that the tenants are going to be.

How did Cerdà translate these intentions into planning the *ville*? Each block of his grid originally consisted of two big, shoebox-shaped buildings facing one other with a big open space in between; these *intervalos* were to take up at least 50 per cent of the ground in each block, so that lots of light and breeze could circulate throughout. As the plan evolved, the two facing shoeboxes were connected on the sides, creating a four-sided building with a huge interior courtyard – the 'perimeter block' of planning jargon. A perimeter block equal on all four sides differs from a palace courtyard with a main building with side-arms and an entrance wall in front. The move from *intervalo* to perimeter was forced on Cerdà. So much open space for the poor in his original plan was treated as an impossible luxury, as in La Barceloneta, a workers' suburb outside Barcelona in which, by 1900, almost all of the plots of land were occupied by building mass. Cerdà's generous original provision of space affirmed, on the contrary, workers' rights to air, light and space.

Cerdà paid close attention to the underground infrastructure of water beneath the streets of the grid, attuned to advances in sanitation displayed at the Great Exhibition at the Crystal Palace in London in 1851, particularly to the efficient flushing toilets devised by the engineer-inventor George Jennings. Cerdà sought to apply some of the same principles of managing waste to sewer systems underground.[19]

As regards the social problem of the additive grid, evolution rather than intention came to the rescue. Initially the *intervalos* were meant to be the sociable spaces, while the streets would serve vehicles. To accommodate turning vehicles, Cerdà made a little diagonal slice at the edges of his blocks, so that turning corners became rounded, easy and smooth. Just as a carpenter chamfers a table leg to soften its edge, Cerdà chamfered his grid to accommodate speeding carriages. This shaving of the edge may seem trivial, but it proved immensely consequential socially, because the *cité* which arose in Cerdà's *ville* lay just there.

The change began when the ends of each block were capped during the 1860s. Now there was a continuous building mass around all four sides, enclosing the *intervalo*. The function of the chamfered corner changed in tandem with this enclosure. The perimeter block's chamfered edge now created a new, wonderfully hospitable site in which people could gather. The octagonal-shaped site did not so much push vehicles out as invite people in: traffic, parking, drinking and lounging were all mixed up at the corners – still evident in Barcelona today.

A space thereby became a place. Sheer scale in part made the difference between a boulevard café, along Haussmannian lines, and a café located in the octagonal of the Cerdian grid; the Paris boulevard cafés were far bigger and their clientele less local. The difference in speed was as important as that of scale: as the corners clogged with people, they became places in which to slow down, rather than spaces in which to speed up. Most important, these sociable spaces were not

spaces of spectacle in the Haussmannian sense; they were neighbourhood scenes rather than gathering points for strangers coming from
all over the city.

Monoculture Cerdà's legacy is in many ways admirable: he sought
to build a city for all, with the grid as a space of equality and sociability. But Cerdà's idea of the *ville* also embodied a danger: the additive
grid as a monoculture. The danger is apparent in farming, where
monocultures exhaust the soil and are subject to rampant diseases,
whereas biodiverse fields are healthier and more resilient. This logic
of biodiversity applies to urban environments as well. Plans made of
additive parts, meant to repeat on an ever-expanding scale, are pecu-
liarly subject to ills of a social and economic sort, because once one
block begins to degrade, there's no reason other blocks, exactly similar in form, will not succumb.

The vulnerability of Cerdian idea appears dramatically in commercial property: an assemblage of uniform buildings, as in London's
Canary Wharf, succumbs to boom-and-bust cycles, since the devalua-
tions which apply to one building apply to other, similar structures.
As the housing analyst Anne Power has shown, there are social consequences of monoculture, as can be seen on British public housing
estates. Problems which begin in one building – a disruptive neighbour
or drug-taking among children – spread quickly, 'like a plague', because
there is no reason why any other part of the estate should be different
socially as well as physically. A peculiar disease of perimeter blocks
built for poor people on the Cerdian model is that courtyards can
become clotted with interior additions or storage shacks, the shrunken
space then admitting less air; dark and dank also means dangerous in
such a space. A uniform environment easily sickens, as it has in perimeter housing estates from Moscow to Vienna to London.[20]

The tragedy of Cerdà's visionary work is that he meant none of this
to happen; his project aimed at equalizing the *cité* through equalizing
the *ville*. The remedy seems clear: the alternative to monoculture in
the built environment is a collaging of different building types,
people and activities, which may appear visually and socially a mess,
but in the long run will prove more resilient than a single-species
environment. Open-systems thinking counsels exactly this kind of

mixing; the whole then becomes greater than the sum of its parts. Put another way, the fabric does not tear so easily. How then to build this stronger urban fabric? The third giant in urbanism's first generation thought Nature suggested an answer.

Landscape When Alexis de Tocqueville first came to America, in 1831, the usual way for a foreigner to journey to New York was to sail into the harbour from the south, a route which afforded the voyager a sudden view of the crowd of masts along the packed wharves, behind which were offices, homes, churches and schools. This New World scene appeared to be a familiar European one of prosperous mercantile confusion, like that of Antwerp or the lower reaches of London on the Thames. Tocqueville instead approached New York from the north, along the coast. His first view of Manhattan on 11 May was of its bucolic upper reaches, still in 1831 undeveloped farmland dotted with a few hamlets. At first what excited him about the view of the city was the sudden eruption of a metropolis in the midst of a nearly pristine natural landscape. He felt the enthusiasm of a European coming here who imagines he can plant himself in this unspoiled landscape – that America is fresh and simple and Europe is stale and complex.

After that fit of youthful enthusiasm passed, New York began to disturb him. No one seemed to care about the natural environment in itself, and the buildings in the city were treated just as indifferently, people scurrying out of offices and restaurants and shops without much minding or even noticing how they were made. Throughout his American journey, Tocqueville was struck by the lightweight character of American settlement – nothing was made to last, nothing was permanent. The reason was that the American 'new man' was too driven to settle; 'keep moving' was the frontier mentality.

Though it was one of the oldest cities in America, New York's planners indeed treated it as if it, too, were a city on the frontier. In 1811, they imposed an additive grid in one go on Manhattan – from Canal Street, the edge of dense settlement, up to 155th Street – and then in 1868 proposed a second stage which would extend the grid to the island's tip, and in Brooklyn east from its old harbour. The settlers on the frontier, whether from fear or prejudice, treated the

Indians as animals in the landscape rather than as fellow human beings; on the frontier nothing civilized existed, it was a void to be filled up. Planners could no more adapt to the existing landscape in New York than they could in Illinois, even when, practically, some more flexible arrangement than streets in a grid would make better use of a hill or better suit the vagaries of Manhattan's water table. Inexorably, the development in the grid abolished every farm or hamlet it encountered as it spread.

The third giant of the 1850s generation, the American Frederick Law Olmsted, tried to address this destructiveness by asserting the social value of nature in the city. Like Haussmann, unlike Cerdà, he was not armed with a craft. The scion of a well-to-do family in New England, he dabbled in agricultural studies and literature, his adult life then taking shape as a journalist. A turning point in his life occurred when, as a young man, Olmsted travelled to Liverpool and wrote a book about what he saw. His description of Liverpool echoes Engels' critique of Manchester, yet the young Olmsted had only the conviction that something should be done – without knowing what to do.

Liverpool had been one of the seats of British slave trading – an injustice which had disappeared by his visit – but the city's history sharpened his conscience about racial slavery at home. After his visit, but before the Civil War, he then made a tour of slave states at home, writing what remains today a gripping account. Race slavery in the South had, in his view, produced a terrible irony: the master's lash provoked stoic endurance and hidden forms of mutual support among the enslaved, while it had enervating, degrading effects on the whites who whipped rather than worked.

This consciousness about race turned Olmsted towards thinking about parks as places where the races could mix – off the plantation, in a city. It's not clear why Olmsted thought he could design parks, conceiving suddenly of himself as a 'landscape gardener', or, as we would say today, a landscape architect. This was pure self-invention along Pico della Mirandola's lines. As a maker of urban parks, Olmsted followed in the wake of centuries of architect-gardeners in Europe; as physical constructions, Olmsted's parks owe much to an immediate American predecessor, Andrew Jackson Downing, who in the 1840s developed cemeteries inside cities like Mount Auburn Cemetery in Cambridge, Massachusetts, as gathering places for the living as well as resting places for the dead. Olmsted had a different idea of the mixed uses of a park.

He thought of these racially mixed parks as 'gregarious' rather than 'neighbourly' places, the first being large spaces, bringing together people from all over the city, as against the second, which were small spaces serving only locals and tended to be more uniform in identity. The 'gregarious' park should also be inclusive of Christians and Jews, Irish and German immigrants – all Americans. In other words, inclusion was more possible in an impersonal space of strangers than in the more intimate space of neighbours. In this, Olmsted defined a social ethic for the city. People who differ had better be tied together in impersonal public spaces than in small communities. So problematic has that ideal of inclusion in public space proved that we need to understand in detail how Olmsted sought to enact it in the design of Central Park.[21]

Central Park was begun in 1858 and, in its original form, pretty much finished by 1873. It is the joint work of Olmsted and his partner Calvert Vaux: Olmsted the amateur did the general designing and dealt with the politics and the public, while Vaux the trained architect focused on the underground infrastructure of drainage, and above ground on the park's bridges and buildings. The Park is a tract of land, 843 acres, originally heavy clay with rocky outcroppings, located north of built-up New York. At the time, the 'central' in Central Park was pure fantasy, since it was far from the city. Since the early nineteenth century, free blacks and Irish had farmed the land and created little hamlets with churches and cemeteries. Olmsted's project destroyed this existing, integrated, rural life for the sake of a visionary, integrated, urban life.[22]

Olmsted began his 'gregarious' invitation at the park's edges. The park is lined with low fences and there are many entry points. The planning commissioners wanted big, ceremonial entrances framing the park, which Olmsted contested: more modest gates signalled 'that all were welcome, regardless of rank or wealth'. This seemingly small detail also marked Olmsted's attitude towards the urban masses as diametrically opposed to Haussmann's: stout gates framed the new parks in Paris because Haussmann was obsessed with crowd control. Olmsted rejected the fear that a huge park would inevitably be unsafe at night; therefore Central Park was to be open and easy of access at any time. By the time the park was built in 1873, many distinctive spaces appeared which were not in the original plans, for example spaces at the north-east and south-west corners which could be used casually. Over time, the programming of other spaces became increasingly loose.[23, 24]

So familiar has this park become, its natural landscape seeming to have been always there, that both native New Yorkers and visitors have lost any sense of just how artificial it is. Four thousand men worked over the course of its construction to transport 5 million cubic yards of material to build the hills and open fields we think have always been there. Its amenities are all inventions: a bandstand set in the midst of a new planted forest, a playing field laid out where there used to be scrub. You might imagine a swamp can simply be enlarged into a lake or other water feature. Not so. The swamps have to be drained in order to be reshaped; the hugh reservoir at the Park's north end was fed externally.

The most miraculous artifices to me are Vaux's bridges. They are dug down into the land, so that the through-traffic they enable across the park from east to west is not visible on the surface. Vaux's is a different take from Haussmann's on transport: Haussmann put fast-moving traffic at ground level, whereas Vaux sunk it below ground, making the bridges pedestrian walkways. What's wonderful about the pedestrian bridges is the playful variety of forms their mouths take; as you come to the Denesmouth Bridge, it seems as though you are going to be sucked into Hades, while the Gothic Bridge invites children to scramble up and down it over the traffic below.

But Olmsted's vision proved as fragile a plan for mixing social differences as did Eixample in Barcelona. Within forty years, the perimeter of Central Park filled in along Fifth Avenue with individual mansions for the wealthy, at the same time as Central Park West began to be lined with apartment blocks for the upper-middle class. As privilege surrounded the Park, the people inside it became less mixed; the lower classes and the poor did not commute to its pleasures regularly, as Olmsted had hoped, but more rarely on special occasions. Within, the Park began to decay physically. Vaux's infrastructure 'bones' remained good, but the playing fields and ponds deteriorated through neglect. Massive investments were required in the 1960s to rescue the Park from crime and decay.[25]

Still, it remained a provoking proposition: social inclusion can be physically designed, contrary to Rudofsky's belief that the *ville* takes a backseat to the *cité*. What gives this proposal muscle is, I think, the very artificiality of the place.

Artifice Pastoral writers since Virgil have evoked the peace the natural world could bring to those disgusted with the struggle for power or the burdens of life. In a way the relief seems obvious – putting cares out of mind for a while, dwelling instead in a world of ever-blooming gardens, roads meant only for strolls, views and prospects which never fail to please. In this regard, nothing was meant to seem more inviting in eighteenth-century Paris than the vast Place Louis XV (Place de la Concorde). Though exactly in the centre of Paris, and dotted with fountains and statues, it was left to grow into an urban jungle in which people wandered erratically (looking nothing like it does today). The Place Louis XV contrasted to royal gardens built outside cities, like Louis XIV's Versailles or Frederick the Great's Sans Souci palace, which were disciplined by lines of trees marching with military straightness to vanishing points: the kings commanded nature. In the Place Louis XV, nature was left free. But these urban oases were meant at the outset only for an elite. Central Park, so its creator hoped, invited the masses.

As much as Engels, Olmsted knew that the conditions were harsh for the mass of people; Olmsted's park was meant to ease the oppressiveness of the city – but his twist was to think that racial tensions in a city could be escaped, or at least diminished, in such a pleasure-oriented space. People would mix together sociably for the sake of pleasure here, whereas functional places like factories, or even commercial streets, would not promote 'gregarious' impulses. Artifice animates sociability, while reality deadens it. This isn't quite an aery ideal; today, there is more racial contact on the playing fields or among the picnickers in Central Park than in the city's transport or its working spaces. Olmsted hoped his designs would make pleasure's sociable gift via a particular kind of illusion.[26]

Olmsted thought of the park as a theatre – which in itself was nothing new. As in London's Vauxhall and Ranelagh Gardens, eighteenth-century urban gardens housed puppet shows, bearpits and other amusements; in Balzac's day, the gardens within the Palais Royal in central Paris put on a twenty-four-hour sex show. Olmsted was more puritanical, conceiving of his park as offering more innocent pleasures: the theatrical spectacle lay in the uses of natural means to create a vivid illusion: the park as a theatre of nature.

Again, Olmsted was certainly not the first landscaper to think of nature and illusion as sisters. In the eighteenth century, untamed, free-flourishing gardening was dubbed 'English', seeming to be nature run riot spontaneously. The 'boundless garden', in the words of Robert Harbison, lacks an 'obvious beginning or end . . . the bounds are confused on all sides'. These wild English gardens were in fact cleverly calculated illusions. Disorder was designed by mixing species of flowers from different parts of the world, shoving flowers of different blooming periods next to one another, and carefully composing contrasting foliage into a background for the flowers; such planting techniques expressed the same desire to create an environment of seemingly untamed, ever-productive free growth, among which it was, however, also possible to stroll even if one was wearing a wide pannier skirt – by chance nature had also provided a winding alley of crushed stone to walk upon.

The English garden designers saw no conflict between the natural and the artificial. The artifices could be, indeed, transparent illusions – for instance, in the distance sheep might graze, but for some reason they never came close enough to foul the paths with sheepshit. The sheep were kept at bay by ha-has, invisible ditches cut into the ground. People were conscious of, and took pleasure in, this artifice; inspecting a ha-ha was part of the pleasure of a stroll. In the same way, perceptible artifice marks Vaux's bridges in Central Park, with their play of visible-at-ground-level and invisible-beneath derived from the earlier British ha-ha. In sum, the sociable ethic entails a suspension of reality; theatre does the suspending.

The High Line is one modern parallel to the landscape work Olmsted and Vaux did in Central Park. If you were homeless in the 1960s, you climbed up a set of disused railroad tracks on the west side of Manhattan to sleep rough; if you were gay, you went there for anonymous sex; day and night the railway tracks served as a drugs bazaar. 'Everyone' knew the High Line would have to come down; a few people who were not included in 'everyone', notably the architect Elizabeth Diller, thought differently. She noted that interesting weeds sprouted in the crevices of the railway tracks. With the innovative landscapers James Corner and Piet Oudolf, she imagined that railroad tracks + interesting weeds = a new kind of urban promenade. This proposition proved a great success. The High Line now attracts large numbers of natives out for a stroll as well as tourists drawn to the novelty of the place.

One connection to Olmsted lies in the artifice of the planting itself: on this unlikely terrain Piet Oudolf planted species that do not cohabit on the ground. The landscaping combines ruderals, which are fast-growing plants that tend to die young, that is, most weeds, but also annual flowers; competitors which tend to crowd others out, but commit floral suicide by exhausting nutrients in the soil, as many grasses do; and stress tolerators like sea kale which need protection to get going, but once established do well in low-nutrient environments. The planting scheme in the High Line, using a system of tray-shaped enclosures, keeps the three going all at once, producing an illusion of 'natural' biodiversity for the visitor.[27]

In New York and other big cities, parks and playgrounds can be built in other unlikely places, again following Olmsted's tie between artificial and sociable space. I was involved in one such project in the 1980s – a park built over a sewage treatment plant on the west side of Manhattan in Harlem, along the Hudson River. Despite our best efforts, there was for some years a strong whiff of the sewage beneath. However, the kids in the community needed a place to play and adapted to the smell until we learned how to fix it. In urbanism generally, when we speak about 'naturalizing' a condition, what is really meant is that an arbitrary construction like this comes to be taken for granted. 'Naturalizing' means that an artifice becomes accepted on its own terms within the mentality of the *cité*.

Olmsted didn't think in the ecological terms we use today, in which a seamless join between nature and man-made is the aim. There's no smooth integration between the planted and sculpted world of the park with the street plantings, drainage tables or tidal walls of the city's infrastructure. Central Park does contain an immense reservoir, but its functional ecological role proved fraught – the filthy water required an immense amount of expensive purification, and it was abandoned by the end of the nineteenth century. The reservoir makes a gesture of practicality, but that is not really what the park is about. Rather than see Olmsted as a failed ecologist, it makes more sense to think of him both as a sociologist who wants to use soil and plants to bring people together, and as a theatre director of the planted world itself.

The rule of an illusion Frederick Law Olmsted's hopes for racial harmony lay in removing people from labour into a space of leisure; the park was meant to suspend hostilities in the outside world which were felt by rich and poor as well as black and white. This vision has now turned sour in the modern city. In its ever-greater reliance on tourism, the pleasure/consumption economy has become more a focus of urbanism, but sociable mixing is not the result.

It may seem absurd to compare Central Park to the clean-up of Times Square in New York, but in fact they are linked in the effort to create theatricality. For a century the home of theatre in New York, Times Square housed – until two generations ago – a thriving drug culture on its streets and in its doorways, as well as provisioning the city's sex industry in cheap hotels. It was a place of petty robberies and shoplifting (though not of grievous violence; in New York, as elsewhere in America, violent crime is more prevalent in domestic settings than on the streets).

The clean-up entailed the destruction of many run-down buildings in an eighteen-square block area. Though these housed sex workers and sheltered drug addicts, the buildings also contained many small workshops along their grungy corridors: seamstresses working on costumes for the theatres, or cutting cloth patterns to be used in the garment district south of Times Square. The smell of pot in the corridors of these buildings could mingle with the scent of fresh-cut wood, for Times Square also contained thriving businesses which made specialty furniture. Cheap rents made these urban workshops possible. Before the clean-up, hundreds of small restaurants and bars served these workers; Greeks and Italians ran these places, some of which looked like the inside of a refrigerator, others like dusty plastic copies of the 'old country'. They would have been attractive to no tourist, nor did the *New York Times* rate them, though many *New York Times* workers hung out in them in the days when the *Times* was actually printed in Times Square.

In the clean-up, after the rabbit-warren buildings came down, upmarket office towers and apartment blocks arose, and the workshops departed. The costume-makers left for New Jersey, the button-makers became mail-order, and some of the older musical instrument-makers decided to retire, while younger ones retreated to barns in the countryside. Times Square today is a territory for tourists, with the services required by mass tourism: packaged entertainment, chain-store places to eat, standardized hotels. That's nothing to be snooty about, save that few New Yorkers go to this centre of New York by choice. As in London's Trafalgar Square, it looks full of life, but is a black hole for residents. Tourists and locals do not mix, and few package-tour groups mix with each other. Their pleasures are organized and contained.

No one can be held accountable for what happens after they are dead. However Olmsted, admirable even noble in his aspirations, inaugurated a certain emphasis on removing the signs and sites of labour in his planning of sociable spaces in the city, the equating of sociability with artifice so that the city itself becomes a kind of theatre – translated commercially into tourism, this can have a deadening effect on the city's centre.

The great generation of urbanists all sought to shape the *ville* in order to mobilize the city, albeit in contrasting ways: Haussmann sought to make the city accessible, Cerdà to make it equal, Olmsted to make it sociable. Each plan had its limitations. The network incisions Haussmann made in Paris privileged space over place. The fabric Cerdà devised for Barcelona proved a monoculture. Olmsted privileged artificial pleasure in order to promote social integration, but did not succeed. It may seem ridiculous to critique them for not having solved at the outset the huge problems posed by the modern city. None the less, there is an element missing in their plans for the *ville*, which is also absent in the labours of the civil engineers. This missing element is a reflection on the distinctive material of which the cité is made: its crowds. How does this dense human substance relate to urban form?

IV. THE CROWD

At the nineteenth century's end, two writers sought to make sense of density. Both were interested in crowd psychology but in quite opposite ways. One explored a classic sort of crowd, the unruly mob rampaging, letting their passions hang out. The other investigated an experience of feeling crowded which makes people uptight and withdrawn.

The mob Gustave Le Bon was an unashamed royalist who tried to make sense of the excitement which coursed through the veins of mobs, as in the first French Revolution when crowds roamed the streets searching for royalists to attack. Before Le Bon, the mob was treated by reactionary writers as a self-evident horror, a mass composed of riff-raff and the lower orders. To Le Bon the matter was not so simple; a profound change could come over people of a more varied background when fused into a crowd, causing them to hunt in packs like wolves.

The key, to him, lay in how mobs take form, his insight being that, whenever large numbers of people gather, they can 'together commit crimes they would never do alone'. In part this is due to the simple fact that in the mass people become anonymous – they are no longer identifiable singly and particularly individually; the dense mass ensures that the individual cannot be held to account. Psychologically, as a group swells in size, there is an exhilarating feeling of 'us', of release, of being free to do anything; Le Bon says that 'grandiosity' replaces more sober reasoning, as people discover a new shared energy. 'Let's go get the king; nothing can stop us.' This mobilization of crowd energy is inseparable from the creation of spectacle:

behead the king, or just stone any aristocrat who happens along a street; drama takes the place of reasoning.[28]

This analysis of crowd psychology made Le Bon a founding father of social psychology, since he argued that the group has a different set of feelings and behaviours than the individuals who compose it, understood singly. Le Bon's ideas about the vicious mob were taken up by Sigmund Freud from about 1921 on in his writings on group psychology. The mob's capacity to transform individuals – that is, degrade them en masse – became an urgent theme during the Fascist and Nazi 1930s. Elias Canetti sought to understand how this transformation came over 'good Germans' and Ortega y Gasset considered its effects on normally peaceful Spaniards.[29, 30, 31] The crowd suspends moral judgement.

Le Bon himself figured as the analyst of a very dark *cité*, but though cities with their huge crowds would seem the natural home for this transformation, he did not have very much of interest to say about them. Almost any big space would serve, he thought: the entrance of Versailles Palace during the first French Revolution, the forecourt of the Louvre during the second, the halls of the Hotel de Ville during the Commune. A more spatially sensitive analysis came from Georg Simmel, a contemporary of Le Bon, who deduced an entirely different psychology from the experience of feeling crowded, pressed in and pressurized by others.

Feeling crowded In 1903, eight years after Le Bon's book *The Crowd* appeared, Georg Simmel wrote a short essay, 'Die Großstädte und das Geistesleben', to accompany an exhibition in Dresden. The essay is usually translated into English as 'The Metropolis and Mental Life'. The German word 'Geist' is close to what the French call a mentality, in this case a mentality of place. The *Großstäd* Simmel had in mind was Berlin, which made Dresden in 1903 an odd sponsor of Simmel's inquiry, since the place was sleepy-small-town in outlook; Dresden's civic worthies were predictably unhappy with Simmel's essay.[32]

Simmel engaged with the sensory overload which occurs when masses of people press together. He wrote that the basic characteristic of the big-city *cité* is 'the intensification of nervous stimulation which results from the swift and uninterrupted change of outer and inner stimuli' – liquid modernity in the streets. He is describing Potsdamer Platz in Berlin, the hectic crossroads of the German capital; specifically he is describing the crowds on its sidewalks, a mixed, moving mass of shoppers and commuters. Here, in Berlin's middle, a huge space was filled by big department stores and vast cafés, by traffic on foot, in horse-drawn omnibuses and in private carriages, the public transport bringing in Berlin's ever-larger, ever-more polyglot population of young provincials, displaced foreigners and the burgeoning mass of soldiers garrisoned to the city. On the sidewalks, like those in Potsdamer Platz, a sensory overload occurs in 'crossing the street'; here 'the tempo and multiplicity of economic, occupational and social life' quickens.[33]

Haussmann and Olmsted sought, in different ways, to increase the intensity of urban life. Simmel feared it. Too much stimulation causes anxiety: a car honks, your eyes swivel and so you nearly bump into an elderly man who is navigating forward erratically. Your attention is caught a moment later by a homeless person crouching and begging, who, noticing you noticing, makes to rise. You feel crowded by all these sensations, and so, to protect yourself, you put a lid on your reactions. '[T]he metropolitan type of man ... develops an organ protecting him against the threatening currents and discrepancies of his external environment ... He reacts with his head instead of his heart.' You don't freeze when the horn honks; to the rising beggar you give no responding sign, instead marching ahead, avoiding eye contact. You absorb impressions but you don't show yourself to be vulnerable. You display cool.[34]

This is Simmel's mask. The phrase is mine, not his; his phrase is the display of a 'blasé attitude', which doesn't quite do his idea justice, since people are not really indifferent to their surroundings, only acting as though they were. The blasé attitude results in blasé behaviour: you see stuff happening and you move on, you don't get involved. Of course the blasé attitude can become a cartoon, as in the famous – and apocryphal – story of people in Times Square stepping over the fallen body of a tourist who has had a heart attack. Moreover, a soldier might question if there's anything specifically urban about being blasé; under fire, even if comrades are dying or crying out in pain, the competent soldier must keep order in the group by a display of sangfroid cool, by not going to pieces in the eyes of others, no matter what he or she is feeling inside.

The word 'blasé' also doesn't do justice to what Simmel has in mind because he is thinking about anxiety in a large framework. The mask which a person dons for self-protection deploys a kind of rationality. A person step backs and calculates, rather than responds on impulse. 'The reaction to metropolitan phenomena is shifted to that organ which is least sensitive . . . intellectuality is . . . seen to preserve subjective life against the overwhelming power of [the outside].' The great city concentrates these invasive forces in its crowds; they pose a threat to the inner life. Its densities push people to close in on themselves: though over-stimulated, outwardly they reveal little.[35]

Simmel's biography matters to the blasé mentality he describes. He was only notionally Jewish, since his father had converted to Catholicism and his mother was a Lutheran; in Jewish law, because of his Christian mother, he was 'lost to Judaism'. But not in Kaiser Wilhelm's Germany. Though steered towards academic opportunities by Max Weber, anti-Semitism pushed back and he could not get a regular academic post for a long time. However, Simmel shed no tears for himself; nor, he argued, should other German Jews. Jews need a mask: stay cool, keep your distance, do not react visibly to painful stimuli. The outside still hurts – all the more because the hurt is bottled up. The Jew's dilemma Simmel sees as emblematic of modern man or woman. He writes that the 'deepest problems of modern life derive from the claim of the individual to preserve the autonomy and individuality of his existence in the face of . . . external culture, and of the technique of life'; faced with the danger of being typecast, the individual needs a protective mask so that he or she won't feel swallowed up in the 'social-technological mechanism'. Impersonality can protect the self.[36]

This is a majestic, indeed tragic, view of the mentality of urban life. But it's not very explicitly connected to the *ville* – to the built forms which might cause people to feel crowded. To explain the connection, we need to quit Simmel's grand vision for a moment, to recount how feeling relates to a specific urban form – the sidewalk.

The sidewalk There are two ways that feeling crowded can be measured. One is 'footfall density', which counts the number of bodies passing by a fixed spot; in my own planning practice, for instance, a team will clock how many people pass a store entrance every five minutes. The other measure is 'sessile density', the numbers of people who are confined or choose to remain in a place for a more extended period, for example a crowd in a football stadium or a café. Footfall density is not a stable number. Thoroughfares meant for ceremonial processions, for instance, are only intermittently dense with people, of which Gorki Street in Moscow is a good example. From being a messy, mixed thoroughfare in the nineteenth century, Soviet urbanists started in 1937 to transform it into a space for Stalinist spectacle. Its façades, tarted up with the heavy classical motifs favoured by the dictator, contained massive crowds of people only a few times a year, the rest of the time it was an empty frame. Simmel conflated peak use like this with constant use.[37]

He was on more secure ground in associating over-stimulation with sidewalks. Streets which confine density to sidewalks are relatively modern. The wide, raised sidewalk which marked Haussmann's urbanism permitted dense pedestrian crowds to inhabit the streets while protecting them from speeding carriages. Until the appearance of industrially cut paving or macadam roads, there were few such pedestrian channels; the street as well comprised the space in between buildings. Only in the modern period did the raised sidewalk become a general feature in the fabric of European and American cities. This was possible thanks in part to the industrial manufacturing of perforated iron pipes in the 1820s, which allowed a street to drain, sidewalks thereupon being laid at a subtle tilt to sluice water into the street.[38]

The effectiveness of a sidewalk depends on what's beneath it. Early sidewalk-makers dug drainage pipes raw into the ground, but Bazalgette's generation realized that drainage cavities needed to be dug out around them; pipe-within-tunnel is the form still used today. Though a sidewalk had and has to be higher than a roadbed, it cannot be too high, otherwise there are accessibility problems for the elderly and for children; in my practice, our rule of thumb is to peg sidewalk height at 75 per cent of a normal household step, that is, about 16 centimetres.

The translation of 'dense' into 'crowded' derives physically from the compressive effects of sidewalks, in comparison to the looser movements of navigating older, more amorphous street space. Curiously, the narrowness of a sidewalk doesn't correlate well with the feeling of compression, since a wide sidewalk will often be the more populated, and can more easily house sessile densities. Feeling crowded on a sidewalk also varies from culture to culture. Noon-time sidewalk densities in New York's mid-town Sixth Avenue are about 80 per cent greater than those in London's Piccadilly, which can make the London street seem uncrowded to the visiting New Yorker, though insufferably stuffed to the native Londoner.[39]

The other *ville* factor determining how crowded streets feel is the alignment of street lines to building lines. If a building is set back from the edge of a sidewalk lane, the pressure of containment is relieved; this decompression becomes more pronounced when different structures have different setbacks. If, on the contrary, there are continuous street walls, as there are in most of Manhattan, the pressure of containment increases; the street, as it were, doesn't leak. A refinement of this distinction appears when lateral spaces between buildings are permitted, but still the edges of buildings all line up regularly in relation to a sidewalk or roadway – to use another metaphor, the teeth of the street are regular. Regular teeth have been in fact a long-standing aspiration of urban design; as far back as 1258, Roman law decreed that all the houses in the Via Larga (now Via Cavour) and other new streets line up evenly along the street.[40]

A third element in making a street feel crowded has more to do with dwelling than making. This is the tendency of people to want to clump together. The urbanist William H. Whyte found, two generations ago, when studying the spaces around the Seagram Building, Mies van der Rohe's skyscraper set in the very centre of New York, that people would choose to place themselves near to others rather than move as far away as possible. A supposed science called 'proxemics' charts how people choose to clump. Rather than laying down universal laws, proxemics emphasizes cultural specifics, as in the finding of one study that, during their end-of-the-day *passeggiata*, Italians prefer to stand closer to one another than do Norwegians lounging about after work. Variations of proxemics are a matter of common sense: whether Italian or Norwegian, while cruising for sex in a club, you will want to get closer to strangers than when shopping in a department store.[41]

The well-meaning urbanist will seek to satisfy, indeed to encourage, the desire to clump. For instance, by providing benches and other pieces of street furniture in groups, rather than distributing them in a more even but isolated fashion along a street; again, benches belong near bus-stop shelters, not far away from them. When I worked on a park project in New York City, my rule of thumb was to provide enough benches so that six Italian-sized families could gather in one spot. Sociable clumps more often form without premeditation on the planners' part. In Barcelona's dense Las Ramblas – a very long plaza lined by streets – people congregate in clusters rather than try to spread themselves out, though the boulevard was originally conceived for spread.[42]

Simmel wanted to explain the other, dark, unsociable side of the sidewalk. The American novelist Theodore Dreiser invoked the trope of the 'unseeing masses' to describe urban crowds, their coldness and indifference. Simmel didn't take this cliché at its face value. A mass of people will arouse negative feelings of being crowded and compressed; a sidewalk is the physical form which does the compressing. People then don a blasé mask to ward off feeling crowded – but even so, inside they seethe.

About the human DNA of a city it might seem that its crowds compose a triangle. Along one side lies mob behaviour; along another, blasé behaviour; along the third, more sociable feelings. Haussmann's constructions for Paris, in the military logic of those long, wide streets along which cannon could move, responded to the crowd as mob; ironically, the boulevards became instead places where people clumped. Cerdà and Olmsted believed in the sociable crowd, clustered at street corners or away from the street in parks. The triangle image does not convey, though, the complexity of the crowd as Simmel explained it: that experience of density on the streets which drives people inside themselves, shielding their subjectivity.

V. MODERN BUT NOT FREE – MAX WEBER IS UNHAPPY

As we have seen, the medieval adage which runs *Stadtluft macht frei* still resounds when people believe they are free to shape themselves in a city. At the end of the nineteenth century, Max Weber thought the modern city did not in fact provide that freedom – neither to individuals nor to the collective body of urban citizens. Max Weber's writings on cities appear as a chunk of his magnum opus, *Economy and Society*. The whole work is about much more than narrow economics; it's the social science equivalent of Wagner's *Ring* cycle. So far as I know, however, Max Weber never wrote a word about Cerdà, Haussmann or other modern urban designers. Even so, the author was in his own life quite sensitive to the place in which he lived; in between long bouts of depression, he walked its streets and avidly followed the fortunes of its citizens.[43]

The making of Weber's own Berlin followed the crafting of London and Paris. Berlin shared their problems of filth: August Bebel remembered 'waste-water from the houses collected in the gutters running alongside the kerbs and emitted a truly fearsome smell. There were no public toilets . . . as a metropolis, Berlin did not emerge from a state of barbarism into civilization until after 1870.' Once Bismarck had decreed Berlin to be the capital city, this state of affairs couldn't and didn't continue: an extensive sewer system was installed in the late 1870s, the beginnings of an equally spread-out public transport system laid in the 1890s. Massive brick and stone housing sprouted on land which before was dotted by shacks and vegetable gardens. This transformation occurred with great speed; the writer Stefan Zweig reminisced that 'the Berlin of 1905 was not like the city I had known in 1901 . . . it had become an international metropolis, which in turn paled beside the Berlin of 1910'. Even so, the monumental public spaces served as a cosmetic, covering up the fact that most of the city was poor.[44, 45]

To Weber, this capital, huge and showy as it had become, was not really a city. Berlin was but the mirror of a state: all its grand gestures of avenues and parks, the monuments, the ornate façades of buildings, dramatized the new nation. The city had no distinctive life of its own, because it did not control its own fortunes. By contrast, a true city for Weber seemed 'equipped with the following features: 1) the fortification; 2) the market; 3) own court of justice, and, at least in part, autonomous justice; 4) associative structure between different groups; 5) at least partial autonomy or self-rule . . . in which the citizens take part . . .'. In other words, a true city was, like ancient Athens or medieval Siena, a city-state.[46]

One way to make Weber's dry specifications concrete is to contemplate the walls around medieval cities. These walls were thick stone piles with few entrances, as in Siena. When an army laid siege to a city, citizens within and peasants outside sheltered behind them. The wall's gates were the tax-points of the city, the guards at the walls deciding who could trade inside. Within, the self-governing city was not a free market; instead the city regulated the price of bread, spices, bricks and furs. For this reason, Weber believes, the market was usually found in the centre of a city-state, so that traders could be easily observed and controlled. Most of all, the city-state could write and rewrite and re-rewrite its laws, bending them to changing circumstances beyond the walls as well as to shifts among people within. Last year's exile from Florence could become this year's citizen of Siena and then an exile without rights next year, depending on Siena's relations with Florence. In a city-state, *Stadt Luft macht frei* made sense, because the city could set people free – or unfree.

For Weber, citizenship is not a universal condition; rights and powers are place-based. If you don't live in a place, you shouldn't have the right to say what happens there (i.e. in today's terms, foreign investors' powers should be sharply curbed). Conversely, all citizens should enjoy certain basic rights because they lived in the same place – this city-state logic would generate the model for national passports and identity cards.

It's no big stretch to deduce how this view of the past would apply to the present. Weber's ideal type of the city would indict the modern city for its lack of self-control. Most obviously, no citizens voted to create a network of boulevards in Paris, a block fabric for Barcelona, or to locate a Central Park outside existing New York. These plans were arbitrary assertions of power, the first enabled by an emperor, the second by an unelected committee of notables, the third by a committee of planning commissioners who had not exposed the possibility of Central Park to much public discussion. More broadly, according to Weber, modern cities are not self-governing because national states, international businesses and ubiquitous bureaucracies rule. The city-states he admired were democracies in which the citizens had voted, as a whole, for the plans which shaped the *ville*.

Weber's version of the city-state brings out hives in some historians. If you compare Venice and Siena in 1500, for instance, the city on the water was firmly self-controlling, but was an oligarchy, whereas Siena was a failed experiment in democratic self-governance and by 1500 the toy-boy of neighbouring Florence. If there is a large element of idealization in Weber's picture of the city-state, still this kind of description serves a critical purpose. Weber's method is to create what he calls an 'ideal type' of social structures like the City, then explore why reality diverges from the model. Yes, reality is different, but you only noticed, Weber and Weberians riposte, because you have a coherent, ideal picture of City, or Free Market, or Christianity, to measure the crookedness. Here, in the ideal type of city-state, there will be a seamless connection between *ville* and *cité* (though Weber doesn't use those words) because a city-state creates physical forms like the wall which suit exactly how the citizens want to live.

Weber cast the five elements of his city as the rational, functional structure of a self-controlling place. The *cité* as a subjective experience, full of emotional angst, such as Simmel conceived it, is absent from this calculation. Such subjective tone-deafness of Weber's vast project seems indeed to have split him from Simmel. They originally shared a common interest in the qualitative understanding of experience (*Verstehen*), and Weber continued throughout his life to admire Simmel as a writer. But Weber's *Economy and Society* opens with the declaration: 'The present work departs from Simmel's method . . . in drawing a sharp distinction between subjectively intended and objectively valid "meanings".' In this, I think, the sociologist did himself a disservice.[47]

The bureaucrat at his or her desk, dully regulating everyday life via dry, abstract rules, repelled the sociologist – the bureaucrat's own lack of affect seeming to confine others to an 'iron cage'. Though he had little sympathy for the wild, Dionysian revels celebrated by Nietzsche, Weber feared that the real hallmark of modernity was life imprisoned in bureaucratic routine – a fear of too much orderliness which put him far from Engels' and Marx's image of the modern as 'all that is solid melts into air'. His emphasis on self-rule is not a desire for fixed procedure; he admires in Siena the continual rewriting of its laws, the ever-changing pricing of bread and bricks as the needs of the commune altered. Self-governance is for him a work in progress, rather than a fixed set of regulations.

Perhaps this attitude also explains why this mental omnivore had no taste for the urban plans going on all around him – plans which declared the solidity, the fixity, the bureaucratic permanence of the German state, but more widely asserted *the* plan for, *the* form of a modern city. We cannot ask him to spell out this critique, since he wrote only of the distant past; we can observe that his list of the elements which give a city-state life are open-ended in a way which has vanished. The implicit Weberian critique of the modern city is that its conditions do not favour the city as a self-revising, self-governing place, but favour bureaucratic over democratic processes.

Looking back on the birth of modern urbanism, this critique seems wide of the mark. The cities the Great Generation sought to shape were anything but stable places, as is life in the bureaucrat's cage. The Great Generation sought to impose different forms of order on the city, but each form was insufficient to solve the problems it addressed. Haussmann's networked city could not control its crowds; Cerdà's urban fabric could not realize the socialist aim of equalizing the city; nor Olmsted's parks alone provide the solution for a more sociable city. The Great Generation experimented with the city, encountering as any open experiment does, dead ends and defeats as well as successes. After them, in the twentieth century, the sting of defeat eased as urbanism became less ambitious about connecting the lived and the built.

3

Cité and *Ville* Divorce

The Great Generation struggled to connect *cité* and *ville*. Their heirs gave up on this struggle; instead, as in a marriage going wrong, corrosive silences took over; difficulties were not confronted. By the 1930s the two domains were well on the way to divorce. In family divorces, problems which parents can't face will be passed on to their children. In urbanism, this occurred after the Second World War, discolouring debates about how to open up the city.

I. PEOPLE AND PLACE UNCOUPLE — CHICAGO AND PARIS IGNORE EACH OTHER

Chicago Just after Weber celebrated the city-states of the Middle Ages, a group of Americans tried to gain a fuller, more positive appreciation of dwelling in the modern city. The University of Chicago was a good place to do this; since its creation in 1890, it had followed the German university model as a centre for research rather than the English model of a club for civilized young gentlemen. Though the university was located in the leafy south side of Chicago, and built to look like a medieval institution, its sociologists almost immediately left academic shelter. To the north and west of the university, Chicago had become a thriving, mixed, modern city. It served as a railway hub for the whole United States, and contained much more varied industries than did Manchester in the nineteenth century. European workers found refuge here up to the 1920s, when European emigration declined; in that post-war decade African Americans began migrating up from the old, racially paralysed Confederate states. The Chicago School wanted to find out what it was like to dwell in such a complex place.

Its founder, Robert E. Park, worked for twelve years as a crusading journalist, then studied with the philosopher and psychologist William James at Harvard, receiving an advanced degree in 1899. Afterwards he went to Berlin to study with Georg Simmel, seeking to tie the theorist's views about mentalities to empirical research. Park was an impressive figure: once home, he taught for seven years at an all-black technical college, the Tuskegee Institute. In 1914, he moved back to Chicago, magnetized by the city's energy.

Park disliked journalism's quick, slick encounters; instead, his Chicago School adopted field-work methods from anthropology, living in communities for extended periods, asking systematically what was in people's heads. The researchers drew on work done by W. I. Thomas and Florian Znaniecki on how Polish immigrants contrasted their peasant past to the industrial-worker present, interviewing the dirt-poor immigrants intensively and taking their thoughts seriously. By the beginning of the Second World War, the Chicago School had conducted hundreds of such studies, many of which are still, unfortunately, languishing in archives.[1]

Harvey Warren Zorbaugh's book *The Gold Coast and the Slum* embodied how the School set about its work. Tensions between rich and poor living close together on the near north side of Chicago gave the context; Zorbaugh focused on poor people living in the shadow of Chicago's skyscrapers, either in rooming houses or in cramped flats. The voices of the people themselves constitute big slices of his text; they discuss, for instance, the pawnbrokers to whom they resort to make ends meet, and what a poor family can pawn. Zorbaugh listens hard. Compared to Engels a century earlier, he is a much more systematic *flâneur*, working street by street, conducting pawnbroker conversations in each. He is also a more neutral presence than Engels until the end of the book: only then does he indict local politicians and institutions for letting down the poor.[2]

Community The Chicagoans were expert analysers of commmunity, but they were ambivalent about it. One reason for their unease lay in the history of the concept of 'community'. The idea can be traced back to Thomas Hobbes in the seventeenth century. Still famous for describing human existence in a state of nature as a 'war of all against all' (*bellum omnium contra omnes*), he would seem an unlikely godfather to celebrations of community. Yet from observing the behaviour of children in the aristocratic Cavendish family, to whom he served as tutor, he concluded that his charges had a strong desire for 'concord', taking pleasure in one another's company even when scrapping or arguing. To this pleasure he compared the condition of 'union', a more cool, contractual, political bond which restrained violence.

Hobbes's contrast between the sociable impulse of concord and the political need for union directly influenced the nineteenth-century sociologist Ferdinand Tönnies; he sorted out the distinction as one between *Gemeinschaft* and *Gesellschaft*, usually translated in English as the difference between 'community' and 'society'. The one embodies face-to-face, personalized encounters, the other impersonal and instrumental arrangements. The term 'neighbourhood' conveys how *Gemeinschaft* feels – friendly or hostile in daily relations with people not part of your immediate family. In society, in *Gesellschaft*, people don Simmel's mask. They are cool, blasé, with one another. This division is loaded, politically. Neighbourliness, as Tönnies understood it, doesn't address 'concord' at work – not good news if you were a labour organizer – or sociability in impersonal public places, which would be depressing to a parks designer like Olmsted. Tönnies shrunk the *cité*: life is local.

The Chicagoans were unhappy about this formulation for two reasons. The first was that Tönnies put community and work in separate boxes; he thought the work world embodied all that was cold and unfeeling in modern capitalism, and that only on leaving the factory gate or office door did people come alive emotionally. But the Chicagoans found that concord with neighbours often proved weaker than with fellow workers at the factories and slaughterhouses where the men worked. Because of such solidarity, W. I. Thomas argued that left-wing politics should focus on labour-organizing rather than on community-organizing. Thomas was driven out of the city of Chicago in the 1920s just because of his city-orientated politics, and because he was one of the first researchers in America on sexual social norms; he fled to the New School for Social Research in New York, where his work remained in the groove of the Chicago colleagues like Park, who fought and failed to protect him.[3]

Gender was the second reason Chicago had a problem with Tönnies. He thought unabashedly of *Gemeinschaft* as a feminine space and *Gesellschaft* as a masculine space – one reason Hitler was drawn to him. *Kinder, Küche* and *Kirche* (children, cooking and church) established for both sociologist and dictator community as a woman's realm. It's true that Tönnies simply mirrored the values of his own time. Even in cities like Engels' Manchester, where both sexes of the industrial proletariat had to work, the aspiration was that women should stop doing so, if the circumstances of the family improved in any way. So, too, as I found in a study of families in nineteenth-century Chicago, the first sign of upward mobility among the proletariat was female disengagement from paid labour.[4]

The Chicagoans took issue with Tönnies' beliefs in large part because the Great Depression had reoriented people's attitudes. A decade before the Second World War brought large numbers of women to work in Chicago war plants, the Depression had changed the labour landscape. Industrial jobs done by men were more at risk than the service jobs women did as nurses, waitresses, typists, minders of infants and teachers in elementary schools. Charlotte Towle, the Chicago School social worker, found that women who were pondering how to keep their unemployed or under-employed men from drink during the Great Depression moved naturally to a critique of capitalist immiseration in their thinking – though they wouldn't use those terms. If Tönnies shrunk the ethical horizon of *cité* by gendering it, the Chicago researchers found their female subjects in the Great Depression scaling up their consciousness.[5]

Both for reasons of labour and gender, the Chicagoans resisted Tönnies' romanticization of the local as a refuge from society, as though the neighbourhood is like a tropical island in the cold sea. Yet as researchers they focused on local communities. Why?

The School, influenced by John Dewey's belief in experience-based knowledge, created a method out of the recounting of personal experience: gone is Balzac's omniscient narrator, telling the reader what's up, no matter what his characters think. In the 1920s and 1930s, anthropologists, notably led by Claude Lévi-Strauss, explored the narrating of personal experience as a way of thinking about society. This challenged a social-science disposition to treat the histories people tell about their own lives as blind accounts, as innocent narratives in need of interpretation by the expert social scientist. The method of the School was to focus their subjects first on concrete, seemingly minor experiences, then to follow the trail as interpretation expanded. If a situation proved hard for people to make sense of, then the researcher accepted it was objectively so, not a matter of the subject's false consciousness or stupidity. However, the Chicagoans were uneasy about how to relate what they heard to their own politics.

Authorial anger bursts out at the end of Zorbaugh's study about the lives of slum-dwellers; it signalled that the School did not see its own role as entirely passive. The Chicagoans agonized over how to connect to their subjects just because of this. If the people they interviewed were seared by the world, the interpretative constructions people made out of those experiences were often less ideological than the interviewers' own progressive politics. Members of the School (my mother among them) tried to organize communist cells among African American women coming up from the rural south to Chicago, thinking that because these women were economically oppressed, they were ripe for organizing. Robert Park, Charlotte Towle, Louis Wirth and other elders of the Chicago School feared such moves from scholarship to politics, worrying that they would discolour the research itself. More than bow-tie prudence shaped these fears; the fieldworker might turn the poor into those two stock cartoon figures, the hapless victim or the heroic resister. Znaniecki had from the start, before the Great War, argued that a researcher should try to understand how oppressed people survive trauma rather than dwell on the fact that society traumatizes.

If their professional relation to politics remained problematic, the legacy of Chicago lies in how it thickened the meaning of two words: 'experience' and 'local'. They credited the steelworker as a competent subject to analyse his own experience. They showed that in this quest for self-understanding, the localities in which they lived did not induce an island mentality. These were the School's ethical convictions about person and place.

In their stress on complex knowledge, the Chicagoans might seem to have embraced the city whole, its physical forms as well as its people. But they did not. Their work emphasized the *cité*, but neglected the *ville*. They imagined the shape of the city in primitive two-dimensional terms, and thought about three-dimensional built forms not at all. The word mattered more to the Chicago School than the eye.

For instance, Park and his colleague Ernest Burgess created a peculiar two-dimensional image of the city. They used a bull's-eye target to make a map of a city, separating wealth, ethnicity and race, or functions like central business districts, manufacturing locales and residential places, into separate bands. The reason for the bull's-eye target was their belief that social and economic differences radiate out in concentric bands from a central core. The image was misleading. The circle is a tight, minimalist form, whereas, in terms of difference, big cities are made up of messy blobs and odd-shaped rhomboids which together compose a collage of poverty and wealth, functions or social groups.

The Park–Burgess procedure contrasts to the map-making which Charles Booth had undertaken a few decades earlier in poor parts of East London. Booth worked from the bottom up: street by street, house by house, he traced the wealth of inhabitants, showing how complicated a map of political economy could be, yielding no simple circle but rather a collage. Booth then asked himself, is this mere mess? If not, how do the elements in this complex picture interact? Booth's collage provokes reasoning about the image, while the Park–Burgess circle does not. Booth is reflexive rather than symbolic.

Two of the three versions of fabric produced by the founding generation of urbanists – the orthogonal cross and the additive block – were as reductive as the bull's-eye target. The generation immediately following began to query this simplicity and to transform the fabric. By 1900, planners sought to rebalance the unequal weight between street and boulevard, to vary on Paris's Left Bank, for instance, the flow of carriage traffic along the Boulevard

St-Germain so that it could support more pedestrian traffic. In Barcelona, planners began to focus on transforming the façades of the perimeter blocks as these extended through the city, fearing the monotony of the original Cerdian form.

The Chicagoans, on the other hand, did not think too much about how, when and where the bull's-eye target might morph into a blob. Their 'concentric zone theory' tied tight together form and function, imagining that each place in the city had a specific use – housing, industry, commerce or culture. The strict division of labour found in Henry Ford's automobile factories appeared to them also to mark urban space. This mechanistic view of the *ville* came from people who had anything but a mechanistic view of the *cité*.

The lack of interest the Chicago School had in three-dimensional, built form is surprising. By the early decades of the twentieth century, Chicago became the world's capital of modern architecture; it was home to Louis Sullivan and Frank Lloyd Wright, as well as to Daniel Burnham, the inheritor of Frederick Law Olmsted's work as a landscape designer. Burnham's Chicago Plan of 1909 guided Chicago's city fathers in preserving open spaces along the giant lake edging the city. Unlike Haussmann's preoccupation with façades, late nineteenth-century architects in Chicago concerned themselves with tying interiors to exteriors. All reasons to notice the built environment, yet the Chicago School did not notice; it could not see buildings as bearing on its own investigations, nor connect its own rich sense of *cité* to a parallel complexity in the *ville*. 'The city is not', Park said, 'merely a physical mechanism and an artificial construction. It is involved in the vital process of the people who compose it; it is a product of nature, and particularly of human nature.' The word 'merely' is a give-away in this humane manifesto. A city, as the cliché goes, is its people.[6]

The separation of people and places seeped into the Chicago School's politics. Louis Wirth, the most theoretically minded of the Chicagoans, wrote in his essay 'Urbanism as a Way of Life' that a city is 'a motley [mixture] of peoples and cultures, of highly differentiated modes of life between which there often is only the faintest communication, the greatest indifference and the broadest toleration, occasionally bitter strife . . .' Disconnection from and indifference to the physical city only made the problem of social disconnection seem worse.[7]

Planning and architecture usually proceed via propositional thinking. Weber had invoked propositional thinking in the ideal of the self-governing city-state, as a place whose citizens treat its rules as proposals which can be changed or evolved, rather than imposed in fixed form by the outside powers. Propositional thinking is the designer's version of such self-governance. How should a school be made? In a workshop or studio, different propositions are put on the table, analysed, debated and chosen. Outside forces may defeat the result, but the process is inherently a practical exercise, engaging existing reality by thinking about ways to change it.

The politics of the Chicago School did not lead to propositional thinking of this practical sort. By privileging verbal analysis, it was as though they had tied one hand behind their backs: they could not work on concrete proposals for places where 'communication' might be strengthened, or 'indifference' countered, to use Wirth's words; politics became disembodied. They had no idea of how a good school could be designed because they had no interest in design.

Paris Chicago's indifference to the built city symbolized half the problem in the marriage between making and dwelling. The other partner showed an equal indifference, disconnecting *ville* from *cité*.

The emblem for this seemingly absurd uninterest in dwelling appeared, in Park's generation, in a proposal made by the young Le Corbusier to transform part of Paris. In 1925, he published a plan for remaking the centre of Paris, levelling the medieval quarter of the Marais to the ground. Once graded flat, Corbusier proposed erecting enormous X-shaped towers on a checkerboard grid, each tower isolated in its own space.

The Marais at this time was indeed a dank and unhealthy place, a complicated mix of poor Jewish merchants, newly arrived peasants displaced from the Massif Central in France, and long-established Huguenot craft workers; all had found refuge in decayed, broken-up, Renaissance-era palaces like the Hôtel Salé, abandoned by aristocrats who moved across the Seine in the early eighteenth century to what is now the 7th arrondissement. Life in the ruins was complicated; the peasants didn't take well to the longer-established Jews and Protestants, nor these latter to each other – and they all had to share cramped, foetid quarters. Like the plagues which originally generated the Cerdian grid, the Plan Voisin addressed these health concerns by providing light and air around each tower.

Unlike in Cerdà's original plan, the spaces in which people lived and worked were to be lifted entirely above the ground plane, whose streets and highways would be devoted to fast cars and trains; people would not actually walk the streets. Corbusier named the Plan Voisin after an aircraft manufacturer, André Voisin, whom the architect admired for his technological forwardness and who had designed for him a streamlined automobile. All the towers in this *hommage* are the same height, and could be repeated endlessly, covering the Marais, all the Right Bank, or even better, Corbusier thought, all Paris. This was a proposal for an additive grid with a vengeance.

The Plan Voisin seems a brilliant solution, in principle, to the classic urbanist problem of bringing light and air into mass housing. The X-shape tower appears more efficient in circulating air than the perimeter block, where air can becoming trapped inside the inner courtyard. Corbusier knew that for his towers to work, their windows had to open to take in and expel air, but an open window on a tenth storey is dangerous. As is evident from preparatory drawings, he focused on the exact design of the open window as an important detail; the air-conditioned sealed tower was just making its first appearance, but this didn't appeal to him; he was a pioneer in 'passive building' technology.

The daring of the Plan Voisin lay largely in the materials of his towers, for these were to be made of poured concrete used as never before. Concrete is basically a composite of crushed and powdered stone, plus a lime-based cement binder; add water and the muck can be poured into any sort of shape, which then hardens. The Romans used volcanic ash and pozzolans in their cement, which aided the hardening. They were genius craftsmen; from aqueducts to temples, their structures were so strong many still haven't cracked. The Roman builder's art died out during the Middle Ages, particularly the knowledge of how to make good lime binder. In the seventeenth century, as concrete came into favour again, cracking and chipping appeared an issue. Squat concrete buildings proved safer to make than the beams and floor-plates of towers, which remained made of mortared stones (mortar being softer than true Roman concrete).

The eventual solution to this weakness was two-fold: better chemical understanding of lime, and the introduction of rebar, which is a steel rod set inside the concrete. The nineteenth-century engineer François Coignet experimented with reinforcing concrete with rebar, and his countryman Joseph Monier patented it in 1877. But fifty years later, it was still unknown just how much weight one slim vertical, reinforced concrete column could bear. Cass Gilbert's 1913 Woolworth Building in New York, which goes up 800 ft, is a cautious tower in its engineering, built up floor by floor with a large number of supporting posts. Corbusier's Plan Voisin proposed to do away with as many posts as possible, each level an unobstructed space floating in the sky, the reinforced concrete of both posts and poured concrete floor-plates stretched to their structural limits.

If only Corbusier's sense of the surrounding environment had been as engaged. He made an extreme use of perspective in order to render the towers; the perspective on the project is drawn from someone descending in an aeroplane to the ground, about 1,000 metres up. While the architectural convention of looking down on a big built object to see it whole is commonplace, Corbusier has over-stretched this convention, by positioning the viewer so high in the sky that it is impossible to see much detail in his buildings; one notices more the mechanical repetition of the Xs, composing a forest of towers.

The Plan Voisin illuminates, oddly, one aspect of 'liquid modernity': its erasing of past time. Corbusier imagined the new *quartier* to be made of neutral or white-painted poured concrete. The colour is meant to challenge the ways in which time is usually revealed in physical materials. Façades of old buildings or worn paving stones convey that the physical environment has been used; dwelling marks form. White-painted poured concrete appealed to Corbusier because it sends no such signal; buildings can always be restored to like-new condition, as though no one has ever dwelt in them. There's a certain seductive logic to using materials this way: to live your own life, you need to break with the past. If the marks time leaves on materials recall past memories, habits and beliefs, then to live in the present you should scrub these marks away; you should paint the *ville* white. White means New; White means Now.

Manifesto At this point in his career Corbusier hated the messiness of the *cité*, a dislike he centred on the street. In 1929 he declared, 'The street wears us out. And when all is said and done we have to admit it disgusts us.' A few years after the Plan Voisin, Corbusier's acolyte, the urbanist Sigfried Giedion declared, 'The first thing to do is abolish the *rue corridor* with its rigid lines of buildings and its intermingling of traffic, pedestrians, and houses.' Both shook their fists at the Haussmannian boulevard, as it had evolved. Around this time Corbusier coined the phrase 'The house is a machine for living in'; he tried to work out the most efficient way for people to live, then to build it before they moved in. It little mattered that 'Now New' required so much destruction of lived experience: 'the principal aim is manifesto' he declared of his Plan.[8]

As a manifesto, the Plan Voisin denies the *cité* for the sake of the *ville*. The relieving absence of *cité* was consummated for Corbusier in a journey he made to New York in 1935, celebrated in the book *When the Cathedrals Were White*. The manners and mores of people in New York were of little interest; they were, after all, Americans. He looked around, but talked virtually to no one. New York's additive grid, however, seemed to realize the intentions of the Plan Voisin, which he now named as a 'Cartesian' space: 'The streets are at right angles to each other and the mind is liberated.'[9]

In terms of past urbanism, the Plan divorces the functional city from all the stimulations encompassed by the term 'theatricality' – the arousals either of Haussmann's boulevards or of Olmsted's parks. Simmel asserted that functional, rational, blasé behaviour protects against the drama of the streets. Corbusier created an architecture which could actually do the work of de-sensitizing, a blasé architecture, the mechanical 'liberated' from the visceral.

However, Corbusier was in fact a more complicated person than his manifesto against the pulsing *cité* might suggest. Attracted to, then repelled by, Russian-style communism, he sought to develop a more social-democratic verison of the Plan Voisin, and in the 1930s assembled a group of colleagues around him to do this. Nevertheless, they all remained in thrall to the Plan's essence: that a city could work like an efficient machine – that the crooked timber of the *cité* could be straightened. The efforts of this group culminated in what is perhaps the most influential planning document of its time, the Charter of Athens.

II. THE BREACH WIDENS – THE CHARTER OF ATHENS

In July 1933, members of this group, CIAM (Congrès internationaux d'architecture moderne) had assembled in Athens an exhibition of planning ideas drawn from the study of thirty-three cities around the world, grouped around four functions: living, working, recreation and circulation. The aim was to create a functional synthesis. The leading figures in CIAM then boarded a boat, the SS *Patris*, to cruise the Mediterranean while developing the design principles for such a city.

The seas were reportedly calm; the European land mass certainly was not. Walter Gropius, the visionary architect of factories and schools, the founder of the Bauhaus, a comprehensive school of design, was expelled in 1933 by the Nazis, as was the architect-historian Sigfried Giedion. Corbusier, now Europe's dominant architect, grappled with his own radical sympathies, despoiled by the realities of Stalin's Soviet Union.

They went offshore because they wanted to work together intensively, believing that the design of cities should be a collective project combining different sorts of expertise: graphic design, for instance, was to them as important as three-dimensional modelling. They aimed to rationalize the city so that each of the four functions had a distinctive space or building associated with it. Form should represent function literally; that is, by looking at a structure you should be able to understand instantly why it is there, and taking the structures as a whole, how the city works. This was the theme Corbusier asserted most generally in his book *The Radiant City*. He and his acolytes assumed – though not explicitly, because these were sophisticated men of the world, and probably all had views on Nietzsche – that simplifying the city in these ways would make it better.[10]

CIAM believed there is a clear toolkit the urbanist can use, once form truly follows function. In terms of housing, the Charter follows the model set down by Corbusier in the Plan Voisin: 'highrise apartments placed at wide distances apart liberate ground for large open spaces'. Recreation is conceived formally rather than informally: rather than hanging out, 'the new open spaces should be used for well-defined purposes [such as] youth clubs'. In terms of work, the Charter focuses on shortening 'the distances between work places and dwelling places . . . to a minimum', not on the kinds or quality of work people do. The Charter foreshadows the destruction of the mixed boulevard and the construction of the single-purpose highway widely used today, recommending that 'pedestrian routes and automobile routes should follow separate paths' and that 'heavy traffic routes should be insulated by green belts'.[11]

Many of the Charter's guidelines for the functional city, such as reducing commuting times, are just good common sense. Though Corbusier's white-concrete modernism is the enemy of dirty buildings worn by history – that is, by human experience – it certainly is correct that a city cannot be a museum of form, with historical conservation practised for its own sake. But the big problem of the Charter is the split between its visual good ideas and the poverty of its social imagination, a breach prefigured in the Plan Voisin. Though most of the people on the boat had fled totalitarian regimes, they had succumbed on board – by celebrating the functional city – to a brutally simplified form of experience.

After the war, this brutal simplification appeared most dramatically in Brasília, the new capital for Brazil which Lúcio Costa helped to plan in the late 1950s. A protégé of Corbusier's, Costa applied the principles of form–function clarity to a city whose purpose was politics; thus each form had to represent a particular part of the political process. It was soon clear that the shape of Brasília's buildings did little to promote democracy within their walls. More, a larger city almost immediately began to grow around the planned city – a city of poor people gradually creating a place which was socially and economically intense, if also chaotic. In the face of this reality Costa clung to the generic ideals of the Charter: 'there exists, already perfectly developed in its fundamental elements ... an entire new constructive know-how, paradoxically still waiting for the society to which, logically, it should belong.' That latter phrase is pure Plan Voisin; it asserts that the modern *cité* has not caught up with the modernizing *ville*.[12]

From the time of the ancient urban planner Hippodamus, admired by Aristotle, a certain kind of urban planning ignored natural terrain, mapping the city as though no hills, rivers or forest knolls stood in the way. In the making of Chicago, for instance, its original planners treated the icy winds blowing off Lake Michigan as irrelevant to laying out its geometrical grid plan, whereas a less implacable plan would have curved and twisted streets so that they acted as shields against the cold.

So too for CIAM: they were in search of generic plans for *the* functional city. Their onboard proposals did not reflect the actual diversities in existing plans and built forms among the thirty-three cities displayed on land in Athens. Indeed, they argued that the urbanist should not focus on the differing characters of modern Paris, Istanbul or Peking. The Charter is most modernist in declaring 'the re-use of past styles of building for new structures in historic areas under the pretext of aesthetics has disastrous consequences. The continuance or the introduction of such habits in any form should not be tolerated.' In this they meant to shock tender, Romantic sensibilities: in the future, Paris, Istanbul and Peking should look more and more the same, they should converge in form. These cities indeed now do. The Charter proved prophetic.[13]

Once the Charter boat landed, as happens after cruises, intimates on board went their separate ways. Josep Lluís Sert stressed pragmatic aspects of the Charter in his book *Can our Cities Survive?* Younger architects once under the influence of Corbusier moved away from his formalism; the Dutch architect Aldo van Eyck did so in the 1940s when he made a wonderful series of parks for Amsterdam which focus on local character and context. As is true of other artists who do not burn out by explaining themselves, in later life the artist in Corbusier transcended the manifesto-maker. For instance, the Indian city of Chandigarh, Corbusier's late, great urban essay of the 1950s: in Chandigarh, the designer's attention to small details, to unexpected vistas and to erratic movements between complex spaces makes it a place rather than a machine for living. Other late Corbusier creations like the church of Ronchamp are even more haunting structures that defy any easy, functionalist account of their form.[14]

Still, it is Corbusier's earlier, experience-starved beliefs which have passed into everyday urbanism. The Charter served as a planning guide throughout the twentieth century: both Plan Voisin and the Charter influenced big housing projects from the post-war Robert Taylor Homes in Chicago to the mass of towers in Shanghai today; Corbusier's destruction of outdoor street life prefigures the indoor shopping mall. Both Plan and Charter preside over one version of the 'smart city', in which high tech seeks to reduce the confusions which attend living in a complex place.

The reductive consequences of functionality became evident at a conference at Harvard University in 1956, where many of the original sailor-survivors from the boat passed on the functionalist ethic to a younger, American generation of engineers, architects and power-practitioners. Josep Lluís Sert, an émigré from fascism, had now become leader of Harvard's architecture faculty; Sigfried Giedion also taught there; Corbusier, though not present, was, a few years later, to build the university's greatest modern building, the Carpenter Center for the Visual Arts. The Chartists intersected with younger Americans like Victor Gruen, the father of the shopping mall; Edmund Bacon, the planning guru of Boston; political figures like David L. Lawrence, who in Pittsburgh practised grade-flat-and-build development. Liberal well-meaning set the tone; this was the American century at its apex, with all its New World idealism, confidence and can-do pragmatism.

The meeting summed up urbanism as what Dean Sert called 'that form of city planning which deals with the physical form of the city', rephrased in retrospect by the urbanist Alex Krieger as the 'mediation between plans and projects'. Thus was functionalism reduced to professionalism – 'inter-disciplinary exchange' – among people who spoke a proprietary language. Blessed by Harvard, the mediation and combination of technical disciplines which became official urbanism focused on making the *ville* work as a self-contained problem.[15, 16]

Two voices were raised against the prevailing mood. Jane Jacobs, then a youngish writer for architectural magazines, attended the event, and found the assembled dignitaries depressing in their self-confidence. Lewis Mumford was the event's humanist, a great historian of cities and a committed progressive. He ringingly declared the 'absolute folly of creating a physical structure at the price of destroying the intimate social structure of a community's life', which was in fact just what the developers Gruen, Bacon and Lawrence were in the midst of doing, big-time.[17]

Mumford and Jacobs sought an alternative to official urbanism, one which incorporated a city's lived complexities into its built form. Yet only a few years after the Harvard meeting, Mumford and Jacobs parted ways, bitterly, over how to achieve this goal.

III. HOW THEN TO OPEN THE CITY? – LEWIS MUMFORD DEBATES JANE JACOBS

Jane Jacobs became famous as an activist for the campaign she waged against Robert Moses, the dictatorial planner of much of twentieth-century New York who wanted to turn Fifth Avenue into a highway running through one of the city's most loved parks, Washington Square. She persuaded the public to see this proposal as criminal, and eventually New York's politicians relented. A great book then explained why she had been so persuasive. In *The Death and Life of Great American Cities* (1961), she argued against conceiving of the city as a purely functional system; she asserted that big master-planning inevitably suffocates community; she spoke for mixed neighbourhoods, for informal street life and for local control. Her books – she wrote many more than this one, late in her life taking a philosophic turn – put her squarely in the Chicago School ethnographic tradition. In later books, she was interested in the complexities of how neighbours respond to one another, what they say and don't say. Like the Chicagoans, she came to sympathize with the reasons people don't get involved in politics, even though she never stopped urging them to do so. She became a hero to my generation.

She also put Lewis Mumford's back up. He attacked her in the name of socialism, asserting that to fight capitalist top-down power you need a sweeping, countervailing force. More, Mumford thought that people, in order to fight, need to see what an alternative vision of the city might look like, an image which shows what they are fighting for. He believed in design. Though Jacobs and Mumford were both left-leaning politically, Mumford leaned towards Fabian socialism, which emphasized policy-making, while Jacobs was a maverick with strong anarchist inclinations. The debate between them concerned the relative balance between the built and the lived, *ville* and *cité*. Mumford credited the urbanist as central planner with a much greater political virtue than did Jacobs.

Jane Jacobs embodied her urbanism, at least as I knew her. (Introduced by our mutual editor Jason Epstein, I knew her casually during the time she lived in New York; oddly, she and I had more encounters after she moved to Toronto.) In New York I would run into her when she held forth in the White Horse Tavern in Greenwich Village, a bohemian haunt in the 1950s and 1960s, free from its current tourist taint. Then it was a noisy, smoky place with a mixed clientele of artists, dock workers, meatpackers, gays and nurses from a nearby hospital; its food was barely edible, but the atmosphere was socially nourishing. Here, Jacobs pronounced on architects I had never heard of, or detailed devastating gossip about local politicians, especially the cronies of Moses. Unlike the quintessentially self-obsessed New Yorker, however, she was observant, curious about who other people were and what they were doing – in this bar and in the various coffee shops which she toured weekly. Jacobs' writings convey the same curiosity about people's doings that she had in person; in her pages, trivial communal incidents, petty jealousies of merchants, or the watchful observation of strangers – what she calls 'eyes on the street' – animate the life of the community. In this she was the direct heir of the Chicago School: her aim was to open the city, from the bottom up.

Lewis Mumford (whom I knew better at the time) was not a relaxed, curiosity-driven urbanite; in fact, thinking our city too politically corrupt and physically degraded, he had fled New York to Amenia, a small town upstate. Soured on New York, Mumford was also consumed by the conviction that he had not been given the recognition he deserved, even though by the 1950s he was in fact a famous writer. Jane Jacobs was his particular bête noire; he first tried to stop publication of her book, then wrote a condescending review of it in the *New Yorker* magazine, entitled 'Mother Jacobs' Home Remedies'. His venom was self-destructive, putting off most readers at the time, who as a result did not judge his views on their own merits.

Much as I disliked Mumford personally (a dislike which he returned), he deserves a hearing today because he sought to open the city through making the *ville* according to a particular socialist plan. His ideal was the 'garden city' which his mentors had built variously in Britain, America and Scandinavia; these were meant to be places where nature and building would coexist in well-designed equilibrium, as would the balance between home, factory, school and shop; garden cities would heal the breach between *ville* and *cité*, opening up a good life for all.

Jacobs Some commentators believe that Jane Jacobs' emphasis on casual, informal exchanges in the street, or on unregulated processes of urban development, are examples of liquid modernity. Not at all. She advocates informal relations which are slow-growing; this is a question of the rituals of neighbours which develop by chatting at a laundromat or taking children to and from school year in and year out. Slow-time more largely shapes the way she thinks about the political economy. What she calls 'cataclysmic money' is the sort of investment made by speculators and developers in league with architects and planners like Robert Moses, wreaking havoc on communities through big, sudden, transformative projects. Jacobs argues instead for 'gradual money', which is modest in amount, addressing modest everyday needs: building a play place, investing in street furniture or trees, a loan to the local grocery for a face-lift. In all these ways, her urbanism breaks with Paris – from Haussmann to Corbusier. She celebrates irregular, non-linear, open-ended paths of development. Slow-time dictates in turn a certain kind of urban scale. Small is where slow happens.

She seems, like Tönnies, to emphasize that only face-to-face relations on a street, in a local community, can attach people to the place where they live. Her ideal neighbourhood crystallized in the bohemian West Village. This was not a 'nice' place, at least in my own experience. I lived for a while above Dirty Dick's Foc'sle Bar, an establishment near the White Horse which catered for stevedores during the day and transvestites at night; the stevedores brawled with the transvestites when their paths crossed in the evening or the morning. The Mafia held Jimmy, the bar owner, in its grip; he paid kickbacks to them and to the West Village police, and whenever he missed a payment, one or the other beat him up. Physically, during Jacobs' time, the West Village was run-down, with a visible population of rats on the streets, and many broken water-mains and cracked sidewalks – all of which the authorities did little about. There was nothing romantic about this roughness.

This Jacobs knew; unlike Tönnies, she wasn't a romantic invoking the warm 'we'. But despite the problems, she observed that people wanted to live in the West Village, and asked why it was attractive. In part, *Stadtluft macht frei* applied to the West Village as a place tolerant of outsiders. But the adage also applied to people who were not outsiders. Neighbours left each other free in the sense that, although recognizing one another on the street, or chatting about prices in the shops or the latest outrage perpetrated by landlords, yet people kept their distance, seldom getting to know each other very deeply. She thought such relations good; she privileged what could be called neighbourliness without intimacy.

Jacobs echoes the Chicago School in not paying too much attention to the quality of the built environment. She declared that 'the city is not a work of art', and certainly the design work in the Village based on her ideas is unadventurous, most notably a block of townhouses which are plain and, to my eye, depressing buildings. But for her it didn't really matter: people will nest in, gradually nipping and tucking and adapting these structures according to their ways of living. Form will emerge from the way people dwell. Hers was a version of 'form follows function', in which the word 'function' stands for the host of informal, free, loose activities occurring face to face.

Politically, Jacobs thought the local to be the scale best suited to a certain kind of democratic practice, based on the American town-hall meeting. In the ancient world, Aristotle thought the ideal size of a city should be one in which a shout at one end could be heard at the other (so really the size of a village, according to our modern-day lights), and that a democratic space is one in which everyone can see as well as hear how others are reacting to a speech or discussion. The idea which has survived these antique measures is the primacy of direct democracy, face-to-face, rather than delegated, representative democracy which can be practised on a larger scale. Jacobs believed direct democracy could be built up in a cellular fashion, with each cell being a neighbourhood in which people had, as it were, shouting-distance knowledge of one another. Of the three sorts of urban fabric, her views most suited the courtyard type.[18]

From this measure of democratic form comes the most provoking aspect of her urbanism, which concerns order and disorder. It might seem that slow-time growth and daily rituals of neighbourliness should stabilize a community. Not to Jacobs. In *The Economy of Cities* (1969) she explored the trading and other exchange structures which make a complex city work: there has to be high density, and this density has to be diversified in function as well as population. Combine the two, and unexpected things can happen; time's arrow ceases to shoot straight. As she put it in *The Death and Life of Great American Cities*, 'if density and diversity give life, the life they breed is disorderly'. She was thinking in part about commercial relations, as did Aristotle; put a lot of competitors together and they compete, connive and flourish – which is the logic today of 'innovation hubs'. She was also thinking of politics: it's most alive when debate is open and fractious and things happen. A city has to operate informally for these benefits to appear; the four pre-planned functions of the Charter of Athens will not give a city this kind of fizzy serendipity.[19]

There are resonances to her title, *The Death and Life of Great American Cities*. Psychoanalysis sees those words 'death' and 'life' as more than figures of speech. Freud's writings from the 1920s onwards portray a struggle between the forces of life and death, Eros and Thanatos. In the mythic family of Thanatos, as imagined in classical times, deadliness can take various forms. The Keres, who are

1. Bazalgette (top right), the finest engineer of the modern city, stands above the new sewers he was constructing in London, *c.* 1860.

2. Bazalgette's London sewers composed a network far more tightly connected and efficient than streets above ground.

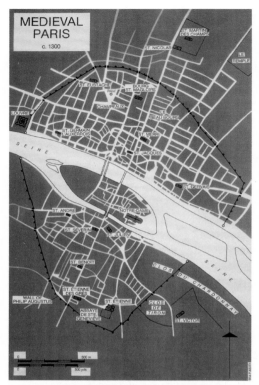

3. In Paris, Haussmann remade the city from above, paying less attention than Bazalgette to the festering city beneath.

4. The barricades posed a political threat: Haussmann built wide boulevards, down which, in times of unrest, two files of horse-drawn cannon could fire into the side streets.

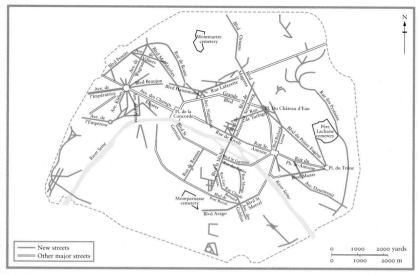

Montmartre cemetery
Blvd Ornano
Blvd Péreire
Ave. de Villiers
Blvd Malesherbes
Blvd de Wagram
Rue de Rome
Blvd Magenta
Ave. de l'Impératrice
Blvd Beaujon
Ave. des Champs Elysées
Blvd Haussmann
Rue Lafayette
Rue de Maubeuge
Grande Blvd
Pl. de la Concorde
Ave. Niel
Pl. Du Château d'Eau
Rue des Pyrénées
Ave. Kléber
Ave. de l'Empéreur
Ave. Napoléon
Blvd Sébastopol
Boulevard de Turbigo
Rue St Germain
Rue de Rivoli
Rue St-Antoine
Blvd Richard Lenoir
Blvd du Prince Eugène
Père Lachaise cemetery
River Seine
Rue de Rennes
Blvd St Michel
Rue St Germain
Rue de l'Odéon
Rue Gay Lussac
Rue du Fb. St-Antoine
Rue du
Pl. du Trône
Blvd Mazas
Ave. Daumesnil
Montparnasse cemetery
Blvd Bernard
Port Royal
Ave. des Goblins
Blvd St Marcel
River Seine
Blvd Arago

N

New streets
Other major streets

0   1000   2000 yards
0   1000   2000 m

5. Haussmann's transport solution divided Paris into three *réseaux*, or networks of boulevards.

6. In the Haussmann street, people mixed socially, as well as circulated efficiently. Progress at the cost of repression?

7. In Barcelona, Cerdà, unlike Haussmann, focused on buildings rather than public space. The housing blocks added up to a geometric street pattern.

8. How the Cerdà building blocks could, in time, fill in.

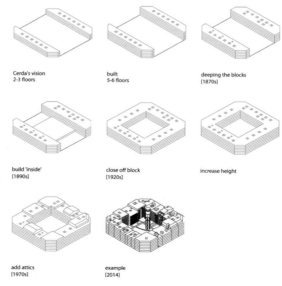

Cerda's vision
2-3 floors

built
5-6 floors

deeping the blocks
[1870s]

build 'inside'
[1890s]

close off block
[1920s]

increase height

add attics
[1970s]

example
[2014]

9. In New York, Olmstead sought a third way of making the city by building refuges from the streets in public parks like Central Park. In such spaces, people of different races, classes and ethnicities were meant to mix sociably.

10. The desolate urban reality outside Central Park.

11. Le Corbusier's Plan Voisin of 1924, a perverse step-child of Cerdà's plan of building the city through uniform blocks. There is meant to be no street life.

12. The Plan Voisin became a model for warehousing and for segregating the poor, as in this bleak New York City project of the 1950s.

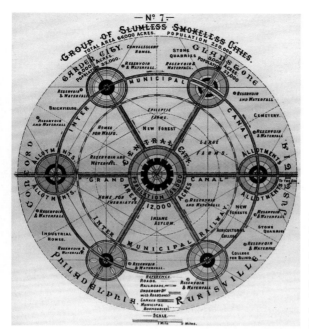

13. Lewis Mumford's remedy for the Plan Voisin: the Garden City. It restores the ground as a plane which ties together all the aspects of living in a city.

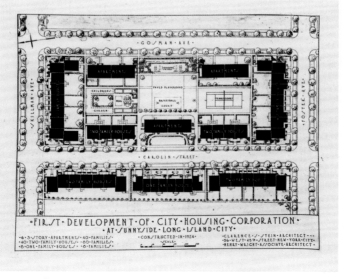

14. Mumford worked on a piece of Garden City in this project in Sunnyside, Queens, New York.

15. Jane Jacobs' remedy for dead urban space: Greenwich Village, New York as a throw-back to Paris before Haussmann.

16. Unlike Olmsted, Jacobs preferred social spaces tied to street life. In the Whitehorse Tavern in Greenwich Village she chats happily with the author, unperturbed by the drunk who had passed out between us.

17. An open space today: Nehru Place in Delhi, used by pavement dwellers, hawkers of stolen electronics and sari sellers, its sides lined by start-up firms.

18. A closed space in Shanghai. Pudong is an upmarket version of the Plan Voisin.

19. From open to closed: the shikumen of Shanghai was once a courtyard form of dwelling, in which people lived mixed intimately together.

20. The closed shikumen: cleaned up, its former dwellers expelled.

21. On a trip to Moscow, the writer Walter Benjamin contemplated the time aspect of open and closed: the past as closed, the present as open. Here is the past, in all its backwardness.

22. Here is the future, exemplified by a modern Moscow building which seemed to embody openness and hope.

23. Feeling caught between past and future, Benjamin identified with Paul Klee's *Angelus Novus*, which depicts a figure, Benjamin says, who 'looks back while being blown forward'.

24. Martin Heidegger's hut in the Black Forest, an emblem of flight from the city, and so from contact with Jews. Simplicity of built form combined with social exclusion.

25. Heidegger inside the hut. Domestic means safe.

26. Paul Celan, the interned poet who wrote a famous poem about the Hut (see p. 128).

27. Edmund Husserl, Heidegger's half-Jewish teacher, was one of the excluded. He was also barred from the library in the University of Freiburg when Heidegger was briefly Rector there.

Thanatos' violent sisters, preside over slaughter and disease. The twin brother of Thanatos is Hypnos, the daemon of sleep, bringing release from anxiety and the suspension of waking cares – the god of dreamless sleep. She wanted to rouse the city from this sleep.

Another way to convey her intentions is to think of the West Village, as she celebrated it, as a kind of Media Lab transformed into urban space, the acme of an open environment. What could possibly be said against it?

Mumford Lewis Mumford countered each of the features of 'Jacobism', hoping instead that certain formal ways of building the *ville* could open up the city. Jacobs' emphasis on slow, small process as a political strategy seemed to him not strong enough medicine to contest the big developers and the construction companies. Spontaneous strikes staged by workers outside the control of unions – so-called 'wildcat strikes' – are gestures of protest which let off steam but seldom effect lasting change. So too is wild-cat urbanism. This criticism is unfair to Jane Jacobs; her bottom-up protests stopped Robert Moses from turning the centre of New York into a highway. Still, about Jacobs' celebration of disorder Mumford cuts close to the bone.

In his view, Jacobs contradicts herself, because she is obsessed with street crime, particularly muggings. Everyone has their stories; there were many, many crimes of this sort in the West Village during the era in which she wrote. Jacobs' remedy for mugging is embodied in the phrase 'eyes on the street', which means surveillance by people who live in the sort of low-rise housing which allows them to see what's happening outside, engaging with the people outside, and, if need be, calling for help. The practical problem with 'eyes on the street' as a general precept is just how much you can actually see: you can't see around the corner, or the next street along.

More than this, her celebration of the non-linear, emerging, dynamic city relies on a sustained spontaneity. Like many people of the Old Left, confronted by the anarchic fizz of the New Left, Mumford thought this an impossibility, the very idea no more than narcissistic self-indulgence. Whether right or wrong about us, his more trenchant critique is that sustained spontaneity is no way to address issues of race, class, ethnicity or religion: there need to be stable rules of conduct which sustain people in the face of the defeats and impasses which attend radical political action. Mumford's disgust with Jacobs' looseness left him with one unshakable conviction. Relying on slow-time, on whatever chance throws up, without a guiding image, life in cities cannot improve. If cities are to become more just, their foundations have to be put in order through design. The *ville* has to lead the *cité*.

Mumford believed he had first seen that design for the *ville* when, as a young man, he went to England to work with Patrick Geddes, a Fabian socialist. Behind Geddes were thinkers like Ebenezer Howard and Henry George; George's utopian work *Progress and Poverty*, of 1879, embodied a non-Marxian socialism in which labour and capital are reconciled by an overarching master plan. What inspired the followers of Howard and Geddes was their belief that good architecture should play a leading role in social reform, addressing the anarchy and neglect which marked industrial slums.

George's utopian hopes are embodied in Howard's garden city. The basic idea of a garden city is to link spaces of work, education, home and leisure tightly together, and to surround these spaces with a protective green belt. The 'city' is actually cities, plural; once a garden city reaches an optimal size it should spin off satellites, smaller places which in turn grow to optimum size, begetting further satellites. Within each satellite, the amount of travel time among the linked activities regulates how big they will become; these cities privilege pedestrian and public transport. Commerce, leisure and schools are near to home, but industrial work is segregated, particularly if the industry is polluting. The life of the *cité* is to be coherent – work, family and civic life are always connected spatially and therefore socially.

This urban ideal has been realized throughout the world. The first, and most famous, garden city was Letchworth near London: Howard's idea was realized by Raymond Unwin and Barry Parker in 1904. Frederic Osborn, Howard's own partner, began a second garden city in 1919 in Welwyn, again outside London. Prominent subsequent American examples are Sunnyside, Queens and Radburn, in the New York–New Jersey area; Greendale, Wisconsin; Greenbelt,

Maryland; and Greenhills, Ohio. Outside the UK and the US, How-ard's influence has appeared in Svit, Slovakia, in the Residencial San Felipe of Lima, Peru, in Alto da Lapa and Alto de Pinheiros in São Paulo, Brazil, and at the other end of the world, in Sunshine, near Melbourne, Australia, and in Thimphu, the capital of Bhutan.

The 'garden' in garden cities matters in this regard. Nature was to be put to use, in giant vegetable plots in the green belts – the garden city planners were the first to envisage urban farming. But more, they thought that through the right designs, nature and the built environ-ment could be brought into harmony. In the early modern era, landscape designers had split into two camps about how to create a balanced environment. One was through geometric discipline. In the late seventeenth century wide ploughs and drum-seeders allowed crops to be grown in long, even rows, matching the straight lines of Le Nôtre's gardens in Versailles. Against this disciplining geometry, the advocates of crop rotation and overplanting created fields that looked unstable or anarchic, but whose shifts were carefully controlled – just as the eighteenth century pleasure gardeners con-trived the English-style gardens in which, as we have seen in Olmsted's work, nature seems to run wild but is in fact a calculated environ-ment. Garden city planners wanted to discipline nature in the manner of the French geometric farmers. The gardens in a garden city reflected their conviction that, to make a city sustainable, it had to be orderly, its farming like its buildings carefully thought out in advance. Sus-tainability happens top-down, not bottom-up.

Like Max Weber, Mumford recognized that modernity poses a deep challenge to cities, but Mumford made a deeper knife-cut than Weber. Mumford thought localism was a form of disempowerment. The masters are happy to leave the people to enjoy the pleasures of a neighbourhood, while keeping control of the city overall. Mumford wanted citizens to assert their own agency by making radical demands, by saying what the whole *ville* should look like, rather than withdrawing into local life. This demand for form is the socialist side of the ideal garden city. Still, citizenship in a garden city does not embody the freedom Weber imaged in a city-state. The inhabitants of the Sienese commune could shape the form of their city, whereas the citizens of Letchworth cannot: the plan is set.

The places created by Howard and Geddes particularly appealed to Mumford as the recipe for a 'sustainable city' – a phrase, if I'm not mistaken, Mumford coined. Though he did not foresee the current climate crisis, Mumford did foresee the urban question it would pose: can climate change be dealt with at the level of the *cité*, say by driving as little as possible and cycling whenever possible? Or does a truly effective solution lie only at the level of the *ville*, as in the moving of power stations away from watery edges in the city? Both matter, of course, but which matters more? Mumford was in no doubt. Big ecological or technological challenges have to be met first and foremost at the level of the *ville*; local solutions, especially voluntary local solutions, are just too small.[20]

Mumford was an analyst of technology as well as of cities – indeed, he is the godfather of one branch of the 'smart city' movement. By 1934, when Mumford published arguably his best book, *Technics and Civilization*, he had moved beyond thinking about how to plan a socialist garden city; he pondered how the effort to wrest form out of flux, beginning in the great technological revolution of the seventeenth century, came to influence the machine culture of the twentieth. In Newton's time, or so Mumford argued, the powers of technology expanded control over the city; now technology has become a self-contained force, displacing people. Mumford knew Norbert Wiener slightly, and admired Wiener's late criticism of cybernetics; he once said to me in the same vein that Aldous Huxley's *Brave New World* should be the bible of every urbanist. In old age, Mumford sunk into bleak pessimism on this account, believing that high tech could not be coupled to socialist politics.

Despite all this, Mumford's technical interests led him to criticize Jacobs' concept of local scale. You can't build an infrastructure, he asserts, by thinking in terms of a bottom-up, cellular framework; you need to think about the system as an integrated whole. To take a current example: Chinese civil engineers try to think in terms of scale in dealing with problems of traffic congestion in a new city outside Shanghai by calculating that, for 40,000 inhabitants, they will need two highways each 10 kilometres long and 36 metres wide, the lanes with no median strip but with verges. These big roads then require tributaries 2 kilometres long and 13 metres wide (the dimensions for a four-lane, two-way street). The tributaries require capillaries of a half-kilometre and two lanes wide. The engineer has to plan in this top-down way to deal with the millions of vehicle trips circulating in and around the new city.[21]

This kind of calculation is Jane Jacobs' Achilles heel. She has no good idea of how to scale up from the local to the urban. It won't do to call, as she does, the city a 'collection of communities'; infrastructure, like roads, electricity or water, needs to be built by scaling from whole to part. Of course, scaling down traffic flows can and has wrecked much of the modern city. But the remedy for a bad kind of big scaling lies in a better way of seeing the city as a whole, rather than trying to work it out bit by bit. Mumford's own urbanism sought a democratic-socialist way to think on a large scale. The issue of scale in political terms has everything to do with hierarchies of value, deciding which are the more important things relative to the less important: how could we ever sort out scarce resources without establishing these hierarchies of value? How could disorder ever sort out what matters in a city?

The Mumford–Jacobs debate is about two different versions of the open city. For Mumford, 'open' means embracing – an embracing vision, as in the garden city, which involves all aspects of people's lives. Jacobs is more 'open' in the modern open-systems sense, favouring a city in which there are pockets of order, a city growing in an open-ended, non-linear way. Mumford has a more closed idea of the *cité*, since he favours orderly and predictable behaviour, but against himself he thinks openly about technology, imagining a smart city which is constantly evolving and revising itself. Jacobs' sense of the *cité* is Chicagoan in her focus on everyday, face-to-face encounters, but pure New York in hating small-town friendliness. Her politics are more open than Mumford's, I would say, because she emphasizes the processes of discussion, debate and resistance, while he provides citizens with the plan for their socialist lives.

Urbanism, fractured In Part One's too-brief survey, I've brought to the fore one particular aspect of urbanism – that it has become a fractured discipline, split between knowledge of building and dwelling. Some branches of knowledge may follow a progressive path, adding to the fund of facts and ideas over the course of time. That has not been true of urbanism. As a result, there is no generally accepted, compelling proposal now about how to open up a city.

At its origins, modern urbanism did seek to join building and dwelling, in the experiments of engineers working mostly underground, and the plans of the generation of 1850 working above it. Perhaps the crooked relation between building and dwelling is just too deep, too structural, for this effort ever to have succeeded. Bazalgette's sewers made the city healthier, but did not thereby make people think more rationally about tuberculosis or plague, as this eminent Victorian believer in progress hoped. Cerdà was a socialist who believed the grid fabric of the city would serve the goal of equality – a good environment for all – but equality declined into monoculture. Olmsted was in his time truly radical, believing racial amity could be achieved by design – but only in a place cut off from the conditions of everyday community and work. It's a terrible irony that the reactionary of the Great Generation, Baron Haussmann, produced streets and public spaces which have worked well socially, but this success is at cross-purposes with his intentions. The theorists of the *cité* were not optimistic that much could be done: Simmel thought the sensory overload in public places would drive individuals inside themselves; Weber argued that, collectively, citizens have lost their autonomy.

The last century withdrew from the great nineteenth-century drama of putting the lived and the built together. True, the Chicago urbanists who studied the lived world of the *cité* were sophisticated – verbally, not visually. Those who dreamed of building the modern were daring, but indifferent to the voices of the people who would live in their dreams. Corbusier's Charter of Athens was a boat-bred vision of the rational, functional city produced *for* people instead of *by* them. The breach which divided Chicago from Paris debouched as a conflict between New Yorkers about whether a city can be made open, by design.

I once remarked to Jane Jacobs, when I was first trying to work out the relation of *cité* and *ville*, that she was better on the *cité* than Mumford, while he was better on the *ville*. This was not while their quarrel simmered in New York, but later, after the Vietnam years when she and her family left for wintry Toronto. Jane Jacobs was strong spice in her placid Canadian home; she remained so even after she became physically immobile. We became friendly in the way New Yorkers are friendly, which is to say we argued whenever I visited Toronto. Perhaps our arguments cheered her up, wakening memories of the earlier, unstoppable flow of talk which attended her weekly excursions. This time she rounded curtly, as I remember, asking me, 'So what would you do?'

PART TWO

The Difficulty of Dwelling

4

Klee's Angel Leaves Europe

I had no answer to Jane Jacobs. Indeed, though I argued with her, she seemed to fill up my imagination and speak for my sentiments, as for many other young urbanists. In the 1980s, I got the jolt I needed to turn a fresh page. Cities in the developing world were then beginning to grow explosively, and about these places I knew very little. I took on work with UNESCO and then the UN Development Programme; thanks to the London School of Economics, I began to spend time in Shanghai, Mumbai and Delhi. My new colleagues, I discovered, found it as difficult to connect *ville* and *cité* as did people from my own background – but difficult on their own terms.

I. THE INFORMAL WAY OF DWELLING – MR SUDHIR IN DELHI

Nehru Place In the south-east of Delhi, a vast T-shaped market has arisen on top of an underground parking garage. Nehru Place came into being because in the 1970s Delhi did not have enough commercial real estate to house its burgeoning small businesses. The government's planning agency therefore allowed the derelict area which was the original Nehru Place to develop. Original plans show the plaza above the parking garage as empty, and lined with low, four-storey buildings meant for office start-ups rather than shops. Today, there remain traces of that intention. The boxy buildings lining the sides of Nehru Place form a downmarket version of Silicon Valley; here, tech start-ups occupy cramped rooms next to computer repair shops and cut-rate travel agents. The open-air plateau, however, has filled up with retail stalls. Here, people sell smartphones, laptops and pre-owned motherboards, also saris and Bollywood CDs, sometimes all out of the same boxes. Crowds surge with shopper energy, and they are mixed. In the multiplex, the same Bollywood film has been cut and edited differently for the three languages in which it is currently showing. Nearby is a huge temple, and also more upscale, pristine office buildings.[1]

People mingle casually on the plateau during the course of the day. Unlike Silicon Valley in the US where everybody makes a point of dressing down sloppily, here the budding techno entrepreneurs flaunt designer jeans and expensive loafers. Yet they do not hold aloof from the heaving market; a very good food stand, for instance, is located outside the entrance to a suite of offices housing a firm which has pulled off an IPO. Rather than lunch in an upmarket place, the sharp young men still hang out around this stand, eating off paper plates, gossiping easily with the stand's half-blind, motherly proprietor.

At night India's ghosts appear in the form of pavement-dwellers who colonize the staircases or spread out under the few trees which offer some shelter against the weather. One night I watched the police try to sweep out these night-dwellers: as the forces of order moved forward, the dispossessed regrouped behind them; once they had disappeared, the pavement-dwellers bedded down again – as the police knew perfectly well they would.

This mixed scene does not quite evoke Jane Jacobs' West Village because, though loose and micro-scale in the character of its daily life, Nehru Place came into being thanks to large-scale, careful planning. Planners have spent big money to provide Nehru Place with its own, efficient metro station, plus a simple and equally efficient bus terminal. Slightly raised above the ground and slightly angled, keeping out rain and draining filth, the elevation of the garage roof – though unlikely to win any architecture prizes – is a master-stroke urbanistically. On top of it, an informal *cité* has become grafted onto a planned *ville*.

It's misleading to imagine, in this regard, that the poor only appropriate unbuilt land. Many places which poor people colonize were previously constructed for a purpose – truck storage, factory and the like; these spaces lost their value for one reason or another, were abandoned and then appropriated. Nehru Place is one version of appropriation; unforeseen rooftop activities have been added to a structure whose original purpose was car parking.

There are four dimensions of informality evident here which mark other fast-growing (in UN-speak 'emerging') cities. Economically, the entrepreneurs do not lead a bureaucratized existence; they have escaped India's legal economy, which had suffocated under a leaden bureaucracy. The start-ups in the four-storey buildings are energetic but failure-prone. Legally, the goods now traded on the plateau are politely described as 'grey goods', which means they have been at worst stolen or, less bad but still illegal, have been diverted from factories or storage facilities, untaxed. Politically, as with the pavement-dwellers and the police, Nehru Place is informal in the sense of not being rigidly controlled. Socially it is informal because of its transience. Shops and shoppers, offices and workers come and go; the stall you remember from last month is no longer there; the half-blind, motherly kebab-seller seems, at least in my experience, the only permanent fixture. Informal time is open-ended.

Versions of Nehru Place can be found in a Middle Eastern souk or a parking lot in Lagos; they used to appear in the squares of almost any small Italian town. In all of them, sellers and buyers can haggle about goods which have no fixed price. Indeterminacy prompts a kind of economic theatre: the merchant declares 'this is my rock-bottom price!' to which the seller responds with something like 'I really don't want this item in red; don't you have one in white?' to which the seller, discarding the 'rock-bottom' declaration, ripostes, 'No, but you can have it in red wholesale.' The Parisian department store put an end to this economic theatre; in their windows, commodities were dramatized, but their prices were fixed. Grey-market goods have revived a certain kind of face-to-face intensity in the city.[2]

I learned this to my cost in Nehru Place. I had first come here, in 2007, to hang out rather than to work. (The LSE was holding a conference in Mumbai that year, and I wanted to see more of India than the inside of a conference hall.) The day before my visit, my iPhone had gone on the blink and someone gave me a tip; a repair genius operates out of an open-air cart near the south-west corner in Nehru Place. I found the spot, but not the man; he had 'been moved on' a young woman nearby said. This peculiar locution my local colleague interpreted as 'he has refused to pay the right bribes'. If I couldn't repair my phone, I might have to find a replacement, which was not an extravagant expense here. Many goods are cheap because, as one merchant said to my translator-friend about a box of new iPhones, all in red, 'it happened to fall into our hands'. It was he who offered to do a deal 'wholesale', in red, and we did it, on an overturned cardboard box which served as the merchant's shop counter.

He sold me a dud. I returned two days later, found him and demanded my money back; the Indian friend with me released a volley of what sounded like quite threatening Hindi, and a new phone was handed over. The iPhone merchant then smiled, as though this was just part of the working day. Rather than a slick youngster, he was a balding, paunchy man, reeking of some sort of perfume which perhaps also 'happened to fall into our hands'. What touched me was a framed photo of two adolescent children he set on the upturned cardboard box.

It was insufferably hot, and I was pouring with sweat; having placated me, the merchant offered tea, the hot liquid somehow assuaging the heat. We sat on either side of the box, stained with the rings of prior teacups; evidently refreshment for assuaged customers was also normal business practice. Via the interpreter standing behind me as we sat, I told the merchant that I was a researcher and he replied, 'I am Mr Sudhir.' 'Sudhir' is a first name, and my host, evidently believing all Americans use them when meeting strangers, used his own, perhaps adding the 'Mr' as a signal that I should treat him with respect.

After selling another red iPhone to a wandering Dutchwoman, his eyes carefully averted from me, Mr Sudhir returned to our conversation. We had already discussed grandchildren, always a bond. His own story now appeared: Mr Sudhir had received a few years of schooling beyond the norm in a village eighty kilometres away, and perhaps this prompted him as an adolescent to seek his fortune in Delhi, however he could. Contacts had put him into Nehru Place, originally in the foetid stalls down in the parking garage which served the most marginal traders: 'In the garage it was hell,' Mr Sudhir observed, 'I had to be watchful every moment.' In time, though, he rose above-ground, occupying one regular spot and becoming known to a few key contacts outside.

As we had talked, I heard other voices. In the 1980s I had made a study of 14th Street in New York with the photographer Angelo Hornak. In those far-off, pre-gentrified days, this big street resembled Nehru Place in one way: 14th Street sold towels, toilet paper, luggage and other everyday goods which 'happened to come into our hands'. The goods were available because freight operations at New York's Kennedy International airport, we were told, 'leaks'. This grey market of 14th Street served as the public realm of working-class New York, as almost all the underground lines in the city converged on it. Out on the sidewalks, in front of the stores, were over-turned cardboard boxes like Mr Sudhir's shop counter.

I became acquainted in particular with a group of African migrants who manned cardboard boxes on 14th Street between 6th and 7th Avenues. They were men just hanging on, earning a few dollars each day, sleeping rough in basement corners or outside, but immensely proud. My passable French served as an entry card to stories of long, erratic journeys from West Africa; of politics or tribal conflicts which had aborted jobs, landed sons in prison, daughters in prostitution. The escape to America was filled with guilt over abandoning home, yet it had not improved their fortunes. Their life's journey led relentlessly downwards, and they were depressed.

Dodgy dealings have led Mr Sudhir in the other direction. Abjection meant to him meant hawking stolen goods in the depths of the Nehru Place garages. He made a move up, both literally and socially, by finding a place in the open space on top of the garage. The fact that he had a business in goods of dubious origin did not detract from his aura of solid paterfamilias. With his regulars, the market offered a chance to establish a 'solid stone' on which his two sons could stand when they took over the business.

It was the same, I learned, with his house. In the course of the twentieth century, as the urban revolution gathered force, the mass of poor people streaming into cities occupied empty land to which they had no legal right; by one estimate, 40 per cent of new urbanites in the year 2000 squatted, building cinderblock or cardboard shacks. Private owners now want their property back; governments see these shack-camps, if made permanent, as a blight on cities. Mr Sudhir, who has squatted for fourteen years, doesn't see it that way. Year by year he improved his house; he wants to secure these improvements by making his tenancy legal. 'My sons and I have recently added a new room to our home,' he told me proudly, building it each night cinder block by cinderblock. An insightful analyst of these settlements, Teresa Caldeira, says these long-term family projects become a disciplining principle for how money should be spent over the years. The collective efforts are a source, moreover, of family pride and self-respect. Mr Sudhir has a family to support, and a dignity to maintain.[3,4]

His situation is a familiar one sociologically, if uncomfortable morally: ethical family values are coupled to shady behaviour. The harsh conditions of survival can put poor people in that position; taken to a more violent extreme, it is the story told in Mario Puzo's *The Godfather*. I cannot say that my sympathy for Mr Sudhir as a paterfamilias made me accept being fleeced by him. Still, I wasn't very angry; need rather than greed drove him, and he wasn't a self-righteous crook.

Our tea should have been an unalloyed moment, one old man sharing with another the fruits of a life of striving. But looking around us in Nehru Place, he concluded our chat with the comment, 'I know I will be pushed out.' This, I should emphasize, was survivor rather than victim talk. 'At our age,' he told me, 'it is not easy to start again. But I have my eyes on . . .' – he named a number of other places where he might set up shop once more, illegally.

What are the forces that seek to push out this admirable con man?

Formal growth Naked power needs clothing to survive; it needs to legitimize itself. The promise of growth is one way to do this; growth wraps together economic, political and technical progress. Those heroic figures of the nineteenth century, the civil engineers, believed fervently that taking control of cities was a moral achievement. In India, colonialism resorted to the idea of progress to justify its subjection of Indians, who, as is true in all colonial logic, were seen as backward. In the explosive growth of cities, the idea of progress still lurks, but now in a subtle form: it is expressed by the belief that places such as Delhi should become 'world-class cities'. When Delhi hosted the Commonwealth Games in 2010, the authorities justified certain drastic changes by saying this was the moment to modernize, to catch up; the city fathers boasted 'Delhi will look like Paris!' Paris is ahead, Delhi is behind. 'Catching up' justifies political and economic power in emerging cities.[5]

Growth appears most elementally as a sheer increase in number. This kind of growth is the most familiar to us because it is how we reckon profit; more cash in hand at the end of each year is good. But growth in a population cannot be justified in this way. In Mexico City, São Paulo, Lagos, Shanghai and Delhi, people arrive as in a flash-flood, rather than in the slow, gradual increase Jane Jacobs thought was good for cities. The sheer size of these flash-flooded cities indeed marks a break from Europe and North America. United Nations demographers peg Delhi's current population at about 24 million, for instance; the biggest city in the world is Tokyo at 37 million. In 1950, by contrast, there were only a handful of cities in the world with more than 8 million inhabitants; London and New York hover today just under 9 million. But the rate of urban growth, rather than the raw numbers, has not marked an abyss between Global South and North. Delhi grows about 3 per cent each year; in the nineteenth century, New York and London grew at a similar speed. The difference is that the Western urban motor is cooling; by 2050, New York and London will have grown perhaps by a further 18 per cent, while Delhi will be at least 100 per cent bigger.[6]

Another point of similarity is why people flood in. While the metropolis certainly glitters for some, most people are driven there. The Irish who came to American cities after the potato famine of 1846 had no alternative but to leave their homes; so too the Jews who fled pogroms at the century's end. One set of statistics suggests that, once the trauma of Partition dividing India and Pakistan subsided, 65 per cent of urban Indians in more recent generations are 'involuntary migrants' from farms and villages to cities of more than one million, while another portrays Brazil's current wave of agricultural and mining land-grabs as decanting more than 70 per cent of the rural population into its cities within a decade. Further, the OECD generally predicts that in the coming two decades most young villagers will have to move to cities of over 2 million to find work; small towns can no longer support them.[7]

One point of difference concerns what happens once people flood into a place. The old narrative for migration was to leave country or village, make a beachhead in town, and then stay there. Today, the pattern among poor people is to keep moving once they become urbanized. Remitting money home, modern migrants – particularly in the Middle East and in the Asian subcontinent – treat the places in which they alight as five- or ten-year work sites rather than destinations into which they integrate for good.

The sheer size of a city seems inextricably coupled to its density, that is, the measure of how many people are concentrated in a given space. With about 25,000 people per square kilometre, Delhi is the fifteenth most dense urban spot in the world, but it's worth pausing to consider what this number means. Small populations can be highly dense; ranked above Delhi's density per square metre is the village of Le-Pré-Saint-Gervais in France. Many of today's giant cities are in fact thinning out in density. Mexico City, for instance, is enormous in the number of its inhabitants, but not dense, as I found when once I left its centre to go to a community meeting on the periphery; six hours after we started, we were still driving. Low-density sprawl marks many African cities as well – which is to say that, in general, size and density are best thought of as independent variables.[8]

Why do cities grow big? The eighteenth-century economist Jean-Baptiste Say answered this question in his *loi des débouchés* (law of the markets), which postulated that 'increased supply creates its own demand', the idea being that an increase, for example, in supplies of milk will spur consumption because the milk is plentiful and cheap. For cities like Delhi, Say's law doesn't work out so nicely: burgeoning population numbers create demand for services which the municipality can't provide.

A more forceful answer to 'why grow big?' appeared in the writings of Adam Smith. As formulated in *The Wealth of Nations* (1776), larger markets will trigger the division of labour in production; a modern example is that great demand for cheap automobiles replaced hand-built coachwork before the First World War, and throughout the 1920s fine-tuned different tasks on the assembly line. The urban analogue to Smith would be that if 10,000 people are targeted for an area which formerly housed 2,000, then the houses themselves will be made according to the division of labour, with apartments of different sizes and shapes, other spaces put to specialized uses, like parking garages dug out below gardens, and so on. In other words, size begets complexity.

A 'megalopolis' derives from this model of growth, in which the division of labour, functions and forms intensifies as the city expands. Usually, the expansion is framed in geographical or regional terms; Beijing is now trying to create a megalopolis by spawning an urban region hundreds of kilometres across, with sub-cities linked together by efficient transport. Unlike the smeared stretch-out of Mexico City, the Chinese idea is that each of these sub-cities becomes a city within its own right, performing a specialized function within the larger Beijing. The American model for this is the megalopolis stretching from Washington to Boston which developed in the last century along the eastern seaboard of the US, an urban region which the geographer Jean Gottmann analysed after the Second World War. Gottmann rejected the concentric circle employed by the Chicago urbanists, replacing it with a complicated Venn diagram of intersecting functions in a territory stretching across 400 miles. Moreover, he argued that economies of scale are achieved if transport, manufacturing and social services are linked across a region.[9, 10]

A megalopolis does not quite describe what Saskia Sassen calls a 'global city'. In global cities, proximity of cities to each other within a metropolitan region doesn't matter much. Instead, there are a set of financial, legal and other specialized service tasks which the global economy performs; these 'global functions' are parcelled out to different cities in a network in which each city plays a particular role, no matter that the cities are far apart. You are, for instance, about to buy a thousand tonnes of copper, making you a Global Copper Player. The price per tonne might be negotiated in Chicago, which has a specialized commodities market. Financing will come from banks in Tokyo, who are sitting on mountains of cash. The legal advice you need might come from London, where, due to its imperial past, specialists have deep experience of differing national legal regimes.

For drilling the copper, you might seek advice in Dallas, where, thanks to its oil industries, experts know all about big-scale equipment. Finally, you may grease the palms of officials in La Paz, Bolivia and Johannesburg, South Africa, where the copper actually is, waiting for you to exploit it. Together, Chicago, Tokyo, London, Dallas, La Paz and Johannesburg perform as one global-city molecule.[11]

There is one huge physical connection between global cities: the container ship which will distribute your copper. Container ships require facilities for unloading and transport on a scale that transcends the industrial-era docks and warehouses of cities like Liverpool, New York and Shanghai; smaller in scale and woven into the fabric of the surrounding city, these are now functionally relics. The Hudson River docks in New York, for instance, were walking and hand-truck distance from the small manufacturers who transformed packages of Egyptian cloth into American dresses; now these dresses, already made in China or Thailand, are offloaded in New Jersey, which itself has almost no clothing industry. The new infrastructure of giant ports disconnects them from the rest of an urban region even as they are integrated into the global economy.

As a result of globalization, an old way to think about political structure has become somewhat outdated. This old way was analogous to the construction of Russian matryoshka dolls, nesting different sizes one inside the next; communities nested within cities, cities within regions, regions within nations. Global cities no longer 'nest'; they are becoming detached from the nation-states which contain them. The biggest financial trading partners of London are Frankfurt and New York, not the rest of the British nation. Nor have global cities become city-states on the Weberian model. The global city represents an international network of money and power, difficult to address locally: rather than face down Robert Moses, a tangible human being who actually lived in New York, today Jane Jacobs might have to send emails of protest to an investment committee in Qatar.

All of these forces combine to threaten Mr Sudhir. Informal local places become inviting targets for global regimes. They are inviting in two ways.

Let's say that you are a Global Copper Player looking to move to investments in real estate: you will follow one of two models. The first is 'opportunity investing'. The opportunity investor is looking for the exceptional deal. You spot a good local deal, even though you live outside the city: you work with teams of highly specialized scouts and service firms; you swoop in to steal a march on slower-moving locals, or seize opportunities to which locals, numbed by familiarity, miss; most of all, you have deeper pockets than the locals do. This was how international property developers from Canada initially got hold of vast stretches of land to build the commercial centre of Canary Wharf in London. The outsiders assembled money from banks and investors outside Britain to put into the abandoned docks; further, the local experts – slick, sharp-suited sharks hired by the Canadians – looked for properties whose owners realized only too late the value of what they owned.

Opportunity investors are hoping to make money out of a particular aspect of open systems, in which a relatively small-scale event can trigger a massive change in the whole. This trigger is what we call in everyday language its 'tipping point'. In a closed system, small events accumulate but they do not tip; rather, they add up step by step in a smooth fashion. The economic point for opportunity investors is that tipping points magnify value in making sudden big jumps. In New York's High Line, for instance, a relatively small investment in weedy plants, street furniture, platform supports and stairs for the promenades produced infinitely greater value in the surrounding land, renovations and new buildings. In an open, opportunity-seeking way of investing, as the venture capitalist William Janeway observes, investors are focused on whether a particular deal can trigger other deals, rather than on whether it is profitable in itself.[12]

Exceptional deals jump-starting growth were easier to pull off in the early stages of the urban revolution; a generation ago, it wasn't clear that cities were going to grow so fast in the south or to regenerate in the north. Today, there are fewer short-sighted owners like those who sold to the Canadians creating Canary Wharf. A more sophisticated model of development has therefore come to the fore.

This is 'core investing'. A plutocrat in Kuala Lumpur may have no way of knowing if a new building in Delhi is a tipping point or not; Kuala Lumpur knows little about the building's relationship to surrounding buildings, to the local community, or to the city at large. And the plutocrat need not care. (I have nothing against Kuala Lumpur, I'm only giving an example.) Essentially, core investing puts money into a set of parameters, a set of specifications. Once you decide on the specs, you look for a place in which to build. The procedure suits globalization because the number of square metres involved, the quantity of materials and labour time can all be decided and then priced at a distance. The core investor is going to treat place just like money; indeed, in many of the sophisticated real-estate transactions, specifications for buildings determine the value of trades, rather than the actual buildings.[13]

In the last generation, core investing has tended to crowd out opportunity investing in cities, just as standardized trading on Wall Street has come to the fore rather than the 'value' investing of financiers like Warren Buffett. Core investing is easier and less risky than opportunity investing; it trades in easily quantifiable terms. Moreover, core investing particularly suits the practice of 'flipping' – that is, investing in the creation and construction of a building and then selling it on before it is actually finished. Whereas the opportunity investor might spot one undervalued building or site, the core investor makes money through large interventions – which are enticing to local governments because they offer the possibility of high tax revenues.

Core investing focuses on projects rather than overall urban plans. Both Haussmann and Cerdà received money to weave an urban fabric, rather than to focus on a single building, street, block or public site. As late as the Charter of Athens or the garden cities, urbanists argued that a plan takes precedence over a project; that argument was the principal weapon they used against private developers. Today the situation is reversed; planners have become the servants of projects – recall that the mantra of official urbanism at Harvard was to 'mediate' the relation of plans and projects, whereas the reality is now a very unequal balance of power.

The 'octopus city', a phrase coined by Joan Clos, director of UN-Habitat, names the consequences of such development. New roads stretch like tentacles connecting parts of the city into which new money is pouring, linking, say, a shopping centre to office towers to new housing; these linkages pass through neglected parts of the city, or bypass slums, barrios, favelas and squatter settlements. The octopus city is an export whose origins lay in Haussmann's network of boulevards that cut through unregenerated, untouched slums in Paris. But the octopus city also represents something new. Haussmann's network was not a piecemeal assemblage of single projects; he had an overall plan he wanted to achieve, and filled it in with streets and buildings. Clos' urban octopus is a beast which grows heads first and then develops tentacles to connect these heads, nodes or centres of development. The urbanist Liu Thai Ker points out that this uneven development has become disguised globally in professional jargon by such tropes as the 'constellation city concept' or the 'policentric' model of a city – tropes which blot out the collective needs of the whole city.[14]

Nehru Place has recently emerged as a target for core investors in the octopus city – attracted in terms of its specifications rather than as a place. A technical aspect of these specifications explains why it is particularly enticing. The FAR (floor area ratio) charts how much built structure lies on a plot of land. Usually, the greater the FAR, the taller the building; to add storeys to an existing structure, a variance in the existing FAR laws is most often sought. In Delhi, the authorities have changed the laws themselves, by raising FARs 150 per cent to 200 per cent on big plots of land. Thus the relatively low rim of the buildings lining Nehru Place may become a thing of the past, as the authorities contemplate lifting the historic 17.5-metre height restriction. If the physical *ville* is able to increase value in this way, the realm on the garage roof is likely to be evicted, the history of the building erased.[15]

For all these reasons, formal growth of the *ville* is Mr Sudhir's enemy. Though he knows this, why isn't he depressed, as his peers in New York's Union Square were? The global Goliath odds seem enormous against this elderly, sedate David.

Though it seems hard to imagine a more unequal society than traditional, caste-bound India, economic development is redrawing the map of inequality. This map is more nuanced than the economist Thomas Piketty's correlation of growth and inequality suggests. As in other countries, India's elite has helped itself to a very large slice of the country's new wealth pie; Piketty's sights are set on that extralarge helping. But this greediness obscures another story. A significant minority are doing better than before, moving upwards from immis-eration into a more moderate condition, which can mean dwelling in more than the UN minimum of 3 square metres of living space per person, or possession of a credit card.

In China, about 300 million Chinese have achieved this status in the last generation as they have moved to cities. In India, a World Bank report in 2015 showed that in the previous decade about 9 per cent of its population moved in this direction; women and young people especially have benefited from urban opportunities. Surpris-ingly, India's rates of upward mobility on these terms are comparable to those in the United States. On the downside, another World Bank study shows that holding on to above-poverty status over time is risky, especially for those who work outside the public sector – in this, India's precariousness is again akin to that in the US. Even a modest downturn in economic conditions threatens this stratum with loss of work; in both urban India and the US, this slice pays too much of its income for a place to live, or struggles each month to pay the interest on credit-card debt. The fortunes of Mr Sudhir's class are thus uncertain, rather than doomed. His values have taken shape around that distinction.[16, 17]

Mr Sudhir's situation is one way today to take the measure of Pico della Mirandola's proposition, quoted at the opening to this book, that man is his own maker. The forces behind today's urban political economy are certainly threatening, but not entirely disempowering for a man at the bottom like Mr Sudhir. He may know full well that rich developers and their political henchmen are indifferent to his fate, but he does not obsess about that fact. He cannot succumb to disabling depression if he wants to survive; he has no choice but to believe in man as his own maker. Indeed, in his emerging city large numbers of people like him are moving from absolute poverty to a more ambiguous condition. This is due, to use Joan Clos' metaphor, to the watery realm surrounding the urban octopus; in the informal economy, left out of top-down, big-project planning, he makes his way, as do people like him, with little or no help from the top.

So long as his circumstances remain ambiguous, he can retain a faith in his powers to deal with them. His belief in family values can be affirmed as *his* values. Ambiguity grounds personal ethics for him.

Would this hold for those, whether in the Global North or South, whose circumstances are less watery?

To find an answer, we might want to look from the top down in another emerging city. Nearer to Delhi than Paris is Shanghai, an Asian city which has served as a model for modernizing. In Shanghai, we could look through the eyes of one of its planners. She was no triumphalist about her powers, instead regretting what she had destroyed in the process of making her city world-class.

II. 'THEY OCCUPY BUT THEY DO NOT DWELL' – MADAME Q IN SHANGHAI

'There was no lipstick in Mongolia,' Madame Q (I have disguised her name) remarked to me as we watched a young architect, one of Shanghai's trendy twenty-somethings, put on an elaborate maquillage. Madame Q's mother was a translator of English, which made her a target in the Cultural Revolution. Since in the mid-1960s all specialized knowledge was seen as bourgeois, inimical to bonding with the people, therefore that knowledge had to be knocked out of a person, therefore the mother was sent north to break stones. The mother did not long survive this baptism. Her orphaned daughter, taken in by a childless couple, developed a more people-proof skill as a civil engineer with a specialized knowledge of building materials.

Shanghai had decayed during the years of the Cultural Revolution, particularly in its housing stock. When Deng Xiaoping allowed people more scope for individual initiative in the late 1970s, Madame Q, along with many of her generation, wanted to turn a fresh page in the city, building it new, big and fast. Madame Q's understanding of poured concrete gained her entry into the lower echelons of city government.

I first met Madame Q at a banquet in 2003. She appears with me in the third part of a film series made by Alexander Kluge, *The Civilization of the City*; onscreen she already shows signs of the ravaging cancer which in a few years would consume her. To me, she had a tragic life, her youth darkened by loss, her middle age cut short by disease, but she wasn't given to self-pity. She did think her professional life was shaped by one big mistake. By the time I first met her, Madame Q was beginning to doubt what she and her colleagues had done; she then sought to preserve as much of the remaining old city as she could.[18]

Government becomes a core investor Shanghai was once an important trading post with the West, with British and French concessions giving a Europeanized aspect to the waterfront, the Bund, where the foreigners clustered. Behind this imperial crust, a vast, purely Chinese city lay in which industry developed in the early twentieth century. Mao Tse-tung stunted that development, but when his successor Deng opened China to the outside again, Shanghai was at first a centre for basic industry; it then metamorphosed quickly into providing higher-level manufacturing, financial services and 'creative industries' – the tech and artist trades of Now and New.[19]

Revival required new buildings, particularly new housing. In 1992 the Shanghai Communist Party issued its 365 Plan, a push to demolish 3.65 million square metres of old housing; by 2000, 2.7 million square metres had been demolished and 1 billion square metres of new housing had been constructed, with hundreds of kilometres of new roads to connect them; the financial district of Pudong rose from virtually nothing. This construction frenzy culminated in the $45 billion the city spent to clean itself up before the World Expo in 2010. As a result, during the early years of the present century China's urban efforts as a whole consumed 55 per cent of the concrete produced in the world and 36 per cent of its steel.[20, 21]

The Plan Voisin entered Shanghai via needle-thin towers, each surrounded by a bit of green space. In 1990, there were 748 buildings in Shanghai over eight storeys; in 2015, there were 36,050, most separated from their neighbours by open space. One upscale example of this Paris-Shanghai vernacular style of architecture today is Yanlord Garden near the riverfront in the Pudong district; cheaper towers follow the same format, each building complete and separate in itself as a 'tower in a park'. The Chinese twist is that the towers are sited according to the geomancy rules of feng shui.[22]

The agent of these changes, the city's core investor, has been Shanghai's Communist Party. The Party had only to give a nod and bank loans or building permits were forthcoming; no Party nod, no action. But the Mao-era of one master-dictator declaring and acting out personal whims was over. Instead, committees and meetings were conducted rather impersonally, and everything occurred backstage; tacit understandings ruled. An elaborate defensive move lay in having private companies do the actual demolitions; that way, if residents protested, the fault would appear as a private one, rather than one for which the Party was responsible. This combination of behind-the-scenes Communist Party power and private enterprise has proved extraordinarily efficient. Once the word *chai* ('raze') is chalked on the wall of a building, it will be gone within a week or two, sometimes just the next day.[23]

Sudden urban destruction is a Chinese tradition which stretches back to the twelfth century, when dynasties routinely tore down the palaces and emblematic buildings of prior regimes, creating new buildings to mark regime change. What's new in the modern era is that erasure happens to more everyday buildings.

Speculative fever in parts of the city has raced ahead of habitation; individual constructions or even forests of new towers still stand empty or are only partially occupied. Indeed, parts of Shanghai are eerie: you can wander literally for hours among ghost towers in which no lights shine at night, and which no people ever seem to enter or leave. Empty buildings are only part of the problem of building so much so fast. 'It will take us less time to get to my office than to yours in London,' Madame Q once boasted about the new, clogged but smooth-running highways. But on another occasion, we travelled on a super-modern highway to a factory at the northern outskirts of town. This road too had been beautifully built, with the verges and centre divider carefully planned, but it had become a highway to nowhere; the factory which was its destination had moved to Vietnam where wages were cheaper. Shanghai now has a number of such beautifully built highways to nowhere, testifying to the danger of a fixed relation between form and function.

If Shanghai is a city which is built too rigidly, none the less the new city is amazing. 'Observe, there is no smell of faeces,' Madame Q once said to me as we walked through a new housing project. Though the city's air is badly polluted as a result of coal-burning electricity plants, modern sanitation has banished Shanghai's age-old threat of cholera. I had expected the construction quality of the forest of new towers to be cruddy, but I was quite wrong. Madame Q and her colleagues have put real money into basic materials, and the workmanship is excellent; this care appears in outside tree plantings as well, which are dug and drained properly.[24]

'Creative destruction' is the theory often cited to describe what has happened in places like Shanghai. The phrase comes from the economist Joseph Schumpeter. Core investing is a good example of what he had in mind in *Capitalism, Socialism and Democracy*: a property like Nehru Place is bought, perhaps levelled flat and built anew, or its people are swept away by gentrification; something new is created which is more profitable. 'Creative Destruction', he declares, 'is the essential fact about capitalism. It is what capitalism consists in and what every capitalist concern has got to live in.' In the Schumpeterian view, the Communist Party would ironically be the instrument of animating this essential capitalist fact. When I put it to her, Madame Q thought this formula too crude; the city had decayed earlier, so there was nothing arbitrary about tearing it down. (In Schumpeter's defence, he was highly critical of breaking things just to put something new in their place; many 'innovations', he pointed out, are neither innovative nor profitable.[25])

Madame Q doubted, indeed, that much Western thinking made good sense of China's cities. I once gave her a copy of Jane Jacobs' *The Death and Life of Great American Cities* to read, thinking she would approve of it. She didn't. The great American champion of small neighbourhoods, of slow growth and of bottom-up politics was too 'American'. Slow growth is only for rich countries. Moreover, Madame Q thought Jane Jacobs naive about spontaneity, which to her meant roving bands of Red Guards during the Cultural Revolution.

Lewis Mumford made more sense to her. Like him, she believed that a city should be tied together by integrating its functions in a formal, orderly way. But the scale of a garden city could not be so easily exported. Garden cities, in Ebenezer Howard's original conception, were meant to contain about 60,000 inhabitants; such a place with so few people would be a mere blip in the Shanghai landscape, or in its newly developing satellite cities, where 3 to 4 million people was to be the norm: you'd need a thousand garden cities threaded together and functionally related to make the Shanghai metropolitan region of 2050. Similarly, Corbusier's original Plan Voisin would have housed, by my rough calculation, 40,000–45,000 people at most. Urban growth of the Chinese sort exposes the limits of either plan in creating coherence for a megacity.[26]

Of the three Western founders, Frederick Law Olmsted and his conviction about the sociable glue of green space was the most provoking to her, because the most troubling. Landscape projects in the new Shanghai have not glued people together; indeed, the forest of towers, a realization of the Plan Voisin on a huge scale, has engineered a social crisis. The social consequences of state-sponsored core investing have been made tangible in one building form. In order to make room for its forest of towers, Shanghai's planners have scrawled the dreaded word *chai* on what was the city's version of an informal settlement, the shikumen.

The target Shikumen are formed of front and back courtyards walled in, with a building separating the two spaces; mass these double courtyards together and you create a cellular fabric. The word 'shikumen' refers to the door at the front of the front courtyard; it is framed in stone in a half-arch or hoop (the literal meaning of 'shikumen'). Put shikumen side by side and you create a lane or alley, called the *lilong* or *lontang*. At the end of each lane is another gate; assemble several *lontangs* in parallel and at their ends you create the sides of a street. One way to imagine the urban form as a whole is that the street is an artery, the *lontangs* are its capillaries, the walled courtyards are blood-cell membranes, and the actual buildings the solid stuff inside.

Though cellular fabric is ancient and ubiquitous throughout the world, locally it belongs to Shanghai's modern history. The Taipei Rebellion in the mid-nineteenth century created a wave of dispossessed people seeking refuge in Shanghai – and local builders spotted an opportunity. Shikumen were originally built as single-family housing, meant for displaced landowners or merchants. After 1900, this type of courtyard began to shelter people poorer than the first wave of residents. The poor led much of their lives out in the courtyards rather than inside tight-packed rooms – for example, routinely cooking meals out in the open.

Poverty and oppression bred improvisation in the courtyards. Food and fuel were shared during times of great scarcity, making for lower rates of starvation than in the countryside. Though Mao-era communists set up a system of neighbourhood spies who monitored the gates, like the proverbial French concierges who reported anything suspicious to the police, the system creaked because, up to the time of the Cultural Revolution, inhabitants of the shikumen wouldn't inform on their neighbours if they could help it.

Informality in the shikumen meant making do collectively – a communism of survival practised in the face of official communism. The collective life marking the shikumen could, it's true, be found in other built forms. Some tall, slab buildings for mass housing had been constructed in earlier times for particular state enterprises; tenants lived in a sort of vertical company town, with communal toilets and kitchens. By the 1990s, though, private ownership by individuals had become the norm and the shared toilets and kitchens disappeared. A 'dwelling' had come to mean an individual apartment, rather than a collective building. It was the collective local life of the city, mostly still embodied in its shikumen – but also now in these vertical company towns – at which the post-Deng era took aim.[27]

Confined to their individual flats, people began to suffer from the ills of isolation. Gross signs of social disconnection appeared, for instance in the neglect of the aged; this grandparent neglect reached such proportions that the government recently declared it a punishable crime. There has been a growing incidence of delinquency among adolescents who lose out in the state's education Olympics – kids who then live in a kind of urban limbo, hanging out in the open spaces around buildings. The isolating circumstances in which people live have led to a rise in rates of depression and, indeed, of suicides in the new, clean tower blocks, taboo subjects which are finally beginning to be discussed openly. The signals of inter-generational disconnection, rising juvenile crime and adult anomie in Shanghai are highest among those families native to the city who have been dispossessed of their established neighbourhood. Madame Q put the problem succinctly: 'They occupy but they do not dwell.' A world-class *ville* seems to have destroyed its *cité*.[28, 29, 30]

'An illustration of life rather than life itself' Just before her last chemotherapy, Madame Q and I sat in an espresso bar sipping coffee which would have done a Neapolitan proud. We were in a renovated *lilong* in Xintiandi, an area sacred to the Party since Mao held the first Congress of the Communist Party in a corner building here. I misunderstood Madame Q at first when she remarked, 'This is not what I wanted.' I thought she was talking about the undignified and useless medical regimen imposed on her. She meant Shanghai.

Starting around 2004, both residents and planners began to think seriously about alternatives to the modernism embodied by the white towers. In part this impulse led to the renovation of the shikumen. Our bar was a beautiful re-creation. Gifted craftsmen had cut timbers and forged iron fittings to make the old building look as if it were in its original state, even though the café was furnished with wi-fi. Other restorations in the area have hidden expensive lofts or flats, behind repointed traditional brick exteriors. The traditional iron latches of many of the restored shikumen are selling points, but the entrances are in fact controlled electronically; as elsewhere, restoration had transformed functional objects into purely symbolic presences.

Renovation of the existing shikumen has meant expulsion of the people who once made it a living *cité*. The gentrifying twenty-somethings who eagerly sought out the shikumen as cool places to be wanted to live in the symbolic aura, but not in the presence of its former gritty, 'real people' residents. The familiar, twinned sins of gentrification and expulsion have been laid at the door of the urban-ist Richard Florida, whose book on the creative classes became, twenty or so years ago, the bible for a new idea of the city. In a dynamic city, the young, the entrepreneurial, the organically minded should rule, and the old, the tired and the dutiful should fade away. The creative economy is meant to be both collective and informal in character, the shared table rather than the closed office – which trans-lates urbanistically into the 'innovation zone', the 'creative hub' in Florida's words. In Shanghai this defines the gravitational pull of the shell-like, communal structure of a shikumen courtyard.[31, 32]

Nehru Place is also a creative hub, located in the shabby rooms of the buildings lining the open space of the market. In its relatively ungentrified state, there is as yet no impulse to tie the influx of the creative classes to the expulsion of others; indeed, much of the stimulation for trendy twenty-somethings here lies mixing in with the non-trendy outside. The long queues around the chapati stand run by the elderly woman in Nehru Place contrast to the strip-lit, stripped-brick interior within the restored shikumen today where only one kind of person sits.

The shikumen is a simulation, that is a copy of what was once here; another kind of simulation imports a building made elsewhere. Of course there is nothing uniquely Chinese about doing so. America's seaside development transposes the colonial architecture of New England to a swamp in Florida; Britain's Poundbury, sponsored by the deep pockets of the Prince of Wales, re-creates a traditional English village; medieval, Elizabethan, Georgian coatings have been applied to structures with up-to-date plumbing. Indeed, it's notable that the architectural firm which oversaw Xintiandi's restoration earned its stripes earlier by faithfully reconstructing Boston's Faneuil Hall Marketplace, once actually that city's basic food market, but now the place where you buy heirloom tomatoes or artisanal bread.

But there is also something special in Shanghai about buying simulations of where someone else, somewhere else, has lived. You can buy a flat in Thames Town (Victorian England plus red telephone boxes; a jumble historically, but no matter); or in Holland Village (a windmill and narrow brick houses); or nearby in Anting German Town (domestic Bauhaus). 'It's like Disney World,' a Shanghai developer recently declared about his own and others' projects. The Chinese film *The World* shows a theme park devoted to simulations of various cities around the globe, a place staffed by unhappy workers depressed by mounting and maintaining these illusions.[33]

Like the international goods flooding into the city, all these environmental simulations are proven brands. They arouse feelings of living in an established place, and by association impart an aura of being rooted. Perhaps people need these proven brands in a city where everything is happening at a pace and on a scale that locals, no more than visitors like myself, cannot comprehend. Perhaps there is a general rule at work: as the political economy rushes forwards, architectural taste looks backwards. True, not only Chinese seek the reassurance offered by the simulation of a proven brand; the Poundbury enclave sponsored by Prince Charles is currently a hot property spot because so many people are drawn, as to the fictional Downton Abbey, to a romantic version of the 'real' England. Yet in China, as is not true in Britain, there is a relentless push to move forwards.

In Shanghai, Madame Q loathed commercial appropriations of the past, out of nationalist sentiment about the 'Chinese mission'. Despite her sufferings at the hands of the regime, she still was an idealist of sorts – like those prisoners in the Russian gulag who clung to the belief that 'if only Stalin knew' they would be freed. Belief in the 'Chinese mission' became strengthened in Madame Q's life as the ideal of a prosperous China became an economic reality. Because of China's actual past, she disliked sanitizing it – but she also believed in China as a leader.

It was ironic therefore that her last work – which she could do only sporadically as the cancer advanced – was to advise on the restoration of the Bund. Before the Communist Revolution in 1949, when Shanghai was a major Chinese shipping and commercial connection to the outside world, the Bund was its epicentre: a waterfront lined with big buildings whose backstreets were grungier, filled with sailors lodging in cheap hotels; here there was also a large colony of foreigners on the run, principally White Russians who had fled the Bolsheviks; the backstreets housed clubs with cheap sex and opium on offer. Near the Bund were mansions which housed the rich Europeans who rarely mixed with the Chinese they controlled. How to convey this rich history?

Madame Q had thought to plaster various buildings on the Bund with interpretive plaques to convey its history; these plaques would have proclaimed that 'so-and-so family suffered from tuberculosis for three generations in this house' or 'in this room, British firms oversaw the importation of opium into Shanghai'. But you can curate a preserved environment in this way only if people want to remember what the place was actually like. Her project foundered; the swarms of visitors here are not minded to remember suffering.

In one of his novels, *Light Years*, the writer James Salter remarks about an idealized American family that it appears as 'an illustration of life rather than life itself'. The illustrations on which Shanghai drew are the city's response to the loss of its *cités*. In the kind of places that Xintiandi and the Bund have become, the sanitized, simplified image rules. Instead of arousing curiosity about what it was like to live in a certain way, the picture forestalls unfolding investigation. Yet sanitized simulation has a sadness built into it. Perhaps Olmsted touched Madame Q because of the sociable illusions he sought to create in his parks. What's happened to Xintiandi is also an illusion, evoking a way of life which was once sociable and shared but now gone. Here lies a great dilemma more generally for urbanism: how to connect to the past – a past whose passing one might regret – without turning the city into a museum.[34]

Simulation versus vernacular 'Authentic' is an elusive concept in building. The impulse to make a new structure seem as though it belongs to another era or another place altogether has in Western urbanism been linked to classical revivals, like the façade of the church of St Trophime in the middle of the twelfth century, built as though it were a Roman temple. Such recoveries are more disturbing visually than they are verbally; a modern poet making use of a Renaissance sestina form would not arouse in all but the most educated reader the sense that this is a very old sort of poem.

In preservation work, the problem of authenticity is how far back to go in restoring an object. Is the object in its most authentic form when it was first made? You might argue over which moment to choose – in work on the Bund the debate was whether to use the 1920s or 1949 as a benchmark, the first being when the Bund was flooded by refugees, the second when the Chinese communist state was founded. But should there be a defining moment at all? Giving a place an 'authentic' identity denies Time its transforming work – as in Colonial Williamsburg in America, or the exact Georgian copies made by Quinlan Terry in Britain.

Few good preservationists now want to make such fixed simulations. Instead, the ongoing history of a place will be excavated layer by layer, or the bandages of a building, such as false ceilings or layers of disguising paint, will be removed, to reveal its past: the preservation aims to reveal the transformations of the original. In the renovation of the Neues Museum in Berlin, the architect David Chipperfield followed that logic by leaving bullet holes in the walls of the museum undressed to convey its history through the Second World War. Were Xintiandi 'preserved' in this way, the damage done by poverty would not be erased from the buildings; an effort might be made to show how structures originally meant for rich refugees in Shanghai degraded into slums for the poor – though uncovering this narrative might make the buildings less desirable to rich twenty-somethings as a place to live. So, too, the structures of the Bund from imperial days through its whorehouse-opium time to the destruction of the Cultural Revolution would be conserved so that these wounds would be exposed.

This is vernacular urbanism. It takes the logic of narrative conservation forward in time, looking for the ways new forms can emerge from the old, but still relate to them. Looking forward, the planner might try to preserve the height of buildings from an early time, even as the façades are allowed to become radically unlike their originals. It is true that fixed simulations are far more popular than vernacular unfoldings. Indeed, historic preservation can descend into a melodrama, pitting David, who protects heritage, against Goliath, who wants to tear down the past and insert those soulless steel-and-glass boxes. David does not demand, 'Build us something better! Innovate!' Instead, he triumphs when nothing changes. In this contrast lies a larger ethical issue.

III. KLEE'S ANGEL LEAVES EUROPE – WALTER BENJAMIN IN MOSCOW

The contrasts between Delhi and Shanghai today perhaps are clarified by a text which addresses neither and was written nearly a century earlier. This is an essay by Walter Benjamin called 'Theses on the Philosophy of History', a writer's take on the dislocations of growth, the forms of nostalgia that have arisen through creative destruction, and the energies stimulated by informal activity – all these themes provoked by Benjamin's journeys to the communizing city of Moscow in the 1920s and his musings on a painting.

In 1920, Paul Klee created the image *Angelus Novus*, a starved, agonized figure with outstretched arms. The writer Gershom Scholem saw the piece that year, bought it and hung it in his apartment in Munich. Walter Benjamin saw it in Scholem's apartment, bought it and hung onto it until his suicide in 1940. Just before killing himself trying to cross into Spain (at Portbou in the Pyrenees, convinced the Nazis would inevitably capture him), Benjamin gave *Angelus Novus* for safe-keeping to the French writer Georges Bataille, who hid it in a dusty corner of the Bibliothèque Nationale. A few years after the Second World War ended, the monoprint came into the hands of Theodor Adorno, who managed to give it back to Scholem, then living in Jerusalem, whose widow ultimately gave it to the Israel Museum in 1987.[35]

So it is an object with a troubled history. While he owned it, Benjamin thought its imagery dealt with the troubles of history. A painter of course might be horrified at being corralled to do symbolic duty, but Klee's title indicates that he too saw his own image that way. The tortured figure hovers over piles of stones and broken objects; a sickly yellow-orange floats like a cloud through the figure, seeping into the sky. In explaining Klee's image, Benjamin first quotes from a poem of his friend Scholem (my translation):

> My wing is ready to fly
> I would rather turn back
> But I would have little luck
> In staying mortal time

Benjamin then writes (since I try to quote sparingly, indulge me here):

The Angel of History must look just like this. That angel's face is turned towards the past. Where we see the appearance of a chain of events, he sees one single catastrophe, which unceasingly piles up rubble and hurls it before his feet. He would like to pause for a moment, to awaken the dead and to piece together what has been smashed. But a storm is blowing from Paradise, it has caught itself up in his wings and is so strong that the Angel can no longer close them. The storm drives him irresistibly into the future, to which his back is turned, while the rubble-heap before him grows sky-high ... This storm is what we call Progress.[36]

Blown forwards by change, Klee's Angel looks backwards. It's an image, I think, formed out of Benjamin's own experience in Moscow during the winter of 1926–7. In a letter to Scholem, Benjamin wrote that the Revolution is 'a force of nature that is difficult to control'. Yet Russians seemed to him to regret the Silver Age before the Revolution; they treasured old pieces of furniture, hid away icons, still obsessed about the Tsar and his murdered family. That winter everyone was hungry and cold; looking backwards to the past would not feed them or keep them warm.[37]

What should a communist city look like? Simulation appeared in Moscow at that time, just as it has in Beijing today. Stalin's Moscow was coming to look like Haussmann's Paris, with vast boulevards lined by buildings decorated like elaborate wedding cakes and subways illuminated by chandeliers – communism driving the people forwards, while the Angel, as urban builder, looked backwards. Neither ideology nor chandeliered subway could disguise, however, the informal economy by which Muscovites fed, clothed and medicated themselves, in open-air markets like Smolensk bazaar. This was, like Nehru Place, a black market which the authorities tolerated; near Christmas-time Benjamin found it 'so crowded with baskets of delicacies, tree decorations, and toys that you can barely make your way from the street to the sidewalk.' The official shops had, however, bare shelves. On 3 January 1927, Benjamin visited a model factory making twine and elastic bands, whose workers were mostly middle-aged women. Modern machines lay next to the workers braiding twine by hand; the machines were switched off for lack of parts and the braiding of threads by hand proceeded as it had a century before. Yet the factory was a hundred times bigger than the workshops in which this craft was once practised – a great modern box, the 'modern' an empty category.[38]

In Stalin's Moscow, Benjamin found reality imitating art, history moving forwards while looking backwards. Today, Klee's Angel stands for another epochal shift, one in which the word 'global' replaces 'communist'. In Delhi, the 'rubble' below the storm of

Progress is its marginal people who, like Mr Sudhir, struggle to find a place for themselves in places where they do not belong. Power stands against them, yet they have made something out of their marginality. In Shanghai, the Angel buffeted by the storm of Progress stands for how certain urbanists and citizens have responded to the city's transformation; unsatisfied with what Shanghai has become, they are turning round and looking backwards, searching the past to give meaning to the present.

5

The Weight of Others

Klee's Angel is an image of ambiguity and confusion bred by the passage of time. We might picture ethics in the city in another way, in terms of how it deals with cultural difference. A closed city is hostile to people whose religion, race, ethnicity or sexuality differs from the majority, whereas an open city accepts them. This black-or-white image sorts out good and bad clearly, and so allows decisive judgement, but in reality matters are not so clear-cut. Difference weighs on the city, confusing both its built forms and its ways of life.

I. DWELLING – ALIEN, BROTHER, NEIGHBOUR

The weight of others On the night of 5 January 2015 a group called PEGIDA organized a protest march in Dresden, the town of Georg Simmel's patrons. PEGIDA translates as 'Patriotic Europeans Against the Islamization of the West'. The signs carried by PEGIDA declared 'For the preservation of our culture' or 'Islam out of Germany', the slogan 'We are the people' twisted an old chant at the end of the communist regime in Germany. Rather than targeting terrorists, PEGIDA hoped to stop all Muslims coming in, because their way of life is supposedly too alien to Western values. PEGIDA and its kindred organizations in Denmark, Sweden and France deny, however, that their anti-immigrant movements have anything to do with the return of storm-troopers. One neatly printed placard, held aloft by an elderly, well-dressed citizen, proclaimed itself 'against fanaticism'. The groups subscribe simply to the view that people who differ so radically cannot live together; the weight of difference is too great.[1]

PEGIDA represents the closed mentality in its purest form, the Other as alien. But this purity was at the time contested. Eighteen thousand people attended the march in Dresden, but only about 250 paraded in Cologne; in Berlin, a counter-demonstration in the name of tolerance comprised several thousands. Less than a year later, Germany opened its gates to masses of Muslims fleeing the civil war in Syria. There were amazing scenes at the Munich train station; bedraggled refugee families pressed against the corridor windowpanes of trains coming in from Eastern Europe gazed out in disbelief at smiling crowds holding up bundles of food and clothing. Many of these bundles were simply left on the quais so that anyone could take them – acts of pure generosity without charity's little sting: be grateful, thank me. At the train station, the Other appeared as a brother; there it was a moment of fraternal connection. This moment was open.

Yet a year later the pendulum swung back – not all the way to the PEGIDA position, but to a fear that this huge mass of strangers in need could not be integrated into society. Foreign newspaper accounts of PEGIDA and Munich stressed the German background for these swings, invoking the Nazi belief in racial purity, the indelible guilt of the Holocaust. But the kaleidoscope of responses to such strangers has nothing German about it, as I saw as a UN Observer in Sweden at reception centres for displaced persons, which two decades earlier had faced exactly the same problem of how to assimilate refugees.

The Swedes were welcoming in the 1990s to many refugees from Bosnia-Herzegovina and Croatia fleeing war in Yugoslavia; they issued about 50,000 temporary permits to stay in the country. The hosts then sought to whittle down this number by drawing a line between involuntary refugees and voluntary migrants. It was a hopeless task: an adult farmer, for instance, could be judged to have chosen to flee from a village threatened by the war – but before it was actually attacked – while his children, having no personal choice in the matter, could be treated as refugees. This legal distinction between political refugees and economic migrants has long been meaningless practically – as for Polish Jews a century ago at America's doors, who, anticipating being raped and killed, decided to flee as migrants rather than wait for the worst so as to 'earn' refugee status.[2, 3]

The problem then morphed into the issue of where the refugees who had been allowed to stay should be settled in Sweden. Culture clashes began right away. One intake centre provided plenty of fresh food, including lots of tasty stew, together with other quality-of-life enhancements such as stylish clothes for the teenage refugee girls to make them feel better. But the stew, wrongly suspected of containing pork, went untasted; the parents forbade their daughters the stylish clothes as immodest. The host's error was to imagine that what we would have wanted, the refugees would have wanted.

One solution to these clashes might have been to concentrate on integration on the job, leaving refugee workers to live at home according to their own lights. (European Union law in fact weakened this solution by insisting that refugees cannot work until their status is defined in a host country, a process which can take months, sometimes years.) But for the workplace to integrate refugees, they would have to learn Swedish. The adult refugees had trouble – as adults do in general with foreign languages – learning enough Swedish to participate effectively in anything but menial work. Meanwhile their adolescent children learned swiftly. This raised a certain anxiety in the refugee community. Adults heard their kids speak a foreign tongue easily, and take quickly to a foreign culture. The more integrated the children became, the more dissociated they might feel from the sufferings and traumas which brought their parents there in the first place – or so many of the parents feared, after being settled for a time. Integration was both a practical salvation and an experiential loss.

How do you dwell in a place where you do not belong? Conversely, in such a place, how should others treat you?

Alien, brother, neighbour This trio of words defines the Other in three ways. The trio has a locus in the writings of three philosophers connected tightly to one another. Their point of departure was phenomenology, as originally framed by Edmund Husserl at the beginning of the twentieth century, a teaching which focused on how human beings experience a sense of being present in the world

(*Existenz* is the German cover term), rather than understanding the world as a realm independent of themselves. Husserl taught *Existenz* philosophy to Martin Heidegger, who altered much of what he was taught. In turn, Heidegger taught Kakuzo Okakura and Emmanuel Levinas, both eventually reworking the ideas of their master. Heidegger attached *Existenz* philosophy to rejection of those whose existence differs; Okakura attached it to an ideal of fraternity; and Levinas to the problem of the neighbour.

Heidegger uses the word *Dasein* for 'dwelling'; it means literally 'being there' – a long-existing word whose meaning he deepened. Throughout his career Heidegger mused about how difficult it is to dwell; people must struggle to anchor themselves in order to counter the 'anxiety', the ontological insecurity, which infects human experience as time flows forward, uprooting people's attachments to places and to one another. We humans are 'thrown to earth', wandering where we do not belong, struggling to embed ourselves. This account of *Dasein* drew on Søren Kierkegaard, but rejected Kierkegaard for finding too easy a refuge in God. Rather, Heidegger's belief is a philosopher's equivalent to Richard Wagner's *Fliegende Holländer*, whose ship endlessly sails the seas, searching for a port it can call home. In order to throw down roots, Heidegger had long sought to get away from the city and find a place to dwell deep in the Black Forest. Here, eventually, he would exclude alien others, particularly Jews.[4]

Heidegger's *Dasein* forms a telling contrast to the use of this word by his student Kakuzo Okakura, who coined the awkward expression in 1919, *das-in-der-Welt-sein*. Okakura formed his ideas by writing *The Book of Tea*, which he composed in 1906, drawing on older tea masters like Sen no Rikyū. Okakura explains that, though the elaborate ceremony for brewing and drinking the tea is strict, there are no depths to plumb once the moves are mastered; it is 'empty of meaning in itself' and thus obliges the tea-maker to contemplate what else is happening or isn't happening in his or her life. Eventually the tea-maker will step back, feeling neither pleasure nor pain, simply that 'I am'. This is also the logic of yoga – a discipline to clear the mind. For Okakura, it applies more socially to the monasteries of Christians which he thought to be the essence of reflective, fraternal places. The retreat enables flight from the turmoil of a city, in order for people to be together calmly, 'strangers bonded by agape', the fraternal bond between people who are not related by blood, as St Augustine preached this doctrine. Okakura would have understood, I think, the scene at the Munich train station as an instance of that same selfless bonding. Okakura ultimately rejected Christianity, and monastic seclusion, arguing that the spirit of *das-in-der-Welt-sein* could be experienced in the midst of Tokyo. The pupil's idea of *Dasein*'s calming power is miles away from the titanic struggle to throw down roots which his master had imagined.[5]

Another of Heidegger's students, Emmanuel Levinas, took up the problem of the neighbour. The Second World War, in which Levinas survived as a prisoner-of-war, coupled with Heidegger's own Nazism, turned him away from his master philosophically as well as personally. Nourished now by the thinking of the Jewish theologian Martin Buber, Levinas sought to create a philosophy of ethics which drew on interpretation of the Old Testament and its Jewish commentators, specifically on the unknowability of God, rather than being centred on Heidegger's philosophy of existing in the world, as embodied in the word *Dasein*. I was privileged to attend a few of the weekly sessions Levinas conducted on interpreting the Torah, but was puzzled: why did he dwell so much on the difficulties of translating Hebrew into French? In time I realized this was exactly the problem addressed by his ethical vision: words turning towards one another, but encountering a limit which cannot be crossed; each language contains irreducible, untranslatable meanings. So it is in life more broadly. In Levinas's view, the Neighbour is an ethical figure turned towards others, but unable ultimately to fathom them – yet you shouldn't turn away, indifferent, just because you don't understand them. And even more largely this is true of the relation of human beings to God – the divine being a realm beyond the reckoning of our existence.

This idea of a Neighbour – turned towards, engaged with the Other who cannot be reckoned – may seem to be far from the usual idea of a neighbour, or of a neighbourhood as a place in which people come to understand each other through everyday encounters, an environment in which people feel comfortable. Nor is the Neighbour a brother in the Christian sense which tempted Okakura; Levinas's ethics are about awe and wonder rather than intimate fellow feeling. Levinas conceives of the Neighbour as a Stranger.

In time, I took from Levinas something he did not intend, and would indeed have disliked: a practical application of this ethical view. The Neighbour as a Stranger bears on the mundane realm of the city. Awareness of, encounters with, addressing others unlike oneself – all constitute the ethics which civilizes. Indifference to strangers, because they are incomprehensibly strange, degrades the ethical character of the city.

Ethical impurity attends the life of all human beings: each of us could, I think, 'understand' the PEGIDA march or appear at the Munich train station. What's harder to do is practise neighbourliness on Levinas's terms.

II. SHUNNING – THE TWO REJECTIONS

There are two ways to shun alien others: flee them or isolate them. Each way can take a built form.

Heidegger flees the city I found Martin Heidegger's hut fairly easily. It was a four-roomed, wooden building in the village of Todt-nauberg, outside Freiburg. The philosopher began constructing his hut in 1922 as a refuge where he could work and think. The village of Todtnauberg has grown in the last ninety years so the hut is no longer isolated, and the villagers, perhaps sensing a tourist opportunity, or simply from local pride, have clearly signposted the way to 'the philosopher's house'.

The journey up Todtnauberg is thrilling. The prospect here is of pines carpeting hills and valleys below and, since you are so high up, of an immense sky. Inside, the hut is simply, solidly made, and beautifully sited between forest and field. Not only is the prospect grand, the house itself is set on the scooped-out side of a hill, so that it looks part of the landscape. The building itself is basically a squarish construction, six by seven metres, covered by a hipped roof, the interior a long living, eating and cooking space running down one half, a bedroom and study down the other half; in the back, there's a primitive bathroom and a drying room (for wood as well as clothes). In the centre of the house is a stone fireplace. The construction is timber framing and is sheathed in wooden shakes; it looks to be built with only a few hand-tools. The structure's austerity is relieved by bright primary colours, yellow and white, in which the window and door frames are painted. Inside, the furniture is as simple and solid as the frame.

Flight from the metropolis has a pedigree stretching back to Virgil. Heidegger's flight reflects in part the Romantic quest for solitude, a line stretching from Rousseau to Senancour to Caspar David Friedrich to Rilke. It might seem that Heidegger's flight from the city was prompted by the same search for solitude which removed Thoreau a century earlier to the woods around Walden Pond in Massachusetts, and sent Wittgenstein in 1913 to a cabin in Skjolden, Norway. After a short-lived term as Rector of Freiburg University in 1933, when the Nazis came to power, the following year Heidegger explained in a radio broadcast why he would not now become a professor in Berlin – he could only think well away from the city: 'On a deep winter's night when a wild, pounding snowstorm rages around the cabin and veils and covers everything, that is the perfect time for philosophy'. Here, freed of other distractions, the philosopher spent his time in a cottage whose rooms contained only the bare essentials: beds, a table, books. Even so, the place was surprisingly full of visitors, mostly students, who philosophized with the Master while walking in the woods or chatting by the fire. Photographs taken in the 1930s show Frau Heidegger cooking at the stove for the philosophers gathered around a rough wooden table, deep in conversation.[6]

However, Heidegger's flight from city was also a flight from the Other, specifically Jewish others. The flight from the city and its human complexities became ever more important to him after he became the Nazi rector of the University of Freiburg. He burned his bridges with acolytes like Levinas and Hans Jonas – a burning and a shaming after the Second World War, which only intensified his desire to flee. After 1933 only Aryan people came to Todtnauberg; Heidegger's Jewish students were either no longer invited or had already fled the country. Away from the city, Heidegger could also get away from painful encounters on the street with colleagues he had repressed or dismissed at the university when Rector; the most personal of these was Edmund Husserl, a Jew and his own mentor, who was forbidden to use the library.

For this reason, after the war Heidegger's hut became a cursed emblem to others. In 1967, the poet Paul Celan, the survivor of a forced labour camp, visited Heidegger here and afterwards wrote a poem, 'Todtnauberg', which, though admiring of the thinker, did not let the man escape its history. 'Whose name did the visitor's book / register before mine?' he asks; in another poem, 'Hüttenfenster' ('Hut Window'), he muses on Eastern European Jews whom the Nazis murdered. The writer Elfriede Jelinek has created a drama called *Totenauberg*, a play on words in which the name of the town is twisted into something like 'Death Mountain'.[7, 8, 9]

There is something perplexing about Heidegger's flight from the city. Freiburg was then a provincial and placid place; the streets of this university town had never seen the strident scenes of bigger places like Berlin. Walter Benjamin thought it bizarre that Heidegger imagined the city as a site of trauma embodying alien (i.e. Jewish), hostile modernity, given the dull place in which he lived; the incongruity is one reason why Benjamin dismissed Heidegger's philosophy as a form of 'Surrealism'. But perhaps the flight from Freiburg is not so inexplicable; for Heidegger, Kant's crooked timber of humanity lived there.[10]

To shun, simplify For all this, the hut intrigued me because of how the physical object it is relates to its politics. The philosophic idea of the hut is as expressed in one of Heidegger's most beautiful, short essays, 'Building Dwelling Thinking'. The absence of commas indicates that these three concepts form one experience: Man should be embedded in nature, in a place he has made for himself without much artifice, in a house devoted to thinking. In the essay, Heidegger evokes 'the simple oneness' of a farmhouse in the Black Forest, and speaks of the builder's craft that has 'sprung from dwelling, still [using] its tools and gear as things'; for the different generations gathered under one roof here there is a shared 'sense of their journey through time'.[11]

It's certainly true that a four-square hut crafted with hand-tools could be made by anyone, and its setting might be enjoyed by any family. You don't need to be a Nazi to want a break in the woods. Yet there is a connection between place and politics here, which can be expressed in the formula: to exclude, simplify.

For urbanists as makers of places, that formula resonates. Exclusion isn't just a matter of keeping out Jews or other Others, it also involves simplifying the look and construction of a place so that the place fits one kind of person, but not others. Mixed forms and uses invite mixed users. Whereas in a stripped-down environment, the more form becomes simple, clear and distinct, the more it defines who belongs there and who doesn't. At the extreme, a hut; at the extreme, Aryans only.

It could be said that in a Heideggerian flight, who the Other is doesn't really matter. Jew then, Muslim now. Flight comes from feeling that the presence of the Other – even in so placid a place as Freiburg – prevents a person from rooting him- or herself. In psychoanalytic terms, the person in flight seeks to build up the ego by eliminating dissonance. It's just that feeling of vulnerability that Simmel described to the burghers of Dresden, another placid place. In such cities, crowd densities are nowhere big enough to be threatening, nor is there a magic number beyond which aliens become an unbearable weight personally. Rather, imagination constructs a disruption from the facts of difference, from how a person looks, talks, dresses, eats, even smells. Absent such detectable signs of difference, the unremarkable Other must be hiding something – the Jew scheming for money, the Muslim seething with terrorist rage. If you are like Heidegger, you can't handle your own fantasy; indeed, the threat you feel grows stronger, the less tangible evidence you have for it. No Jew had ever done him an injury.

In sum, the hut couples exclusion of people with simplification of form. In this, it represents a broad danger: in making clear, direct, simple forms, *Homo faber* practises social exclusion. More, the escape from the city to Nature can mask a rejection of others. Heidegger sought to evade taking responsibility for his actions by fleeing the city and embracing the simple life in the woods; his greatest ethical lapse is his evasiveness.

*

Venice builds a ghetto Exclusion becomes more complicated when you need those whom you despise. In most cities there are 'alien' elements who are necessary to its functioning, from cleaning its toilets to servicing its banks. Within a city, acts of exclusion are more weighted down by place, its spaces and buildings, than they are in a hut; you can't physically get away from Them. Such was the case with Renaissance Jews in Venice. Necessary to the city, their presence gave rise to the ghetto in its classic form.

In 1492, Ferdinand and Isabella, King and Queen of Spain, caused an earthquake in Europe by expelling both Jews and Muslims from their country. For centuries, diverse religious confessions had cohabited in Spain, first under Islam and then under Christianity. In the view of these ardently Christian rulers, sensible of a certain lack of fervour in some of their subjects, the country could become a stronger Christian society only if it contained Christians alone.

Many people escaped to Venice, where, by 1512, the authorities wanted also to exclude Jewish immigrants. But as doctors, peddlers, or small-time moneylenders, Jews filled roles the Christians couldn't or wouldn't fill themselves. Thanks in part to their access to the advanced Arabic medicine brought by Muslims to Spain, the Sephardic Jews who lived in that country were much better than local Christian doctors who relied on spells and prayers. So, too, the Venetians resorted to Jewish networks for trade with the East (which at that time stretched along the Silk Road all the way to China). Most Jews, however, were very poor and unskilled; they filled the niches of the informal economy in the way Mr Sudhir operates today, peddling cheap or used goods below the radar of the Venetian authorities. What the authorities sought was a place in which to isolate this especially degraded group, even while making use of them.[12]

It is easy to imagine today that Jews had always lived in Europe in the isolated conditions of ghetto space. From the Lateran Council of 1179 on, Christian Europe sought to prevent Jews living in the midst of Christians. Rome typified the problem of enforcing the edict of the Lateran Council. It had what is now called its ghetto from early medieval times, as did, elsewhere in Europe, cities like Frankfurt; a few streets in the Jewish quarter of Rome could be gated, but in medieval times the urban fabric was too disordered for Jews to be totally sealed in. Moreover, Jews in most other European cities did not live in tightly packed communities, but rather in dispersed little cells; this was partly a matter of simple safety, since only through self-effacement and anonymity could they protect themselves from persecution.

In Venice, the physical character of the city made possible a more complete isolation. The city's canals are its roads, which separate clusters of buildings into a vast archipelago of islands. In the making of the Jewish ghetto, the city fathers simply put to use the city's island ecology to create a space of segregation. Later, these walls formed by water suggested to Pope Paul IV in Rome in turn how to use walls of stone within the city for segregation; Pope Sixtus V later still enlarged and regularized the first Roman ghetto walls. From this walling-in of social difference, a new principle in European urban design – ghetto space – crystallized as a modern urban form.

'Ghetto' originally meant 'foundry' in Italian (from *gettare*, to pour). The Ghetto Vecchio and Ghetto Nuovo were the old western foundry districts of Venice, far from the ceremonial centre of the city, whose manufacturing functions had shifted eastwards by 1500 to the Arsenal. The Venice ghetto was composed in fact of three places now organized for segregation: the New Ghetto used in 1516–17, the Old Ghetto in 1541 and a third nearby space a generation later. The Ghetto Nuovo was a rhomboid piece of land surrounded on all sides by water; buildings created a wall around its edges with an open space at the centre. The Ghetto Nuovo was distinctive as an island in the city in that it was connected to the rest of the urban fabric by two bridges only. With these bridges closed, the Ghetto Nuovo could be sealed up.

During the day, the drawbridges were opened in the morning, and some Jews moved out into the city, mostly around the area of the Rialto where they circulated with the ordinary crowd; Christians came into the ghetto and to borrow money or to sell food and do business. At dusk, all the Jews were obliged to be in the ghetto, and the Christians to be out; then the drawbridges were raised. Moreover, the windows of the ghetto buildings fronting the exterior were shut every evening and all balconies removed from them, so that the ghetto wall was like the sheer wall of a castle surrounded by a moat. The doors and windows were shut tight so that no light showed from them – the Jews literally disappeared from sight.

This procedure was in contrast to that in the Roman ghetto Pope Paul IV began to build in 1555. Paul's ghetto herded Jews together in one place so that Christian priests could systematically convert them, house by house, with no possibility of a Jew avoiding Christ's word. In this, the Roman ghetto was a miserable failure, as only twenty or so Jews a year out of a population of 4,000 inhabitants succumbed to conversion through spatial concentration. The Venetian ghetto did not aim at conversion; the enclosing of the Jewish community marked the irremediable difference of their being Jewish.

Exclusion of the Venetian sort was seemingly easy. It required only a space which could be totally isolated and sealed off. The essential element of built form is the containing wall. Water made the isolating wall around the islanded Jews then, just as now the 'security' fence made of steel ghettoizes Palestinians. But exclusion of an Other who is nonetheless needed in the city makes this kind of construction not so straightforward; the wall can enable the Other to prosper internally, whereas the dominant culture wants only to maintain it in conditions of bare survival.

Jews gained bodily security, within the walls of the ghetto, so long as they stayed there. The isolated space protected them in 1534, for example, when they were subject to a wave of attacks during Lent; the bridges were drawn up, the windows closed as usual, the police cruised in boats around the islands to make sure crowds of Christian zealots couldn't get at them. The city afforded certain other rights too, like the right to buy food at official (low) prices, only within the ghetto. They acquired place-based rights – of the sort which today a person carries in a passport. Instead of possessing basic human rights as a person, place-based rights depend on where a person lives. This is the Weberian idea, as described in Chapter 2: the city-state defining the citizen. But the city-state of Venice accorded the oppressed rights and privileges only so long as the oppressed literally stayed 'where they belong', that is, they accepted their marginality.

Brothers behind walls? Jews learned how to make a resilient life for themselves in the Venetian ghetto, which became a *cité* as well as a *ville*. In the late Middle Ages, for instance, ordinary Jewish prayers and religious study occurred in the morning, but in the Venetian ghetto these were the times when they were let out. The Jews thus became big consumers of coffee – newly plentiful in the sixteenth century – as a stimulus to stay up at night, the ordinary hours of prayer and study now becoming the hours in which they were incarcerated together.

In exchange for the Jews keeping to the ghetto, the state allowed them to build synagogues. The synagogue, which in the Middle Ages consisted of a congregation meeting in a home, or in a nondescript building, was in the ghetto a building protected by the state; in time, synagogues became sites other Venetians visited as curiosities – a Renaissance version of slumming. Internally, the synagogue building became the defining public institution within the community. Soon 'the' synagogue became several synagogues, representing different confessional groups – Sephardim, Ashkenazi, even a Chinese synagogue for the nineteen Chinese Jews living in Venice in the mid-sixteenth century.

The shared, tight-packed space of the ghetto *cité* was remarkable because Jews were themselves 'peoples' rather than *a* people. The strands of Renaissance Judaism were woven of very different social materials: Ashkenazi Jews did not speak the same language as Sephardic Jews, nor share a common culture, and the doctrinal differences between them were great. Levantine Jews in turn were composed of several schismatic sects. Once ghettoized, constrained to live in the same space, they had to learn how to mix with one another, and to live together.

In part, this involved speaking as 'Jews' to the outside world, co-operating to protect their interests, even while continuing to disagree among themselves. In the Venetian ghetto, as shortly afterwards in the Roman ghetto, the Jews formed fraternal organizations which met in synagogues, but these dealt with purely secular matters concerning the ghetto. Religious differences among different groups of Jews were played down in these organizations, avoided when too explosive, because they were people under a common threat.

The idea that the oppressed will bond in solidarity is both naive and factually rare. Oppression does not beget integration. Rather, solidarity is a necessary fiction to be conveyed to the dominant power: we are strong because united. The oppressed need to learn how to act as though this were true, to act out the fiction, make it believable, otherwise the oppressor will exploit their divisions, divide and rule. Within the ghetto, as happens with other quarantined groups, the mask was dropped – in this case, little middle ground developed theologically between Sephardim and Ashkenazim, nor among the Sephardic confessions.

This is the problem Levinas took up theologically. Considered as neighbours, Sephardim and Ashkenazim have no need, in his view, to find common ground; rather, their 'neighbourliness' lies in respecting the fact that they cannot. His co-religionist Martin Buber had portrayed the presence of the sacred as well as secular Other in people's lives as an 'I-Thou' relationship; God is not elsewhere but here, now, up close, unfiltered. Unlike Buber, Levinas believed the most important element in the 'I-Thou' phrase is the hyphen. God is here of course – but also absent from our experience, because religious truth lies beyond the grasp of belief. If theologically the hyphen represents the neighbour condition, it also represents the neighbour condition among men and women – at once adjacent and separate.[13]

For over 3,000 years the Jews had survived in small cells mixed among alien, oppressive peoples, sustained in their faith no matter where they lived. Now 'being Jewish' became a shared spatial identity, even as Judaism continued to divide Jews religiously. The circumstances of ghettoization forced upon the Venetian Jews a necessary fiction – that of speaking with one voice. The space of the ghetto forced on them habits shared in common, but dwelling together also prompted them, along Levinas's lines, to think of themselves as neighbours.

As for the oppressors, hut and ghetto represent two ways of shunning people. The simplified space represented at an extreme by Heidegger's hut allows no room for anything other than a stripped-down existence: there is no complexity of built form, paralleling the social ethos that there is no room for strangers in a place. Exclude to simplify. The ghetto is a complex space designed to use the Other practically while pushing away their presence socially: to exclude, contain.

These extreme pairings matter because *Homo faber* can turn unintentionally into an oppressor. The exiles on the Charter of Athens boat were hardly seeking to build a Nazi space – they were for the most part Nazi victims. But they felt the appeal of simplifying and reducing form to its bare essentials, as in the famous modernist cliché 'less is more'. Paring down to the bare essentials in a physical dwelling invites paring down the lives of those within. So, too, I think it is no accident that Corbusier's Plan Voisin became the prototype for housing projects and social estates like Cabrini–Green in Chicago or many of the *cités* built outside the Périphérique in Paris: places which concentrate blacks or Muslims in a bare and bleak form of dwelling.

The Christian authorities in Venice justified ghettoizing Jews in the name of their own security, since the Jews were seen as impure beings physically as well as morally – Jews were thought to carry syphilis in their urine and plague in their breath as well as being Christ-killers who used Christian boys for blood sacrifice. The Venetians needed protection from them, so they thought. But this was hardly an 'innocent' – if that's the right word – desire for security, since during the daytime Christians and Jews mixed at close quarters in the city. In the same way, the threat of violence posed by one's maids and gardeners is not the reason the bourgeoisie of Delhi are building gated communities, because these subaltern bodies are present every day, working within the gates.

III. COMPARING – CLASS UP CLOSE

The answer to shunning the Other might seem to tear down the walls, and bring those who differ close together. This happy proposal doesn't do much sociological work, because differences are not all the same. Class differences are not experienced today in the same way as are cultural differences of race, religion or ethnicity. When people of different classes mix together up close, invidious comparisons are drawn; inequalities hurt personally. The reasons why seem to take us far from thinking about the city – but today, invidious comparisons have an urban setting.

Invidious comparisons Class has become personalized, and class differences a source of invidious personal comparison, as a result of a new idea of the working self: meritocracy. Unlike inherited privilege, the meritocratic idea is that where you stand in society should depend on how well you have proved yourself at work. Particularly – if everyone is given a chance – how good you are will justify whatever you win in life's rat race: meritocracy combines a belief in an equal start with the legitimacy of an unequal outcome.

The origins of meritocracy appeared as early as the mid-seventeenth century, when Samuel Pepys and other British naval reformers argued that officers in the navy should be created and promoted on the basis of ability alone, rather than purchase or inheritance of a commission. In the eighteenth century, the writers gathered by Denis Diderot to create the *Encyclopédie*, the great compendium of arts and crafts, expanded the idea of meritocracy, by arguing that all sorts of crafts and work-skills should be included in the ideal of 'careers open to talent'. That was also Napoleon's phrase: 'Every soldier carries in his knapsack the baton of a Marshal of France.' The *encyclopédistes* elevated manual labour in civil society, arguing that the skills involved in becoming a good cook were no way inferior to the skills of a diplomat or politician. Theirs was an equalizing vision, in that they believed most people are capable of doing good work, if they are properly trained and given a fair start. For these eighteenth-century work radicals, meritocracy was open to all.

The belief in individual merit then took an odd turn. Even as the conditions of industrial capitalism did little to equalize the starting points of young people – in many places, getting an economic foothold became harder – the unequal outcomes were justified as the result of talent, or drive, or some other personal quality, rather than by circumstances individuals could do little about. This has persisted into our own day. As in adult workplaces, so in schools, meritocracy breeds a highly personalized search for talent: too often in a classroom, teachers will neglect nineteen pupils in search of the outstanding individual; as in adult workplaces, rewards come only to those who stand out, who are exceptional, with few or no rewards to more ordinary workers who are doing a good enough job or who have put in long service.[14]

As revealed by a varied body of research, it is the people who lose out in this scheme who most personalize class. In schools, Paul Willis has shown, the nineteen adolescents left behind feel personally stung by the outstanding one, reacting to his or her promotion with a mixture of aggression and shame. When Jonathan Cobb and I interviewed working-class unemployed men some forty years ago, we found they harboured the fear that they could have prevented being out of work, even though the objective fact was that the steel plants in which they worked had gone bankrupt or moved to China, if only they had made smarter choices in school. In white-collar skilled work, as I found a generation later when interviewing IBM engineers who were not promoted, employees often spoke about having made the wrong career choices or having been fools to have believed that sheer hard work would yield them a reward at IBM. Rationally, you may know the cards are stacked against you, but still there's that unspoken, personalizing sting.[15, 16]

The personalization of class represents one version of the old idea of *Stadtluft macht frei*: where you stand indicates what you have made of yourself in a place cut free from inherited or traditional limits. In Flaubert's *Sentimental Education*, to take a great literary example, there is nothing in principle holding back Frédéric Moreau's rise in the city; his is not a rags-to-riches story, but one of a person whose money and manners should rocket him upwards. That doesn't happen; Flaubert, with the relish of a sadistic surgeon, cuts through his circumstantial excuses to reveal that Frédéric is demoralized precisely by making intimate comparisons to others, using the smallest details of behaviour, dress and beliefs. He is not an appealing protagonist, and we share some of Flaubert's relish in charting his fall, but what resonates is that Frédéric cannot disown his failure emotionally.

What is the *ville*'s relationship to this personalizing of where one stands in society? The classic ghetto casts light on this modern issue.

It's striking, poring over old prints of Paris, to see, even in the grandest *hôtels particuliers*, shacks in the courtyards housing the blacksmiths or carpenters who serviced them; in the more bourgeois buildings constructed by Haussmann, the courtyards are lined street-side with drapers, grocers and florists servicing a neighbourhood. Within households, many servants were needed to cook, wash and clean; these servants constituted the biggest slice of the working class in Paris and London up to the First World War. However, if all these classes lived up-close physically, class itself wasn't personalized. Master and servant lived cheek by jowl without any thought of making personal comparisons between themselves. Class was an objective phenomenon, something the servant could do little about. *Stadtluft macht frei* didn't apply to their relationship.

The last century altered the urban class structure in a surprising way. On the one hand the urban working class became more diverse: domestic service ceased to constitute so large a slice. Manufacturing in the early nineteenth century had been located on cheap land in the countryside or in small towns; a century later large industries were migrating to bigger cities, location near complex transport networks of rail, road and port becoming more profitable than cheap isolation. The urban service sector also began to grow after the 1880s, as big offices replaced small ones, and these routine white-collar jobs became sources of upward mobility for male blue-collar workers and entry-level work for women with secretarial skills.

But as the class structure became more convoluted, the city also worked as a centrifuge, separating the classes spatially. Ghettos began to appear in a modern form. Working-class suburbs emerged in big cities as early as the 1880s, growing ever larger as transport networks developed. The Park–Burgess map of Chicago's ecology would have made more sense if the circular map had shown blobs in its outer bands of wealth where clerks, plumbers and skilled artisans made homes in leafy suburban islands. Within the central city, working-class districts became ever more homogeneously working class only in the last century; Charles Booth's maps of Spitalfields in East London at the end of the nineteenth century show a much more varied economic base than do surveys made a half-century later. In Paris, the first half of the twentieth century saw a similar shift in the northeast arrondissements from being areas which were dominantly working class to areas which were homogeneously working class.

What we call 'gentrification' is much more than artist-trendies colonizing colourful neighbourhoods, media-trendies following in their wake, attracting digital billionaires still struggling with pimples who price out both the natives and the first pioneers. Gentrification is more fundamentally a process by which the bottom 70–75 per cent of an urban population becomes vulnerable to expulsion by the top quarter of people in a city, either through raised rents or by poor homeowners being seduced into selling out. It's worth noting that some natives 'stubbornly' hold on, as a recent business magazine

THE WEIGHT OF OTHERS

described it, determined to stay where they were born or simply to hold onto an accruing asset. But enough are forced or decide to leave, then disappearing for the most part from the centre of the city, to its further, cheaper reaches. The outcome of this gentrifying process strengthens the equation of class difference and physical separation.[17]

Thus the experience of class in a city today combines close-up personal experience of inequality with an increasingly distant and segregated physical experience. Urbanists speak of the 'death of distance' to describe the effects of informatics via hand-held devices; you are always connected, always related. Class is coming to be experienced as a kind of 'death of distance' in the *cité*, even as the *ville* becomes more composed of class ghettos.

IV. MIXING – THE MASK OF CIVILITY

Where I live in London may seem to qualify as the sort of iconic mixed neighbourhood celebrated by Jane Jacobs. Here lies Saffron Hill, once the setting of abject poverty in Dickens's *Bleak House*, later a street of Italian-owned warehouses and offices. About fifteen years ago, the street suddenly beckoned gay couples, or singles of whatever sexual preference working in the financial City nearby, and a few displaced New Yorkers. Attracted by industrial spaces newly converted into lofts, my spouse and I were among the first of those carrying the Gentrifier Virus.

Intractable elements, however, stand in the way of the neighbourhood gentrifying further. A street beyond Saffron Hill is the diamond centre of Britain – Hatton Garden – packed with Hasidic Jews cutting and dealing gems in the buildings lining the street, selling retail to hordes of young English couples who seem a bit wary about buying from men wearing felt hats and unpressed black suits, the men speaking Yiddish to one another and pidgin Polish to the bruiser private guards who police the shops. A further street, Leather Lane, contains one of the oldest open-air markets in central London, selling cheap handbags, underwear, cleaning supplies and ethnic foods to immense crowds at lunchtime – a reminder to me of street markets in Delhi.

Capping the wreck of the gentrifying dream is the Bourne Estate, a public housing project on the other side of Leather Lane. Though the older buildings in this project are worn, the Estate is carefully tended by residents who are a mixed lot of old, native-born English working class, middle-aged Indian families, and a diverse group of younger people from across the Islamic world.[18]

Communities like mine chug along without their diversity being a problem until something upsets everyday life. For us this happened when a big storage facility for jewellery was robbed in Hatton Garden. It took the police a few weeks to manage the arrest of professional and surprisingly elderly burglars, but in the intervening time rumour ruled the community, and ethnic tensions rose to the surface. Interviewed by the press, people were asked who they thought had done it, and a common response, often delivered flatly, came back: 'someone local'. Away from the cameras, some of the diamond-cutters remarked, in the safe space of the Leather Lane kosher café, that the multi-ethnic police didn't care if 'Jewish property' was stolen. Equally irrationally, a discussion in a halal café canvassed the possibility that 'the Jews' had staged the heist in order to get insurance money. Rumour inflated prejudice: a dry-cleaner, a devout Muslim, told me he had heard through the grapevine that 'the Jews' were going to pin the burglary on his nephew, and asked me for the name of a good lawyer. Before the burglary I heard casual anti-Semitic remarks sometimes when I went to the halal café, but they were just that – casual. I shrugged them off before; now I was seriously offended.

When minor events like the Hatton Garden burglary are inflated by rumour, they can trigger violent confrontations in mixed communities. Classic cases have been pogroms in Poland sparked by the death of a Catholic child, blamed on the magical powers of Jews and their beastly religious ceremonies; Indian cases involve rumours of Muslim cow-murder; in Pakistan, with whispers of the deliberate tainting of halal meat by Hindus. These eruptions rebuke the well-meaning belief that knowing your neighbours better will stabilize communal relations; in cities as different as Smyrna, Delhi and Los Angeles, where groups which have coexisted for years, or generations, a small event inflated by rumour may make people suddenly unable to stand the sight of one another.

A sweeping solution to these irruptions is the 'good fences' argument articulated by the sociologist Robert Putnam. He concluded, based on a large-scale survey of attitudes, that people respond positively to those who differ so long as they live far away. Face-to-face exposure in a mixed community is sometimes like rubbing salt into a raw wound. His findings chime with Robert Frost's line in the poem 'Mending Wall' that 'Good fences make good neighbours'. Putnam is observing, not advocating, just as Frost's poem (so the critic Thomas Oles observes) develops an ironic stance against the piece of homespun wisdom it seems to advance. But the import, none the less, is to suggest that increasing the geographic distance between different groups is more likely to make them tolerant than mixing them together.[19, 20]

My neighbours took a different tack. They made use of light, superficial civilities which smoothed contact between different groups; these became inflated and exaggerated after the breach. In a newsagents run by two Indian men – themselves master diplomats in dealing with diverse customers – the diamond craftsmen, usually on mobile phones speaking Yiddish or Hebrew, made a point of showing politeness to Muslim mothers who popped in from the housing estate ('please, go first, after you') and resolute baby-cooing ('so big for seven months'). The Islamic community also made an effort; at the urging of our local imam, Palestinian flags flying outside flats in the housing estate disappeared. Yiddish grunts of greeting and the reappearance of the Palestinian flags signalled the crisis was over.

The little courtesy embodies Jane Jacobs' precept that 'superficiality is no vice'. You ask how a neighbour is doing without really wanting to know; you are merely sending a signal of recognition. Such small courtesies are also cousins to Simmel's blasé mask, in that they are bland and impersonal. For the sake of healing a breach, of re-establishing a social connection, people hide how they really feel about one another.

The back-story here predates Kant's invocation of the cosmopolitan as a person able to rise above the human differences which make for the 'crooked timber of humanity'. The original French meaning of *cosmopolite* applied to diplomats who were praised if they acquired the capacity to move easily from place to place, culture to culture; Bishop Bossuet in the seventeenth century spoke, for instance, of the much-travelled Swedish ambassador to France as 'un vrai cosmopolite'. Sir Henry Wotton, British ambassador to Venice at the beginning of the seventeenth century, was described as a man who knew how to lie well for the sake of his country. Outside this professional channel, cosmopolitanism marked a class distinction: the peasant or manual worker appeared to be narrowly local in outlook, while the urbane upper-class gentleman and lady seemed more mentally well travelled.

Towards the end of the eighteenth century the word 'cosmopolitan' was democratized. Americans know this shift in the person of Benjamin Franklin, who, both at home and abroad as America's representative in France, was known as a simple and plain person able get along with anyone. 'Do not enquire too deeply into your neighbor's business,' a Massachusetts primer for young ladies advises, 'that she not enquire too deeply into yours.' A primer for boys written about the same time, at the opening of the nineteenth century, counsels, 'it is unmanly to gossip'.[21]

Ease in the company of strangers had long been associated with living in a city; in Old French, the word *urbain* means both the life in a city and the courtesy extended to visitors from another city. In a modern mixed community like ours, these usages are combined in the mask of civility: superficiality, deceit, impersonality. This trio is the alternative to Heideggerian withdrawal from others, the isolation and fencing off of others, or personal comparisons which cut too close to the bone and lurid fantasies about the Other's malign power. So I would say it was right of my neighbours to strap on the mask of civility – at least until the burglars were caught. But surely behaviour which combines superficiality, deceit and impersonality cannot be right in any ethical sense. How could we trust someone wearing only the mask of civility?

The philosopher Russell Hardin notes that trust involves a leap 'beyond certainty' about what to expect from another person or group; we take their behaviour, as we say, on trust. Verbal trust, as in 'my word is my bond', means that things need not be explicitly spelt out. Implicit trust is open-ended, even though it is not blind; we look for clues of what Hardin calls 'trustworthiness', we look for the tones of voice or hand gestures which are those of a 'trustworthy' person; 'he seemed the "sort of person" you could trust'.[22]

Trust has a different character from the Hardin model in a mixed community wearing the mask. Rather than looking for character traits in the other that signal they are trustworthy, you trust that they will not draw attention to the differences separating you. Imagine the following conversation in the Indian newsagent's: 'Speaking as a Jewish diamond cutter, I'd say that's a big baby for seven months', to which the other replies, 'Speaking as a refugee mother from Lahore, I can tell you that most Muslim babies are this size.' A nonsense exchange because the personal information is irrelevant; more, this exchange would not build their *mutual* trust – it would instead emphasize the fact of their differences. Whereas a satisfied smile, a tickle of the baby's nose, builds the bridge.

Which is to say more generally that mixed communities work well only so long as consciousness of the Other is not foregrounded. If something causes that foregrounding, then the weight of others is felt closer up, and mistrust can set in. Silence begets trust. The superficial ritual is a way to reunite a community which has come close to the trigger condition.

I've tried in this chapter to get beneath the pieties which seem to trivialize the understanding of difference. Exclusion can come, as in Heidegger's hut, out of a deep-felt desire to unify and simplify one's life. In the city, closure of the sort erected around the Venetian ghetto failed to reduce Jews to bare existence, but produced among the excluded themselves a kind of neighbourliness which did not unify them. In terms of class today, close-up, invidious comparisons coexist with a ghettoized *ville*. In a mixed community, the rituals of getting along sacrifice truth for trust.

There is, unfortunately, a simple, perverse way to lighten the weight of others.

6

Tocqueville in Technopolis

One solution to lightening the weight of others is to make life easy for all, thanks to modern technology. Technology will solve what sociology cannot, sorting and smoothing the relations between people. Bill Mitchell in the Media Lab was an early believer in this solution, convinced that the smart city could set right social relations. Since he wrote *City of Bits*, 'the' smart city has in fact become two different kinds of city. In the one, advanced technology prescribes how people should use the spaces they inhabit; the *ville* dictates to the *cité*. In the other, high-tech coordinates but does not erase messier activities in the *cité*. The prescriptive smart city does mental harm; it dumbs down its citizens. The coordinating smart city stimulates people mentally by engaging them in complex problems and human differences. The contrast fits within our larger frame: the prescriptive smart city is closed; the coordinative smart city is open.

To draw out this contrast, we need first to reach back into the Ice Age of technology, the 1830s.

I. A NEW KIND OF INDIVIDUAL – TOCQUEVILLE ON DETACHMENT

It might seem odd to take Alexis de Tocqueville, the nineteenth-century writer and statesman, as a guide to the perils of the smart city, though he was prophetic about such issues today as 'post-truth' mass media and populism. His powers to foresee the modern polity derived from a journey he made as a young man to America in 1831. The French Revolution of the 1790s had nearly guillotined his parents, who were minor provincial aristocrats. A brief revolutionary uprising in 1830 in France led him to fear the killer crowds would appear again. Moreover, he was tired of Europe, and so contrived with his friend Gustave de Beaumont a fact-finding mission to American prisons which would allow him – at least temporarily – to leave. He had his adventure, riding horseback through endless wilderness, hanging out in saloons, eavesdropping on town meetings, as well as visiting prisons.

The first volume of *Democracy in America*, published in 1835, shows the young writer still haunted, however, by the past, by the destructive passions of mobs, as Le Bon later analysed them. Tocqueville's book described how the mob-crowd of his parents' generation had morphed into the 'tyranny of the majority' of his own. Like the street mob, the majority, once installed democratically in the offices of state, is not content to rule in a measured way over the minority; it is filled with a passion to universalize its will, so that the 51 per cent pay no heed to the voices of the 49 per cent. This was the political umbilical cord connecting democratic America to revolutionary Europe.

Five years later, Tocqueville changed his focus. In the second volume of *Democracy in America*, published in 1840, Tocqueville measured America against his own country in his own time, a France which he saw as a bourgeois, money-grubbing society – the milieu from which Haussmann sprang. After a decade of Louis Philippe's reign, the country seemed to Tocqueville to have gone soft. Comfort and complacency ruled; people had become uninterested in larger engagements. When he wrote his second volume about American life, he had in mind this disengagement at home. The crowd as mob gave way to a new image of a mass of individuals, detached from society at large, comfort-driven and inward-looking.

This was his crystal-ball moment, so far as the uses of technology today are concerned. 'Individualism' is the key term in his insight; indeed, it is a word which he coined, and which he evokes as follows:

> Each person, withdrawn into himself, behaves as though he is a stranger to the destiny of all the others. His children and his good friends constitute for him the whole of the human species. As for his transactions with his fellow citizens, he may mix among them, but he sees them not; he touches them, but does not feel them; he exists only in

himself and for himself alone. And if on these terms there remains in his mind a sense of family, there no longer remains a sense of society.[1]

This inward-looking sort of individual wants a cosy, easy life, in contrast to the rugged individualism of American pioneers. A rugged individual backpacks while Tocqueville's sort of individual prefers guided tours. Faced in a foreign city with the choice of a Starbucks or a local café, Tocqueville's new man heads to Starbucks; he doesn't have to make the effort to discover and select among an archipelago of local-owned cafés. So too with strangers; 'he mixes ... but does not feel them'. Familiarity rules.

Tocqueville calls the relations between detached individuals an 'equality of condition'. This phrase does not quite mean what it might seem. Tocqueville was under no illusion that incomes would become more equal in the American future, or that democracy would level power politics. By 'equality of condition' he sought to convey that people will come to want the same things – the same consumer goods, the same education, the same standard of housing – to which they have very unequal access. Equality of condition was unbeautifully labelled 'the massification of consumer taste' by the sociologist Theodor Adorno; Tocqueville enlarged massification to codes of behaviour.

The two phrases, 'individualism' and 'equality of condition', mark Tocqueville as a dark prophet of technology – not that he ever, to my knowledge, wrote a word about machines. His ideas explain why the hand-held device and the screen are individualizing machines, and why the standardized programs running on hand-held and computer screens create an equality of condition in communications. These insights can be pushed one step further: his explanations of individualism and equality of condition combine to explain why smart cities can become closed. The devil in all this is what we call 'user-friendly' tech. It passifies.

II. A NEW KIND OF GHETTO – A GOOGLEPLEX

Because of my association with MIT, over the years I've had occasional contacts with various software developers, beta-testing certain programs – the idea being that, if I can use them, anyone can. I had a brief, unhappy fling with Google, testing out a program designed to help people cooperate online. The gee-whiz claims made by Google have always aroused my suspicion; still, I've wanted to peer into its lair. Since the software firm is obsessed with protecting its secrets, the corporate headquarters is difficult to get into; however, thanks to a former student who was just quitting the firm in New York, I had a chance to tour with her inside.[2]

In the city but not of it The Googleplex in New York is a shell renovation. An old building, formerly housing offices for the Port Authority of New York, has been hollowed out, then remade, in order to provision the creative activity inside which has made Google an industry giant. In New York, the Googleplex has faced certain challenges due to its location. Sited just above Greenwich Village, across the street on one side is a reminder of the Other, as the Other used to be in New York: a string of bars, whorehouses and cheap flats along Eighth Avenue. The New York Googleplex also contains, on the ground floor of the old Port Authority building, certain activities which cannot be related to the interior renovation. There is a large health clinic serving the whole West Village rather than just those Google employees who have suffered a psychotic breakdown due to stress. There are also, at ground level, retail banks orientated to the street, and even the vestiges of the light industries which once were concentrated in this part of town thanks to its cheap rents.

Google is proposing, in time, to create an entirely new structure, designed by the fashionable architects Bjarke Ingels and Thomas Heatherwick, whose most notable urbanistic feature will be a glassed-in, rooftop garden, this 'public space' entirely relieving Googlistas from exposure to their physical surroundings. But for the moment the street constitutes a kind of dirty envelope.

The inside is meant to be self-contained. Famously, once inside any Googleplex, everything is available that an employee could desire: you can get your laundry done here, visit the doctor, exercise in a gym, sleep if working late, even watch a movie if you need to chill out – a richly furnished work environment. This is not down to kindliness on the part of the employers; the twenty-four-hour services are the principal means of focusing people on life inside, minimizing non-corporate distractions. All Googleplexi, sprinkled over the globe from Silicon Valley to Munich, are gated communities designed to extract labour from otherwise unattached twenty-somethings; once people have spouses, partners or children, they will want to spend less time on site. For these people, Google provides – as in Silicon Valley – big white buses to chauffeur them to and from the office, thus extending working hours via absolutely reliable internet connections. This Googleplex formula derives from the classic company towns of the industrial era like Pullman, Illinois, in the US or Port Sunlight in Britain, both built in the 1880s; like them, the Googleplex ties a tight time-knot between working and dwelling.

The Googlistas are poster-children for the 'creative classes'. This term, invented by Richard Florida, is now defined by the US Bureau of Labor Statistics as people who mostly work in advertising, media services and tech start-ups outside universities; the number of independent artists, musicians and poets is relatively minute: the creative classes are more distributors, middlemen and branders than actual *Homo fabers*. Pursued by investors, celebrated by politicians as the answer to urban stagnation, the creative classes are an elite which does not do much for the mass. In fact the reverse. As Nathan Heller has pointed out, in 2014 a traditional business like Citibank employed about 250,000 people, whereas Facebook, with a higher valuation in the stock market, employed about 6,000.[3]

In a big city, the company-town idea behind a Googleplex translates as an island within the city which nevertheless has a significant effect on the territory around it. Most notoriously, Googlistas and their kind drive up house prices in Manhattan – just as in their other epicentre, the San Francisco region – currently (2017) by 16 per cent annually in the places they favour. Buildings like the Googleplex serve as a draw for the kinds of clothing stores, restaurants, gourmet gadget shops and the like which also send up commercial rents, which in turn force out local, cheap or sleazy places like those lining Eighth Avenue. Ironically for a group celebrating creativity, the look of a creative-class watering hole is instantly recognizable: large espresso machine, Parsons table, Lightolier X-50 track lighting . . .

The Googleplex is an icon of privilege in a more personalized way.

Twenty years before my New York Googleplex lookaround, I had interviewed youngsters in Silicon Valley for a book on high-tech work in the
new economy. In that primal age, tech start-ups had a certain odour, a
smell amalgamating stale pepperoni pizza, Diet Coke and sweaty socks;
this fragrance was chilled but not dispelled in air-conditioned rooms in
which nobody bothered to open the windows. There are no teeming
streets in Silicon Valley, but the tech start-ups were small and, as in
Nehru Place, the aspiring geniuses spent a lot of time with people in
other firms, looking at what the competition was doing, occasionally
cooperating and conspiring. Start-up failures spurred the need to look
around and outside. Then, as now, the rates of failure were high; only
about 7 per cent of tech start-ups last for more than two years in America. Then, as now, emailing a resumé was unlikely to get you a new job;
you had to connect with people face-to-face.[4]

This tech culture was based on the premise that there's enough
largesse to go around, so that no stumble will prove fatal. But as
noted in the Introduction, the political economy of high tech has
drastically changed, moving from an open, Wild West state to a more
closed condition. As monopoly has become the dominant fact of life
in the tech world in the last twenty years, firms like Google, Apple or
Cisco Systems will snap up, and often then shut down, start-ups that
might become competitors. Monopoly capitalism makes an ironic
frame for the architecture of Googleplexi, for these buildings are
meant to stimulate free exchange of ideas inside, even as the firm
destroys free markets outside.

What makes the Googleplex a Tocquevillian environment is its
absorbing interior, its intimacy – the Googleplex in the city but not of
it. This contrast came home to me as soon as we stepped outside. We
left after touring the workout area and laundry room, sampling the
sushi (very good), watching people staring at their screens (it was very
late at night, but many people were still at their desks). On the street,
a rent-boy, one eye bruised, flashed me a questioning glance; radios
and TVs blared from the apartments above the all-night bars on
Eighth Avenue; my ex-student and I grabbed a sandwich in an inex-
pensive café favoured by gossiping cabbies working the night shift.
We were now in the city.

*

Detached creativity Buildings modelled on the Googleplexi are meant to suit best creative industries. The question they pose is whether an inward-turning environment really encourages creativity.

By taking down walls within a building, it used to be thought, the office designer removes as well the mental 'silos' in which employees can become isolated. But sheer open space does not in itself enable creative exchange; office architects like Frank Duffy critique the idea of the open-plan office in which there is a sea of desks at which anyone can sit anywhere anytime – 'hot-desking'. In such a neutral environment, people tend to fall silent, staring at their screens rather than making informal comments to one another. An open plan needs to be carefully furnished to stimulate them; the space needs to be made more characterful; it needs to become what Duffy calls an 'office-scape'.[5, 6]

The Googleplex is a particular version of office landscape. The design in part creates informal social spaces where people can meet easily, chat over a cup of coffee and think together; more provocatively, the office-scape stages these creative encounters in unlikely spots. In Google, as in many other high-tech companies, cafés and workout rooms have replaced the traditional watercooler as informal sites for exchange; social spaces are integrated into high-traffic areas, rather than being removed into a separate social zone. Placing toilets adjacent to a jumble of food trolleys, work-stations and sofas is a clever touch, albeit non-standard design practice, since after relieving oneself a person is likely to be physically relaxed. The purposeful design of informality produced workspace of a sort entirely foreign to the standard office. The jumble of pool tables, food trolleys, low-slung sofas and work-stations makes Googleplexi look like high-class fraternity houses. Indeed, the Google formula for building a creatively stimulating office takes form around the idea of a campus; John Meachem, the architect-guru who masterminds Google's architecture, imagines a Googleplex as a 'loosely structured' university.[7]

'You can't schedule innovation,' David Radcliffe, a Google space planner has declared; thus the office-scape strategy is to stage 'casual collisions of the work force'. In the new campus Google is building in Mountain View, California, nine new buildings are rectangles, each with a bend in the middle, rather than being shoebox straight; the idea is that at these bends those 'casual collisions of the work force' will occur. Within single buildings, as in New York present and future, odd-angled corridors similarly stream employees towards intersections where the casual collisions will happen.[8]

All of which seems to evoke Jane Jacobs. Indeed, the New York Googleplex is located just above the streets in Greenwich Village she wrote about; at first glance it looks to be filled with the same pulsing, spontaneous, casual collisions outside which she celebrated. The difference lies, I think, in the infantile, play-pen aura of the interior, so unlike the grim street outside or the disorders with which Jacobs was engaged. Blocked? Play ping-pong; tasty sushi is always available; use the chill-out rooms whenever you are tired; a doctor is on call twenty-four hours a day. The workspace parallels the supportive environment touted by very expensive private schools. The expensively made supportive office now serves as the model for design in 'innovation zones', as though the nicer they are, the more creative people will be.

The Googleplex office negates a key aspect of creative work: encounters with resistance. All demanding labour of course prompts efforts to overcome obstacles, but an office, as much as a laboratory or an artist's studio, should allow people to dwell on difficulties. Fun offices with lots of distractions and escape routes don't necessarily help blocked people get to grips. By contrast, in the MIT Media Lab there were all sorts of nooks and paperboard shelters; it looked a mess, and unfriendly to boot, but as an environment spoke of serious work happening. There were no relieving, cosy distractions. In the larger *ville*, the Media Lab looks like start-up districts before they were designated 'innovation zones'. This is more than a matter of style. A messy space littered with half-eaten pizzas and, in my lost youth, cigarette butts sends a signal of creative engagement which tidy, homey environments with pleasure on demand do not.

John Dewey analysed resistances and obstacles as creative spurs; in *Art as Experience*, he observed that, 'Without internal tension there would be a fluid rush to a straightaway mark; there would be nothing that could be called development and fulfillment. The existence of resistance defines the place of intelligence in the production of an object of fine art.' As in art, so in life: resistance prompts us to think. Of course, no one wants to invite or invent difficulties; the stimuli they provide come unbidden, from outside, invading the zone of controlled labour, to then be dealt with. The trouble with the Googleplex is that the interior has been insulated, made a complete, self-sufficing realm; outside reality checks and resistances are excluded by design.

As I now want to show, all thinking, not just creativity, suffers when resistance is minimized technologically.[9, 10] This reduced cognition affects in turn the character of one kind of smart city.

III. FRICTION-FREE TECH — WHAT 'USER-FRIENDLY' COSTS USERS MENTALLY

Bill Gates coined the term 'friction-free' to describe user-friendly technology. Friction-free design should be seen as embodying the second aspect of Tocqueville's prophecy, the 'equality of condition' which is the appearance of massified taste, in this case the terms on which people want to consume technology: easily available and usable by all.

In a mechanical device, the engineer certainly wants to minimize the frictions and resistances which wear down the machine. The digital domain of 'friction-free' differs from the mechanical imperative of reducing wear-and-tear. The term applies particularly to technology which is easy to use but whose workings are largely inaccessible to the user, as in computer-dominated automobiles whose innards are too complex for the ordinary driver to engage with: you use what you don't understand.[11]

The programming guru Peter Merholz fleshes out this mindset by explaining how creators should relate to consumers; the designer should actively seek to hide the complexities of technology from its users. The former head of the Xerox PARC research centre John Seely Brown exhorts his colleagues to 'get the technology out of the way' in use and to make the experience seem 'seamless'. The Facebook boss Mark Zuckerberg converts this exhortation into a social formula, one embodied by the slogan 'frictionless sharing'; his program is meant to diminish the hard, frustrating effort to make a friend or get a date. In all, friction-free becomes user-friendly when the user does not have to think about 'why?' The sting in the tail of this ethos is that the technology becomes difficult to scrutinize critically; the user knows whether the technology does what it says, but is prevented rather than assisted by experts from pondering *why* it does what it does. A contrast is the open-sourced Linux platform, its kernel (the program's DNA) much more transparent, but also much more demanding. To use it well, you have to know a lot more about principles of programming than you do in using more mass-market products.[12]

There are technical paradoxes built into friction-free programs. The most notable is a tendency towards 'over-featuring', which means the ever-increasing numbers of bells and whistles assuring people that they can do anything they want at a touch of a button; there is a programmed answer for every problem. 'Over-featuring' appears in word-processing programs like Microsoft Word, where the sheer number of options can slow down the writing process. In more technical work, over-featuring appears in CAD (computer-aided design) programs meant to cover all options from initial sketching to final materials specification; here the programs inhibit visual focus by offering too many possibilities to focus on.

To be sure, using without understanding is an age-old dilemma. The ancients used garlic as an effective medicine without understanding anything about its chemical properties. Fortunate violinists in Stradivarius's time played his violins without understanding why they sounded so great; today, the sonic properties of these instruments still remain something of a mystery. The ethos of friction-free tries to push these technical puzzles aside. It promotes making tech tools easy to use, at the same time they can be made to do anything. Demands won't be placed on the user. This appeal is just what Tocqueville feared: the clamour of complexity silenced by comfort. But in the tech realm the user pays a big mental price for succumbing to such salesmanship.

Friction and cognition A slew of technology critics have criticized the dumbing-down effects of living too much online. Among them, the psychologist Sherry Turkle has observed youngsters obsessed with computer games. The sorts of disputes kids have on real playing fields about who plays fair or what should be the rules of play do not occur when they sit down in front of the computer; they are absorbed within the frame of predetermined rules which ensure the game can go forward. Nicholas Carr has argued that multitasking onscreen disables people cognitively, shortening their attention span and so leading them to avoid situations which demand prolonged attention to be understood. Both are saying that certain experiences of technology disable cognition of a sustained and questioning sort. Friction-free computer culture can be a narcotic diminishing physical stimulation, with disturbing stimulations in particular being repressed: if you don't like what you see, press Delete, go to another window.[13, 14, 15]

We need to refine this critique, for not any and all tech has a villainous effect on the brain. Merholz's idea of hiding complexity from the user, in order that the experience is free-flowing and easy, does so in particular way: it deflates 'generation effects'. This term refers to the effort of analysing information which is incomplete, contradictory or difficult – information which is open in character. A number of studies show that making that effort means people retain information longer and better than if it is complete, clear and easy to access. Generation effects also can teach people how to become good mental editors, weeding out dross like over-featuring.

Norman Slamecka began the study of generation effects in the 1970s by studying how remembering words and phrases works, the memory of them being greater if a person has to fill in the blanks of partially missed information. In our time, Christof van Nimwegen has studied generation effects by devising a video game called *Missionaries and Cannibals*, the hungry pursuing the devout through forest, savannah and river. Van Nimwegen provided his subjects with either defective, imperfect software or a kinks-free, free-flowing program. He found that people who used the clunky software became much more adept at playing *Missionaries and Cannibals* than people who had the glitch-less program, learning more thoroughly which moves would prove important and which ones were dead-ends.[16, 17]

Modern-day cognition researchers are drawing on an insight which can be traced back to the philosopher Charles Sanders Peirce, writing at the turn of the twentieth century. He named as 'abduction' a process which 'supposes something of a different kind from what we have directly observed and frequently something which it would be impossible for us to observe directly'. Abduction is what-if? knowledge. An example in the Media Lab auto project was a technician's question one day: 'What if I brake by pulling up the steering wheel rather than pushing down a pedal with my foot?' Other people explained this couldn't work because the body is programmed physiologically to push rather than pull in order to stop. 'So what?' the technician replied, 'I am not talking about my body as it is but as it might be trained to be.' Abduction forms the realm of counterfactuals. Peirce believed it plays a critical as well as an imaginative role. We can't know the value of anything unless we take it apart mentally, disrupting the taken-for-granted character of reality. Religious belief might have served him as an example of this reality test, as it did for Peirce's colleague William James. What if God does not exist? You cannot be a truly committed religious believer unless you have gone through the process of experiencing that counter-factual doubt.[18]

On tech terrain, when something is easy to use we aren't inclined to ask, what if it were different? Once tempted to turn on the 'grammar check' function on my word-processing program, I was amazed to see how instantly it caught the many oddities in the ways I construct sentences, but the program didn't suggest imaginative or unusual solutions to these faults – 'grammar check' in Microsoft Word doesn't operate in a playful, what-if? spirit. ('Check', dictionary-wise, means both to monitor and to inhibit.) This deficit might seem countered by the huge array of editing and formatting features in the program: you can do everything with just a few flicks of the finger from setting up a poem to organizing a film script to incorporating tables, images and text. But the menu itself is just the problem: it offers predetermined forms for each function – you can choose only what's on the menu. This contrasts it to older DOS programs like WordPerfect 5.1, a writing tool more difficult to work with, since it had relatively few defined features. But it was a satisfying tool to use because it did not inhibit experimenting with sentence construction or text formats. Its pathetically limited spell-checker meant unlikely words could be conjured without restraint – James Joyce would have hated Microsoft Word and embraced WordPerfect 5.1. The same contrast appeared in the Media Lab. To its denizens, experiments which are easily formatted as Yes/No hypothesis tests are second-rate; the first-rate kind of experiment is in terms of unknowns, possibilities and what-ifs.

This contrast between clear-easy and ambiguous-what-if is explained by the generation effects studied by Norman Slamecka and his colleagues. Incomplete knowledge leads to asking what-if questions, because the questioner has treated reality as undetermined; it's up to you to make sense of it. Another track of cognition studies – dealing with contradictions – arrived at this same end. We owe this work to Leon Festinger, the psychologist who developed the modern understanding of 'cognitive dissonance'.

This term refers to a situation in which there are contradictory rules of behaviour, or rules which are confusing. How will the subject respond? Festinger was a man of the experimental laboratory, making use of animals – he preferred pigeons – but he was thinking always about the application of his findings to human beings. He recognized, though, that cognitive dissonance, a condition which he created for the pigeons, is a painful state that people create for themselves.

Aesop's fable 'The Fox and the Grapes' is a classic instance of this. The fox sees a cluster of grapes high up, which he cannot reach; unable to snatch them, he decides they are not worth eating because they are probably sour – though he has no way of knowing this. The fable is the origin of our idea of sour-grapes thinking; the frustration of not getting one's way justified by thinking 'I didn't want it anyhow.' But the fox still does, really; if the grapes fell to the ground he would devour them greedily. One way out of this bind, Festinger writes, is for 'the person to try to reduce the dissonance and achieve consonance'. This mentality can mean that 'when dissonance is present, in addition to trying to reduce it, the person will actively avoid situations and information which would likely increase the dissonance'. That's the negative side of cognitive dissonance: the subject avoids its complexities whenever possible. The fox craves grapes but in time comes to lie about his craving: 'I really don't like grapes.' Any ex-smoker will recognize this line.[19, 20]

There is also a positive way to respond to frustrating or contradictory experience. Knowing of my interest in complex environments, Festinger led me one day through a laboratory filled with caged pigeons trying to peer around obstacles hiding their watering tubes, or to make sense of feed troughs the experimenters had angled oddly. Some pigeons were simply disorientated by these scenes – were I caged, I know that I would have been. But others behaved differently, becoming more alert when confronted by dissonant circumstances. Their attentiveness, Festinger said, was not just visual: these pigeons heard faint sounds better, and their sense of smell sharpened; their memories improved as well.

The reason is, Festinger said, that these birds had developed the capacity to focus on the dissonance itself. They explored resistance, thereby developing what he called 'focal attention'. He explored how such attention works even when animals' food or safety is not directly under threat, yet their environment has been changed in a puzzling way. In various experiments, his lab found that such environmental changes raised anxiety levels (as measured by heartbeat and hormonal rates), yet still the tenacious pigeons wandered about, sometimes pecking at an impediment to test it – if they were anxious, they were also invigorated, curious birds. Most telling, Festinger found that these pigeons became more intelligent creatures than their disengaged peers.[21]

Festinger once observed that 'we care most about those things we have struggled to understand'. He believed that humans, like other animals, become more cognitively alert by struggling with complicated realities, rather than walking away from them, as in Aesop's fable, or among Tocqueville's individuals, or online. I wondered how exactly Festinger's precept might apply in cities.

The experiments from which Festinger's theory is constructed deal with outright, immediately evident contraries: the pigeon pushes a water lever, and instead a few kernels of grain come out. Whereas ambiguity rather than outright contradiction ruled the streets of Balzac's Paris, Park's Chicago, Jacobs' New York and Mr Sudhir's Delhi. Street life in all these places was on the surface fluid, with crowds of strangers coming and going, an experience of casual sightings, of few deep, illuminating exchanges. Yet through the application of focal attention, pockets of order could be detected in this stream. Even though the street was a sea of black, Balzac's Parisian would seek to deduce from the details of a stranger's clothing his or her class; in Park's Chicago, Zorbaugh found that momentary eye-contact served as an index of whether someone was friend or foe; in New York, 'eyes on the street' scanned the Village looking for people who seemed likely to cause trouble or commit crimes; Mr Sudhir was constantly on the lookout for customers, for what competitors were up to, and (as I later learned) for undercover police whom he would have to bribe. The sociologist Elijah Anderson calls such efforts to infer order from fluidity 'the code of the street' – apprehending, in open-systems terms, 'pockets of order'.[22]

Whereas the ethos of friction-free suspends our focal attention on the particularities of a specific, complex place, even at a trivial level, as in choosing a Starbucks rather than searching for an out-of-the-way local café. More gravely, stereotypes of the Other – as a black or a Muslim – are friction free; discerning the particularity of a black man or Muslim woman who does not fit the stereotype takes mental as well as emotional work. And for an experience to be friction-free, it must be withdrawn from the clamour of contending interests – the interests of other people or, perhaps worse, contending interests within oneself. As with Aesop's fable, or Tocqueville's new individual, complexities and differences which don't mesh easily with our desires are suppressed, ignored or lied about. The result is cognitive loss.

The cognitive goal of Festinger's lab work was to discover the conditions in a cage which stimulate an animal's desire to focus on complexity rather than disengage from it. So too in a city. In the modern city, how might high tech make us smarter, or dumb us down?

IV. THE TWO SMART CITIES – PRESCRIBE OR COORDINATE

There are two kinds of smart city, closed and open. The closed smart city will dumb us down, the open smart city will make us smarter.

Prescribe The closed smart city is a Googleplex enlarged, filled with Tocquevillian individuals, fuelled by user-friendly technology which stupefies its citizens. In this dystopia, as the Dutch planners Maarten Hajer and Ton Dassen write, 'urban technologies will make cities safer, cleaner and, above all, more efficient . . . Smart cities will "sense" behaviour via big data and use this feedback to manage urban dynamics and fine-tune services.' To them, as for the technologist Adam Greenfield, such a smart city is really driven by the politics of centralized control that prescribes how people should live; this tech-nightmare is dramatized in Dave Eggers' novel about Google, *The Circle*. What does it look like on the ground?[23, 24, 25]

An hour's drive to the south-west of Seoul, the smart city of Songdo is being built from scratch, on land reclaimed from the ocean. As of 2012 it housed about 30,000 people, but the settlement is expected to triple in five years. As in Shanghai the speed of development has no parallel elsewhere; for every new house built in America's vigorous sun-belt cities, eighteen houses are built in new cities in China and South Korea. Above ground, Songdo looks like a leafy, wavy version of the Plan Voisin; its towers are surrounded by parks, as in Shanghai, though this new landscape is softer, lushly planted and generously spread out.

Originally, Anthony Townsend writes, Songdo was conceived as 'a weapon for fighting trade wars'; the idea was 'to entice multinationals to set up Asian operations at Songdo . . . with lower taxes and less regulation'. Tech entered the picture, Greenfield says, when big tech was added to make the city more attractive. Companies like Cisco and Software AG bid for work, and the results were to make the environment ever more regulated technologically, even as they boasted less regulated markets.[26, 27]

The control centre for the smart city of Songdo is an eerily calm place. It's called the 'cockpit', a word which doesn't quite ripple off the tongue in Korean, but represents the aspiration of Songdo's planners to create a model for other places, one based on steering a city the way you would pilot an aircraft. The cockpit was in place from the beginning. An array of giant screens shows what's happening to the city's air quality, electricity usage, traffic flows; technicians sit in swivel chairs, watching the screens, occasionally noting something, making a correction, but not speaking very much. There is no need. The formulas which run the machines which run the city work well; technicians showed me around with a quiet pride.

Songdo's soft look betrays the fact that the green, the little ponds, the wavy grid, are all calculated for environmental efficiency and saving. Pointing to a map in the cockpit, a technician told me the exact amount of CO_2 absorption occurring in a particular park – a fantastic calculation to me, but then I grew up using slide rules. There is a one-way flow from the central command centre to the sensor or hand-held smartphone; the sensor, hand-held or hand-holder, reports information, but the control centre makes the interpretation of what it means and how the hand-held should act upon it. This is the way Google Maps and other familiar programs operate, but the scope of control in Songdo is much greater. One big employer clocks where its employees are by monitoring smartphone use. In less Big Brotherish uses of technology, like the orchestration of traffic lights, a whole, if smallish city now operates at the command of the cockpit – or more precisely, at the behest of the big-data assemblages, interpretative algorithms and monitoring of machines which are displayed visually in the room. Such cockpit control embodies the prescriptive model of a smart city.

Songdo's sister smart city, Masdar, is near to and financed by Abu Dhabi. Masdar is meant more as a smart suburb, its 40,000 residents complemented by 50,000 daily commuters from Abu Dhabi. The United Arab Emirates, all huge consumers of energy, are concerned about shrinking their ecological footprint. As in Songdo, urbanists are bent on showing the way forward to others. In Masdar, as master-planned by Norman Foster, relatively friction-free energy use comes from renewables like solar; in planner-speak, the plan is that 'synergistic efficient urban design by means of passive design elements is being applied', making savings of 70 per cent compared to Abu Dhabi nearby. The way to make these good things happen is by 'scaling up and integrating advanced sustainable technologies' which only a computer capable of handling big data can do. Masdar is known for experiments with self-drive vehicles. Its buildings, designed by Foster, are of much higher quality than those in Songdo – and much more expensive.[28, 29]

I had been in Songdo when it was first being developed; later, felled by a stroke, I fielded a team of lively young researchers to see how the city had turned out. In the early days they were amazed: 'For its engineers,' one reported, 'this is a space largely built around a fantasy of ubiquitous computing. It is envisioned as a machinic [*sic*] space in which algorithmic logic, human inhabitants and a lot of black boxes produce networks of entanglements.' Then they became unsettled: 'Homogeneous, heavily monitored and centralized, Songdo offers none of the markers of diversity or democracy lauded by ... the polis ... This space is a nightmare for many urbanists and a fantasy for many computer corporations.' By the end of their visit it seemed to them a 'ghost town', 'arid', 'inert'. Their discontent had little to do with the absence of clubs, drugs or drink; unfortunately perhaps, my researchers are morally upstanding. And anything but technological Luddites, they are just the sort of sophisticates to whom the advertisements for this city of the future should have appealed.

What affronted them, I came to see, was that Songdo is not smart at all. It operated in a stupefying way; my brainy assistants felt the place insulted their own intelligence. Generation effects, abductions and focal attentions played no role in its design; instead, user-friendly ruled. It might seem that smart cities of the Songdo type should also share a Googleish embrace of serendipity – but exactly not. Prescription is meant to foresee, in advance, how the city will function, to lay out its workings precisely in space and built form. Smart cities of the Songdo type fear chance. As one of my assistants put it, the smart city 'litened' the experience of place.

In part this suspended sense of place owes something to Corbusier. The Plan Voisin was a manifesto for the mechanical age, in which form and function fitted tightly together. Lewis Mumford's *Technics and Civilization*, published in 1934, cautioned against soulless technology along Corbusier's line; still, his version of the smart city was also of a place in which form and function mesh perfectly mechanically – everything has a place and a rationale, all the elements of living are laid out precisely in the tight radial design. Today's smart cities bring form–function tight-fit into the digital age, aiming to become self-sustaining environments.

A too-tight fit between form and function is a recipe for technological obsolescence. As people do things differently, the fixed form will no longer serve, or else a new tool will render old skills obsolete. This caution against locking form and function together applies to smart-city experiments, as Norman Foster found when devising docking stations for his new automobiles. Since the time he and his colleagues began working on the project, the electronically autonomous automobile had evolved; now it could accommodate four or five passengers rather than the one or two people imagined in the early prototypes. The docking stations were now too small. An efficient tight-fit assumes the design will foresee every circumstance in which the object will be used, how the environment will work, how people will dwell. As in Shanghai's roads to nowhere, the calculations can prove wrong.

Technological efficiency does not necessarily beget financial success. In Songdo, many of the towers are dark, since the worldwide recession has discouraged buyers. In the Emirates the bursting of the financial bubble has put the luxury experiment which is Masdar temporarily on hold; Suzanne Goldenberg calls it 'the world's first green ghost town'. Below ground, much of the high-tech kit thus transmits nothing. A video of the cockpit sent to me showed this uneven development on one screen as pools of black amid flashing patches of activity. Songdo's economic fortunes show up too as black patches on computer screens. Built-from-scratch, prescriptive smart cities are indeed luxury goods; the cost of constructing them is rising rather than falling. The obvious planning question is why a country like India – so full of people who have no clean water to drink, no proper sanitation, no local health clinics, etc. – would seek to follow this bankrupting path, by planning 100 spanking new smart cities.[30]

The fundamental question about smart cities is why they have a stupefying effect on those who live in them. In part this is because, as my researchers found, they are so easy to live in. They are very user-friendly. Beyond this, the planning itself is not experimental but static in the sense of always seeking a homeostatic balance in its components; the what-if? alternative, the intriguing possibility which leads to a dead end, are not pursued because the ecology will then be disrupted and unbalanced – as though the city were having a technological heart attack. In this way, the prescriptive smart city privileges problem-solving over problem-finding. In good science, the researcher wants to know the side effects of a new drug; in good craftsmanship, the carpenter wants to foresee the problems that arise in varnishing a cabinet after working out how to fit together two differently grained woods. Problem-solving and problem-finding are linked – so long as you are curious. But the prescriptive model deadens curiosity; in this sort of smart city, you don't have to be.

The stupefying smart city has an ethical dimension. Most map programs as currently configured, for instance, show the traveller the fastest, most direct way to get from point A to B, and the majority of them solve this problem by putting travellers on highways. Problem over? The prescribed highway from A to B may well avoid a slower street on which there is a shuttered factory, a wonderfully crowded market or a woeful slum settlement. On the highway, you are making a journey, but you are not learning much about others during the course of your journey. You are moving through space rather than experiencing place. Prescription tells you what is the most efficient route; people neither have to ponder what if it were different nor what is the most experience-rich route.

Of course, much of the daily round has to be framed in terms of sheer efficiency. It's a question of balance: the prescriptive city becomes unbalanced in divorcing functioning from questioning. Norbert Wiener foresaw this danger: in old age he came to fear that his brain-child would prove a monster – 'big data' (Wiener coined the term), controlled by 'Big Brother', can reduce people's lives to digital bits of needs and desires serviced by a few monopolies. Tech as Big Brother has perhaps become a cliché, but Wiener feared something deeper: by using machines, people would stop learning. They would become stupefied. The prescriptive smart city is a site for this stupefication.[31]

Must it be so?

Coordinate Using technology to coordinate rather than control activities makes for a very different kind of smart city; the technology is cheaper and focuses on people as they are, in all their Kantian crookedness, rather than on how they should be. And coordinative tech develops human intelligence.

These virtues are achieved through organizing networks in a certain way. A closed network is usually defined as limited access, whereas an open network will include everyone; the divide online occurs when a paywall, for instance, limits the people who can read a particular newspaper. In the smart-city realm, the difference between open and closed networks concerns feedback. In a closed urban network, the sensors read citizen behaviour, as in speeding or electricity usage, whether the citizen wants to be read or not; feedback is involuntary. In an open urban network, the single citizens or citizens groups have more control over feedback. The coordinative smart city honours limitations on its own data, then processes and relates that information to other groups.

An early example of an open urban network occurred in Porto Alegre, in Brazil, home to participatory budgeting – a bottom-up way of distributing economic resources, inaugurated by its mayor, Olívio Dutra, in 1989. The process began in loose neighbour assemblies which debated how to spend money on schools, health clinics and local infrastructure. Access at this level was totally open. The data, never perfect, was organized so that it could be debated. Conflicts between neighbourhoods were dealt with by elected representatives who had report back to their neighbourhoods. This system flourished for about twenty years before becoming somewhat squashed by top-down power, but even more by the sheer scale of people who wanted to be included in the process as the city grew in size. In Brazil, as megacities emerged, negotiations between a very large cluster of localities began to lose coherence and stretch out endlessly throughout the year. Moreover, the vast wave of migrants which create a megacity were often not integrated into the organizations and assemblies required for participatory budgeting.

Enter the smart city, via the smartphone and big-data assemblage. Huge 'inputs', i.e. shifting votes, can be handled, as changes in the distribution of funds over many communities are calculated in real time. Rather than prescribing, big data now make it possible to coordinate participation at a megacity scale. Citizens communicate online if no longer face-to-face. The data is still organized as debatable, and problematic. A kind of chatroom operates at the local level to assemble views, with proposals appearing online as well as responses. This feedback is what elected representatives are to represent at meetings with other communities, in dividing up the spoils – such as they are in relatively poor communities. The resulting budget is binding, though the city council can suggest, but not require, changes. Something like this system is now installed in over 250 other Brazilian cities.[32, 33]

One of Lewis Mumford's criticisms of Jane Jacobs was that you cannot built up scale in a city, in its *ville*, by local action in the city. The Brazilian experience is a way around that problem: the World Bank has found that localities tend to spend money on infrastructure, particularly on sanitation, electrification and health facilities; these solid projects allow neighbourhoods to share resources, such as health clinics, with other neighbourhoods, or to be integrated with the city, in electrification and water systems. The budgeting *cité* has focused on the large *ville*. It would seem that here, far away from Berlin, Max Weber – had he lived long enough – would have found a kind of city-state in which the citizens control their own fortunes.[34]

As in budgeting, so too the actual design of the smart city can follow an open, coordinative form. The computer game *SimCity* was an early version which aimed at generating urban *villes* through interactive high tech. The ForCity project in Lyons, France, uses sophisticated 3-D models to show what an urban future would look like, drawing on big data sets to construct detailed images of urban future fabric. Though they require expert inputting, ForCity models can translate fairly directly commands such as, 'Show possible three sidewidths for a street of X population, with Y footfall density and Z sessile density.' Thus it's possible for both citizens and planners to practise abductive reasoning, asking what-if? questions, and compare possible responses. The difference between this procedure and pre-computer modelling presented to a community meeting is that previously whenever people wanted a specific aspect of a plan changed, the planners would have to leave the room, recalculate and redraw their plans, then convene another meeting. Now they can stay in the room, since the machines can compute changes very fast.[35]

In both these cases, the use of technology helps people choose; in urban design, high tech can enable people to generate the forms about which they have to make choices. In smart cities of the prescriptive sort, data is pre-packaged, and simplified along user-friendly lines, so that the consumer of this data has little input into its production. More open urban design seeks to prepare data so that the users can themselves see alternatives and make decisions.

Today, systems can self-organize, analysing and responding to changing conditions. There is a difference between closed and open systems in the way they study themselves. Think of a CCTV set-up: in a closed feedback loop, there are elements of self-correction in the angles and zoom-focus of the cameras, but the people running this closed system do not think 'I should stop spying' if they see lovers kissing. Whereas in an open system, the cameraman, out of tact if not embarrassment, would turn the cameras off. In less poetical ways, open systems entertain self-criticism by accounting 'noise', that is feedback of information which doesn't serve to maintain harmony and balance, which doesn't fit in; the flow of such information is held in the system's memory. Some open-source software accounts noise, and so do some versions of the 'smart city', like the traffic-systems modelling in Rio, while other 'smart cities' do not. These are closed, as in Songdo, in the sense that they are programmed to discount data which cannot fit into predetermined algorithms. Songdo's algorithms are self-correcting, but not self-critical.

In the prescriptive model, technology digitally organizes the city as a total system. Urbanism then enacts the system physically; the urbanite has then but to play by the rules, which are designed to be user-friendly. Systems of prescription are hermetic, while systems of coordination are hermeneutic – meaning that the complex calculations required to make the city work are, in the prescriptive smart city, hidden away from city-dwellers, just as Peter Merholz wants, whereas in the coordinative smart city, people have to get engaged in the data, interpreting it (the hermeneutic) and acting on it, for better or worse – a coordinative smart city can make mistakes.

All of which forms a political contrast: the prescriptive smart city is inherently authoritarian, while the coordinative smart city is democratic. Democratic deliberation doesn't mean much in Songdo, simply because there was little wiggle room built into the plan itself. Whereas in Curitiba people practise democracy technologically.

To return to where we began, Tocqueville pairs in my mind with a writer of a different bent. This was Robert Musil, whose great novel *The Man without Qualities* dissected Habsburg Vienna as a mythical, though in its corruption and stupidity, hardly a magical place. I pair the two writers because, whether ethnographer or novelist, both had an exceptional engagement with the daily stuff of experience; they were both Chicagoans in temperament. Musil and Tocqueville also pair as prophets. In Musil's case, his forecast derives in part from his formation as a gifted engineer. An early defining moment in the novel comes when he compares Vienna in decline with a future dominated by the 'obsessive daydream' of a 'super-American city' where technology meant 'Air trains, ground trains, underground trains, people mailed through tubes special-delivery, and chains of cars rac[ing] along horizontally, while express elevators pump masses of people vertically', a technopolis whose algorithms are based on 'exhaustive laboratory studies'. In this city of the future, 'Questions and answers synchronize like meshing gears; everyone has only certain fixed tasks to do . . .' – a cartoon of the Charter of Athens. But this technopolis works only so long as 'one doesn't hesitate or reflect too long'.[36]

This is a version of the stupefying smart city, a place that works well so long as you don't think too much about it. Musil's novel probes its nature, as novels do, in terms of character. It focuses on a nameless protagonist who is a liquid person – pliant, easy, adaptable; sociable on the surface, underneath not much involved in the life around him; such a combination defines a man without qualities. He is the brother of Tocqueville's individual. By contrast, a person with qualities (in German, possessed of *Eigenschaften*, which is hard to translate: prickly, particular, rough) is more engaged in life; his or her character has developed through experiencing obstacles, doubts and remorse. This is the realm of people who have, in Musil's words, indeed 'hesitated' or 'reflected too long'. Their understanding of life is deep just because it has not been happy or smooth. As this vast novel unfolds, the man without qualities increasingly worries that life is passing him by, that the quality of his experience is 'lite', that his easy understanding of reality is thin.

How then can the city be opened up, so that experience becomes denser?

PART THREE

Opening the City

7

The Competent Urbanite

Part Two has pictured three ways a city can impoverish people's experience: fast-track growth on the Shanghai model; recoil from those who differ; the stupefying effects of misused technology. These urgent problems also sharpen Jane Jacobs' question to me, 'So what would you do?' In Part Three I am going to answer her – with a big caveat.

Issues like recoil from people who differ have no 'solution' in the sense that there is social medicine you can take to cure yourself of this disease. Fear of others constitutes instead a chronic illness which has to be managed. Just as the symptoms of a chronic illness can be put in remission, so too the civic body can enjoy long spells of vigorous health – as when people who differ are able to live together. Even so, the collective body never escapes the threat of relapse.

In this chapter I investigate some ways in which urbanites might better engage with the *cité*. In the following chapter, I explore what forms in the *ville* could help them do so. Finally, I present certain ways to bring *cité* and *ville* together. As will appear, my answers to the question 'So what would you do?' are guided by treating the healthy city as an open system.

I. STREET-SMARTS – TOUCHING, HEARING, SMELLING A PLACE

Since my wife has spent her life in planes, the logistics of getting to Medellín in Colombia proved easy. Apart from business, why go there? People told me this city, once famous for its drug wars, was now home to some amazing new civic architecture. Particularly in the barrio of Santo Domingo, where there is a library-community centre consisting of three elegant, modernist black blocks, designed by Giancarlo Mazzanti in 2007. The library, called Parque Biblioteca España, lies high up a mountainside coated with shacks housing tens of thousands of poor people, mostly rural refugees from Colombia's civil wars, the rural violence coming from government battles with self-styled revolutionaries called FARC, battles which seem finally to have ended. The library, an architectural jewel, is easy to access thanks to a giant funicular which goes up the mountain; French-designed, its shuttling cars have cut from hours to minutes the time poor people require to get from the slums to work in the centre of town.

Medellín's then mayor, Sergio Fajardo, had built this and other libraries in the slums, knowing that the poor are usually given grungy, purely functional buildings in which they cannot take any pride. To have people 'take ownership' of their communities, you have to build something worth owning. Therefore he spent money on star architects to design libraries for people who are becoming literate, rather than commissioning a new, world-class opera house. He was a good mayor.

Outside the Playa de España, one small, under-nourished boy took my hand and another took the hand of my wife. These were our 'official' guides, wearing T-shirts proclaiming the fact; they had given this guided tour many times before, earning a little money and getting to practise their English. When Saskia spoke fluent Spanish with them, they seemed a bit annoyed; we were the gringos, they were the insiders, a divide which established their status. The boys – eight, ten years old, scrawny though scrubbed – also presented themselves as our protectors; guiding me to the ramp leading to the library, one of them said, 'You are safe if you stay with me.'

Privilege protects the Googleplex from the city, whereas these young people in the slum need to know more about the environment in which they live; there's too much insecurity and sheer lack for them to take the environment for granted. Still, these kids have remained kids: they could be bribed by the ice creams Saskia offered them so that I could sit and rest, and they were calculating in the open, brutal way all kids are: 'Señor, another fifteen minutes costs you a dollar.'

In Santo Domingo men are hanging out on the streets because they are unemployed, gossiping because they have nothing to do; markets are full of unappetizing, spotty fruits and vegetables too old and withered to sell elsewhere. But the barrio, if unstable and at times dangerous, is no theatre of misery. Though the roofs here are often rusty corrugated tin, and the walls unmortared cinderblocks, the pathways in front of these buildings are swept scrupulously clean. The 'probity' of a house is also signalled by window boxes outside homes and bars; there are lane after lane of these well-tended boxes, mostly filled with geraniums and pansies. As in many barrios, here people are constantly improvising to compensate for what they lack, tapping illegally, for instance, into the electricity grid. It is this making-do aspect to which our guides were particularly attuned; in a long account of who was currently selling cheap bottled water, and indifferent to my boredom, my child guide became absorbed in life as he juggled it.

Though too small to be of much use in shielding us from the adolescents and young adults sizing up our smartphones, the confidence our protectors exuded was justified. They knew every alley and byway of the barrio, and, as we found when we stayed on with them after the official tour, they were pleased that we were interested in the environs of the library. They gave an exhaustive description of dangerous and safe streets which would have done a policeman proud.

Holding my eight-year-old guide's hand, I felt his slight, restraining, cautionary gesture whenever we turned a corner. On a later visit at night to the barrio, I noticed that as my protectors rounded corners they would slow down a bit and survey the lights on in the houses lining the street. If the houses of friends whom they'd just seen were in darkness, my protectors would then stop: why wasn't this family at home when they were supposed to be having supper? Once I asked if anything was wrong; 'no,' one ten-year-old protector replied, 'but there might be'.

Street-smarts are not optional. In the barrio, a glance held a moment too long will be taken as an aggressive challenge, inviting a fight. To know how to behave instantly you have to go through several experiences of eye-contact before you know whether another's stare is hostile or beckoning. Once it has become engrained, your response time will be instinctive and swift; visibly calculating how to behave invites trouble.

Kids in Santo Domingo are constantly fact-checking and updating their survival tactics, because the slums of Medellín are fast-changing environments, with a shifting population of incomers from different parts of the country. As the human rights campaigner Tom Feiling observes, violence has somewhat subsided since 2010 because the drugs economy has shifted to Colombia's coastal cities; the construction of the funicular spanning Santo Domingo has made it even safer for people to get to work in the city centre, releasing them from trudging the miles of ill-lit lanes. So the local is in flux. That means nothing can be taken for granted on the ground – which here is still a place for petty robbery and mugging rather than full-blown drug wars. The little kids might be likened to sailors who have learned how to navigate variable and often heavy weather.[1]

Embodied knowledge Street-smarts frame the concept of embodied knowledge – a very general concept which takes a particular form in cities.

Most of the actions we perform we don't think about consciously – we couldn't do otherwise. Imagine taking a walk and thinking, 'Now lift the left leg, now lift the right one, now the left again, now . . .' Instead, once we have learned to walk as toddlers, we engrain this behaviour into an unthinking habit; it enters the domain of tacit knowledge. In developing a skill like hammering a nail, something similar happens: the craftsman learns how to grip the hammer shank, and the best amount of force to apply, given the weight of his or her own body. Once created, this behaviour enters the tacit realm as something a person knows how to do without self-consciously thinking about what he or she is doing. This is, however, only the first step of embodied knowledge.

Behaviour of a tacit rather than an explicit sort was not a foreign concept to the psychologist William James and the philosopher Henri Bergson, founding figures of 'consciousness studies', who both argued against the sharp Cartesian dualism which separates mind and body.

To explain the process by which people dwell in their physical sensations, James developed the concept of the 'stream of consciousness'; the sharp word in James's phrase is 'stream'. A stream flows: thinking, feeling or dwelling is never static. James criticized psychologists before him for speaking of mental 'conditions' and 'states' as though these were solid lumps or fixed images of being. Even when contemplating a painting hung on the wall of a museum, James says, consciousness is 'streaming' because the viewer's attention is shifting, waxing and waning, jumping to memories of other pictures.[2]

A stream of consciousness implies awareness of context – where you are, who is with you, what you or they are doing when you have a particular thought, feeling or sensation. This awareness of context is what embodies a thought: it is a matter of sensing the physical circumstances within which we are thinking; the 'thought' becomes full of sensate associations. Only when these circumstances change does consciousness begin to stream; it does not flow, as in Descartes, independently, of its own accord.

Bergson does not think about consciousness in quite this way. In Proust's famous tasting of the madeleine, a sustained memory from the past is triggered by a momentary physical sensation – a small cookie kickstarts the vast project of conscious recovery of a territory of experience far, far away. Bergson's idea of *durée* is sometimes likened to this cookie-consciousness, but is just the opposite. *Durée* is all about consciousness of the present, and of living wholly in the here and now; it differs from feeling, as in the phrase of the novelist L.P. Hartley, that 'the past is another country'. Bergson is not as concerned as is James with the contexts for and settings of consciousness, rather of awareness just in itself. But he is interested in how felt contradictions jolt people into feeling 'I am here, now' in a way that familiar recognitions do not. He is the father to Leon Festinger's belief that 'we care most about those things we have struggled to understand'.

In their separate ways, James and Bergson are philosophers of street-smarts. And both pose the same problem: what jolts our consciousness? That happens when tacit knowledge becomes insufficient to cope with reality. A second phase begins.

Something is not quite right: a light is out when usually it is on.

The context can no longer be taken for granted. Or there is a sudden, strange sound of bells: should you stop walking? In carpentry, the workman does not think self-consciously about lower-arm weight until an unexpected knot hidden within a piece of wood makes him or her ponder how much lower-arm force to exert. Similarly in surgery, a routine cut through tissue will have to be recalibrated if the surgeon feels an unexpected dense knot. In both cases, the craftsman is focusing on the problematic. The habit is dredged into consciousness: behaviour has entered the explicit realm, one in which the actor is more self-conscious.

It turns out that the strange sound came from an ice-cream truck, something new to Medellín; once taken in and re-embodied in tacit behaviour, the unthinking response will not be exactly as it was before: this sound of this particular bell conveys a call for pleasure, so go quickly towards it. The process of tacit-explicit-tacit means that the repertoire of walking behaviour has become enlarged in a visceral rather than a self-conscious way: one can act in a new manner without having to agonize over the question of what one is doing. Just as the craftsman has tested a different hammer hold, the street-smart person has pondered; both then reinscribe the behaviour in the tacit realm. This is the third phase of street-smarts.

The sniffing out of possible danger by Medellín kids compares to a kind of danger-management which Sara Fregonese describes in Beirut during the violence of its long civil war at the end of the twentieth century. There, people normally put flags outside their houses to identify who lived within; when gunfire sounded streets away, these flags would disappear, so that a roving militia could read nothing about the people of the street. The street-wise interpreted a clear clue – the sound of gunfire – and took clear action in response. In the barrio, the clues were less dramatic and required more interpretation.[3]

Street-smarts of that sort focus on the small detail. We recall that Balzac's idea of how to read a person's character lay in analysing details, for instance, deducing whether a man is a gentleman or not by looking at how the buttons on his sleeve are tailored. The kids are applying that character-reading to a much more urgent purpose.

They are not assaying the importance of a fact by relating the detail to its whole surroundings, as in: 'It's quiet, but so what? All the people on this street know each other, are good neighbours, and anyhow there was an electricity failure last week.' That would be a contextual assessment. Here the detail nags, no matter the context; it clamours to be understood in itself.

In psychology, clue-reading like this is labelled 'spotlighting', a label derived from *The Principles of Psychology*, which William James published in 1890. His 'spotlight' version of attention asserts that the brain lights up a central object, problem or person to dwell on, and pushes aside objects, problems or persons who seem not central to the problem at hand. He wrote that 'concentration of consciousness . . . implies withdrawal from some things in order to deal effectively with others'. We speak Jamesian language when we say we 'zoom in' on a problem.[4]

Spotlighting provides a certain order to the stream of consciousness. You don't, as it were, just go with the flow, but notice, i.e. spotlight, the odd outcropping or a jutting rock as consciousness moves forward. You spotlight, in James's view, when normal expectations are ruptured. James believed the stream of consciousness itself to flow erratically rather than steadily, occasionally drying up, sometimes flooding, often deviating from the straight path of if-then deductions. James's idea of the flow of consciousness thus might be better likened to walking in a slum street than to swimming in a stream.

James's view of spotlighting contrasts diametrically with 'apperception', a venerable idea derived from Leibniz, in which a difficult or dangerous problem is illuminated by setting it in an ever-larger framework. Leibniz zooms out; James zooms in. In daily social life, spotlighting gives a particular structure to brief conversations on Santo Domingo's streets, and more lengthy discussions in its cafés. I thought my bad Spanish accounted for what seemed jerky changes of subject; there was a thread I couldn't follow. But Saskia corrected me; there would be a flow of inconsequential chatter and suddenly a verbal spotlight would be shone on a disturbing detail, like the sound of a gunshot which seemed to come from a strange kind of gun; others might not discuss right away this illuminated fact, but it would be noted, stored away, returned to later in the conversation or in another conversation. The highlighted sound is not particular to Medellín; spot-lighting in the same way occurs in the Mitre, my local pub in Clerkenwell; after our jewel heist, the usual trivial conversations were peppered with sudden, telling eruptions spotlighting 'the Muslims'.

Embodied knowledge has a second aspect. To say that we 'grasp something' implies that we physically reach out for it. In the familiar physical gesture of grasping a glass, the hand will assume a rounded shape, suitable for cupping the glass, before it actually touches the surface; the body is ready to hold before it knows whether what it will hold is freezing cold or boiling hot. The technical name for move-ments in which the body anticipates and acts in advance of sense data is 'prehension'. Prehension involves acting on an anticipation.

Newborn babies begin to practise prehension as early as the second week after birth in reaching for baubles in front of them. In the first five months of life, the baby's arm develops the neuromuscular capacity to move independently towards what the eye sees; in the next five months, the baby's hand develops the neuromuscular capac-ity to shape itself into different grasping positions. By the end of the first year, in Frank Wilson's words, 'the hand is ready for a lifetime of physical exploration'.[5]

Prehension constitutes a twist on the process of abductive reason-ing described in the previous chapter. It provides an answer to the what-if? question. The body imagines in advance what it would be like to do something. To be sure, anticipating what something is like before experiencing it can be a bad thing. In the case of the PEGIDA demonstrators, wild imagining ruled their anticipation of what Mus-lims are like, before actually talking to any Muslims; so too, an earlier generation of Christians imagined that Jews buried children alive, without actually having seen it happen. Prehension can take a more benign form, however, in expanding one's understanding of the physical environment.

Prehension makes possible the judgement of size and of dimensions in urban space when looking straight ahead rather than to the side. As we move forward towards a distant person or building, we begin to reach out in advance to make sense of what we are seeing; it's the equivalent of thinking the cup is hot or cold before touching it.

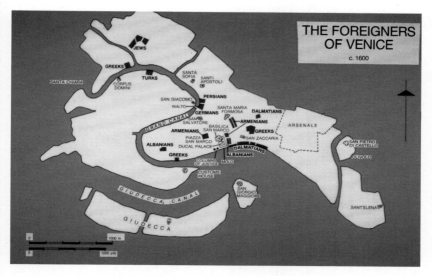

28. Segregation rather than flight is a second way to close
a city. In Renaissance Venice, foreigners were obliged to
live in buildings isolated from citizens. The Jewish Ghetto
is at the northen periphery.

29. The single bridge connecting the Ghetto to the city:
open during the day, shut at
night, guarded always by the
authorities.

30. A corporate, self-imposed version of the Ghetto: the Googleplex in New York, isolated from the street life outside.

31. No reason to leave the building: work and recreation pleasure spaces combined. The firm provides cleaning, medical and other services within.

32. Closure and the 'smart city' 1: in Masdar City, UAE, a single control centre regulates all aspects of the life of the city. It recalls Corbusier's description of the Plan Voisin as embodying the city as 'a machine for living'.

33. Closure and the 'smart city' 2: The city of Songdo in South Korea. Its carefully designated social spaces are a failure; residents prefer places which have arisen informally and do not fit logically into the urban plan.

34. Open and closed in climate change: in the wake of Hurricane Sandy in 2017 in New York, a proposal by Bjarke Ingels Group to create a huge berm – a built-up mound of sand – around the southern tip of Manhattan.

35. The berm is meant to shut out traumatic climate change and mitigate the power of future storms so completely that people can go about their normal business.

Wetlands and their capacity for gradual transformation form a critical part of the design.

Wetland adaptability over time is a function of soil accretion, which itself depends on using tidal sediment transportation patterns.

How does soil accretion work?

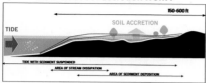

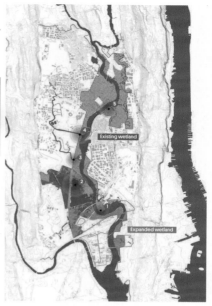

Data points

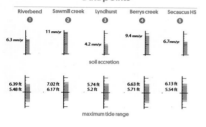

36. In a project created in part by MIT, the emphasis is on adaptation rather than mitigation. This would create a wetlands berm across from Manhattan that rises and falls as storms wax and wane.

37. The result is that the berm shifts in form, rather than remaining as a fixed construction as in the B.I.G. project. The MIT project is more open because of its adaptability.

38. Opening isolated communities: a cable car in Medellín gives residents of a poor area who were formerly isolated access to the whole city below.

39. In this same community, a library run by its residents has connected those who formerly lived isolated and in fear of one another.

40. In Mumbai, an internally open street mixes working and dwelling in the same space at the same time – street life as Jane Jacobs celebrated it in New York.

41. In Naples, the presence of outsiders, in the form of tourists, brings life to a previously dead street. Images 38–41 make clear that 'openness' can be achieved in a variety of ways.

42. The boundary is a closed edge, as in this extreme case in São Paulo.

43. The river of moving traffic is as impermeable a boundary as a solid wall.

44. The open border at the edge of Borough Market, London.
This is a porous space.

45. This edge in Mumbai is both open and closed. The train behind the
street is a danger zone which residents of the street fear and keep away
from, while the street is multifunctional, full of people, at all hours.

46. Place marking: an arbitrary marker of value made in Medellín by the simple, informal gesture of putting a plant in the opening of dwelling.

47. Place marking: an equally arbitrary marker of value, but much more calculated and architectural.

48. A context-specific intervention: street furniture
generated by the larger construction of steps.

49. A non-specific intervention: these coloured chairs and tables could
be put anywhere, and so could add value to any space.

50. The Dutch architect Aldo van Eyck created a park in Amsterdam out a former traffic intersection. 'Open' is created by appropriation.

51. The resultant park has a dangerous edge, where the kids play close to traffic. Van Eyck thought city children should learn how to manage such risks, which they cannot do if they are isolated physically.

52. Van Eyck's appropriation suggests other ways to make use of found spaces in the city. Here is the underbelly of a highway on the west side of Manhattan, once an empty space save for a resident population of heroin dealers and addicts.

53. The insertion of a grocery store underneath the highway, which then served both black Harlem and the mostly white Columbia University community.

54. Incomplete by design: in Iquiqui, Chile, the architect Alejandro Arivenna builds the bones of a good structure and leaves its completion open to the poor residents.

55. When completed, the result is an architectural disaster but an economic and sociological success. 'Open' is not an aesthetic measure.

56. Co-production as an alternative to incomplete by design: in a train station project in Lyon, constant interchange between designers and users produces better results. Here is the station before …

57. … and after.

58. Accretion and rupture of form is a fundamental rhythm in building cities. The rhythm poses an ethical dilemma. This building in Battery Park City, New York, simulates apartment houses elsewhere in Manhattan, whose residents led quite different family and work lives than people do now.

59. By contrast, the Tour Montparnasse in Paris ruptures historic fabric around it. It is awful – and honest to our time. How should urban design mediate nostalgia and truth?

Children in Medellín exercise prehension in calculating what lies ahead before they turn a corner, and adapting their bodies to that, relaxing if they smell food and know that Mrs Santos is at home, cooking, or walking more slowly and carefully if they smell or hear nothing.

Limits on street-smarts The anthropologist Clifford Geertz put in place a certain idea of local knowledge. In contrast to earlier generations of anthropologists, whose aim was to describe worldviews and cosmological understanding, Geertz believed these big concepts developed, if at all, bottom-up; the ways people cope with immediate issues can gradually become expressed in the way they frame 'life' in general. The rituals which orient people also begin in a place-specific way, so Geertz argued, rather than being fished out of the air. This is why archaeology intrigued Geertz, though he never practised it: in ancient times, *where* something happened seemed to him the first step in understanding *what* had happened. Similarly, *where* is the first thing to assess in order to understand *what* in modern times.[6]

This is equally the view of Colombia's greatest novelist, Gabriel García Márquez. His pictures of small doings in small places morph into fantasies and myths which sustain generation after generation of poor people. Local knowledge begets tradition. If this view of local street-smarts makes for great anthropology or art, it has not proved of equal value for our young boys in navigating Medellín. Local street-smarts are not enough to guide them.

The most important building project in Santo Domingo was the construction of an efficient funicular taking people from the steep hillside barrio to and from the city below, where the jobs, churches, sports fields and shops were located. Before the funicular, it was not possible to live in the Medellín barrio divorced from the larger city; the labour market was internally thin, and so people were obliged to trudge long hours up and down the mountainside in search of it. Yet people's outlook could remain ghettoized. In just the same way, in New York up to the Second World War, many elderly Italians seldom left their communities mentally, save for men travelling to work. Santo Domingo opened up thanks to the funicular – it particularly affected young people in the Medellín barrio. They could travel fast down the barrio, then on level ground move fairly freely around the city thanks to cheap bus transport. More recently, the smartphone has connected them to the world beyond; whether stolen, borrowed or purchased, it is now here, as elsewhere, the urban adolescent's most necessary tool.

This widening horizon is overcast. The adolescent older siblings of my guides know that there's no future for them within the insulation of the barrio, and many of these adolescents want to get out of the city entirely. The whole city is now open to young people in terms of seeing other ways of life up close. Would the street-smarts young people learn locally enable them to cope? As in Delhi, so in much of Latin America: local knowledge gained in a village does not prepare them to cope with a big city. Within the sprawling city itself, the same discontinuity can mark the gap between barrio and metropolis. Mr Sudhir negotiated that leap thanks to his connections, and it's true that in Medellín the drugs trade used to create a similar bridge. But these days in Medellín the route out of the local is not channelled this way.

One afternoon in Medellín, I was quizzed about New York by a very young 'assistant librarian trainee' at Mazzanti's library who was just sixteen. She knew the streets of America were not paved with gold, but still she hoped to go north in a year, whether legally or illegally. She asked how long the daily siesta was in New York, and whether she could work as a late-night librarian after school. My answer, that no one takes siestas in New York, seemed bizarre to her (and indeed it is); she was also taken aback that an illegal immigrant could not moonlight at a public library. So she switched cities, asking about the siestas in London and the possibilities of working as a non-documented night-librarian there.

A generation ago, Mexicans faring across the border recounted to the sociologist Patricia Fernandez-Kelly how little lessons learned at home could be applied abroad. The challenges of finding work, resolving legal status, installing oneself in an apartment, commuting, getting health care, etc., are of course always arduous for people who are economically marginal, and the famous 'helping hands' in extended families can help accommodate newcomers only so much. But Fernandez-Kelly's informants stressed that coping behaviour learned in the past didn't prepare them for the present just because their local knowledge was too context-dependent, and so not easily portable. Street-smarts have to be relearned each time a person moves.

The trainee librarian's survival in a complex environment beyond the local seems similar to the prospect facing the Bosnian refugees I encountered in Sweden, or to that of Syrians today in Germany. How do you get beyond the limits of your knowledge in a place you don't know – especially if you are unwanted stranger?

I liked and admired this youngster for her determination to better her circumstances, so much so that later I served as her sponsor to Britain. I decided to do so when she declared 'I can handle it.' I believed her. When the immigration authorities here turned her down, I was dismayed but she wasn't. She is now an assistant part-time librarian in New Zealand. I wondered how her admirable determination had been put into practice – how she managed to flourish in a foreign context. She has somehow learned to transcend her local knowledge. As she is so far away, I can't find out from my assistant librarian how this happened. So I have tried to think in a more general way about how local knowledge might be broadened, as people move around the city.

II. WALKING KNOWLEDGE – TAKING ONE'S BEARINGS IN UNFAMILIAR PLACES

Walking Walking has long meant more than simply getting from A to B in Google Maps fashion. From ancient times on, the physical effort of walking on foot deepened the experience of a long-distance pilgrimage or a short-distance visit to a shrine; the long or difficult route increased the aura of the destination. Early in the Renaissance, in 1336, Petrarch climbed Mt Ventoux in France, just to experience it; finally arriving at the summit, he happened to open a volume of St Augustine, falling upon this passage: 'People are moved to wonder by mountain peaks ... but (in walking itself) they are not interested.' Petrarch agreed, in the abstract, that the physical exertion of walking in itself had no spiritual value. Still, the walk was not wasted time, he thought; the physical effort involved took his mind off the demands and pressures on him down below, and this suspension of 'valley-cares' provoked in turn reflection on how he lived. As we would say now, the walk put him in touch with himself – but like Pico della Mirandola, Petrarch did not quite know what getting in touch with one's 'self' meant.[7]

Modernity made this connection between walking and introspection even more perplexing. Rousseau's *Reveries of a Solitary Walker*, published in 1782, portrays walking as a spur to contemplation; just for this reason Rousseau liked walking in the country, without the distractions of the city. A contrary kind of walker appeared in the person of Rétif de la Bretonne, Rousseau's contemporary, who walked the city like a miner prospecting for gold, hoping to enrich his self through immersing himself in unfamiliar scenes. In *Les Nuits de Paris*, a kind of diary he kept of his rambles in the city from 1785 on, Rétif used the dense life of the streets to stimulate his own, largely pornographic, desires. And in Rétif's wake, Baudelaire in the next century was stimulated by Parisian whores and beggars, the city's ruined palaces and ruinously expensive restaurants; they seem to mirror, to reveal, something in himself – but what? The very complexity of the city made it hard to say.

The figure of the *flâneur* is born of this perplexity: walking the city to know oneself, somehow. This figure contrasts to that of the ethnographer – as embodied by the researchers of the Chicago School. A ethnographer studies others; a *flâneur* searches for self in others.

The stimulations of walking have appeared quite differently to a more prosaic figure – the planner who seeks to organize movement. As noted in Chapter 2, the freely moving body became a goal of city planning in the late seventeenth and early eighteenth centuries. These planners wrapped themselves in the mantle of biological science, particularly William Harvey's analysis of blood circulation, which became the model for laying out streets as arteries and veins, and free-flowing traffic as analogous to a healthy circulation in the body. Walking lost its value in this scheme, and the sidewalk became less important than the carriageway, because freedom of movement was equated with speed of movement. This was in one way illogical: in a hurtling carriage you sit immobile, whereas your blood pumps when you use your own two feet. The planners had transferred the biological value of moving freely from the human to the mechanical, yet there was in the *ancien régime* a good reason for the switch: the immense economic and social gap between people who could afford a carriage and people who could not, and so were forced to walk. The city of fast, free movement was a city for the privileged.

What does 'free movement' entail? Here there is a distinction between the *flâneur* who wanders, not quite knowing why or where to go, and the person with a definite goal in mind, like getting from home to work or, in another vein, cruising for sex. The same split between aimless and purposeful appears between the casual tourist and a critically minded walker like Iain Sinclair, who foot-travels with the aim of illuminating where and how the city has abandoned its poor, or highlighting the stupidity of planners. Rebecca Solnit thus distinguishes between a wayfarer – the walker on a mission – and a wanderer.[8, 9]

The wandering *flâneur* is a friend of the night, because it is at night when the city's secrets come out. As well as shielding thieves or prostitutes, night has been the time when the huge homeless population of London and Paris took over the streets, as later happened in Delhi's Nehru Place. The advent of gaslighting did little to transform the crawling out of the hidden city, since gaslight was dim and the penumbra of cast gaslight usually small, no more than 5 to 6 metres across in the mid-nineteenth century. Even now, when sodium lights cast a uniform orange-yellow pallor over the streets, night is transforming; figures are drained of colour, and the sodium lights create their own shadows.

The wandering *flâneur* is a more open spirit, I would say, than the purposive wayfarer, because his or her knowledge of places and people can expand in unforeseen ways. But what exactly is he or she learning? This is a practical question for people like the youngsters in Medellín, who are now able to wander the city: how can they break out of the limits of the local, as just described, by walking the city – rather than Googling or watching YouTube?

Lateral accounting I speak as something of an expert on the mental consequences of walking. When I began the journey of recovery from my stroke, I was interested to note the effect of walking on my thinking processes. Moving around first helped lift me out of the fog of fatigue, that exhausted half-consciousness which clouds the patient emerging from an attack. Losing one's balance and falling over was then the problem; the newly walking patient addresses this danger via an exercise called the Romberg Manoeuvre, which steadies the body upright. Once you begin to walk, a Vestibular Rehabilitation Programme (doctor-ese for learning to walk straight) trains the head to turn to the right and then the left every three steps, the body thus moving steadily forward even though it is looking sideways. These first walks are about 20 metres twice a day; you lift your legs high when walking, and at each third step, as you turn your head to the side, you slap your thigh. (I do not recommend practising this, as I once did, in a park; you are likely to attract police attention.)

This exercise, resembling a bit soldiers on parade in front of visiting dignitaries, offers one clue about the relation of bodily motion to perceptions of space. In Vestibular Rehabilitation, the combination of forward movement and sideways vision works best if you focus on specific doors, pots or other bodies as you turn the head. Those objects seen at the side enable the stroked person gradually to establish the dimensions of his or her surroundings; near and far, high and low. This is lateral accounting. It makes you see objects to the side afresh, as though you had not really noticed their character before.

Lateral accounting happens to the healthy *flâneur* as well, who practises something like Vestibular Rehabilitation when exploring the city. He or she takes in new 'data' at the sides of visual consciousness; lateral accounting provokes dimensional measuring, and the healthy *flâneur*, like a recovering stroke patient, can see objects at the edge of consciousness more vividly. How does this sorting and sifting to the side work?

Peripheral vision is natural to most animals. In humans, the cone of vision is 60 degrees, whereas the depth of field is shorter in range, so we are always taking in more information than is in focus. In addition, the human animal has trouble making careful, individual scrutiny of more than seven objects simultaneously. At a walking pace, the Jamesian 'spotlight' in the brain therefore tends to narrow to three or four objects in accounting laterally. By contrast, travelling in a car at 50 mph narrows consciousness to a single signifying object. At a walking pace, the spotlit objects are 'round', in the sense that we can dwell on them, studying their contours and context, whereas at a speeding pace the single spotlit object appears neurologically as 'flat' – a fleeting image with no depth or context. In this sense, walking slowly produces a deeper lateral consciousness than moving fast. Lateral accounting is one of the criteria for distinguishing place – a site in which you dwell – from space – a site you move through. It establishes the basic cognitive claim for privileging cyclists over motorists – the cyclist knows more, neurologically, about the city than the motorist.[10]

Lateral accounting explains a certain perplexity that Parisians of Haussmann's time felt in the fast-moving coaches and trains that were then coming to shape travel in the city: they saw more of the city but noticed less about particular places when travelling at speed. There were few guidebooks to the city written from the vantage point of travelling in trains; *Baedeker's Guide* of 1882, for instance, plots out walking tours for tourists, but treats train travel as of no use in understanding the city. Of course, rapid transport is vital to navigating the city – but cars and trains are also cognition-impairing machines. Just here is the challenge for planners of the *ville*: what if they make no provision for walking knowledge? No sidewalks, no alleys, no benches, no public water-fountains? No public toilets? In failing to provide these, they will have dumbed-down the city.

Positioning On a Google map, the 'my current position' pin orients the viewer in space; it answers the question 'where am I? fairly precisely. A more complex kind of reckoning 'where am I?' is necessary to experience in an unfamiliar space.

The psychologist Yi-Fu Tuan takes up this problem by analysing how people learn to walk through a maze. When people first enter a maze, everything inside is pure space, unmarked and undifferentiated in terms of the maze-wanderer's understanding of where he or she is. The first time the maze-wanderer finds an exit from the maze, by blind groping about, he or she knows there is a 'spatial narrative', that is, a beginning and end organizing his or her movements, but doesn't know the 'chapters' which compose this spatial narrative. In time, wandering about repeatedly, the *flâneur* learns to make certain moves, to take certain bits of path which can guide him, because they contain what Tuan calls 'landmarks' – a statue on a plinth would be an obvious landmark, but a tree with diseased leaves or a hidden hole in the path where you almost twisted your ankle would serve equally as points of reference. These create the chapters in the narrative of movement.

Tuan's view is that movement in space cannot be a one-time event, but rather something that has to happen over and over: the wanderer has to repeat his or her wandering to learn how to navigate. Moreover, Tuan's school argues that in choosing orienting landmarks the *flâneur* thinks critically about which objects or images would best orient him- or herself – in other words, which objects or images stand out from the uniform, homogeneous plants that make up the maze. These exceptions lie at the side of vision, as the terrified *flâneur* stares down the perplexing, seemingly uniform tunnels. Tuan's school thus fleshes out Festinger's work on cognitive distance and focal attention: with enough experience, the person, in moving about, becomes able to focus on very particular and non-obvious clues to orient him- or herself. In our terms, there is a lateral accounting which enables prehension of the sort that leads people forward towards an exit they cannot at the moment see.[11]

Quite another way of orienting oneself appears in the work of the geographer Michel Lussault. He is interested in the way walking establishes the relation of near to far. Looking at a map, you know a petrol station is 1,000 metres away from you, but that's only a number; you have to make some kind of physical effort yourself in order to say whether the petrol station is far away or near to you. Obviously people couldn't walk 1,000 metres, let alone 10 kilometres, every time they want to use the words 'near' and 'far'. He argues that while this is true, at some time in a person's development a physical effort made sense of the number which represents near and far, even if you've only once walked a kilometre. You need to walk up/down in the same way as near/far. Were your only experience of height travelling up and down an elevator, 'high' wouldn't mean much to you as a measure; at some point you would have had to climb at least one flight of stairs to use it. Just as a craftsman puts together physical experience with the mental understanding of words like 'tight' so,

Lussault argues, are geographies constructed. In learning the dimensions of a new space, the walking or climbing body provides an initial measuring stick.[12]

Here are two different accounts of how people can orient themselves by moving around unfamiliar places. It might be objected that very, very few *flâneurs* could walk across Delhi or New York. How then to quantify the word 'big'? In cities this question is really one about human scale.

Scaling Measures of human scale in the built environment would logically seem to be based on the size of the human body. This way of defining scale began with Vitruvius and is most familiar to us in Leonardo da Vinci's famous image of a body, arms and legs stretched out, creating a perfect circle within a square. This is the measure of a static body. In our own time, the geometric version of human scale is embodied most famously in Corbusier's Modular Man, which shows a figure with one bent arm raised. Corbusier sought in this image to reconcile the metric and the inches-and-foot systems of measurement; the focus is on the mathematics of the body. The image of Modular Man can be used by architects to create human-scale in tall buildings, calculating the vertical multiples of Modular Man; Corbusier elaborated this procedure after the Second World War, though the modular measure appears in several buildings of the 1930s. The point is to rationalize the body's size, not to treat it as a living organism.

Another way of thinking about human scale was put forward by the great architectural critic Geoffrey Scott, who declared, 'We project ourselves into the spaces in which we stand . . . filling them ideally with our movement.' Scott was enamoured of the Baroque for just this reason, especially the swirling sculptures of Bernini, their stone bodies twisting and bending, their draperies swirling. From this aesthetic appreciation of the moving human form, Scott asserted that we 'project human scale', by imagining our body movements writ large in space – Lussault's concrete, sensate experiences blown up by the imagination. Superman and Batman's leaps create this kind of scalar projection; so, once, did Jonathan Swift's *Gulliver's Travels* (for both super-big and super-small travellers). With practical architecture in mind, Scott argued that the passage through rooms, from rooms into streets, up and down stairs is a better guide to designing spaces that feel human-sized than calculating room size or street width in relation to fixed images of the human body itself. Movement matters more than geometry.[13]

Lussault's precepts about near and far appeared in the work of Allan Jacobs (no relation to Jane), a planner for the city of San Francisco in the 1980s. For this Jacobs, the 60-degree cone of vision ruled. At the top of this cone, he argued, the roofline of buildings should always be visible. Using the 'Jacobs rule' guides some planners in turn to determine the width of a street. The wider the street, the taller can be the buildings lining it, so long as you can always see the rooflines from the ground. In San Francisco, the Jacobs rule privileged the low buildings because the streets are narrow, whereas a pedestrian walking forwards in the Champs-Élysées in Paris can see the tops of buildings which are much higher as he or she moves along. What Allan Jacobs disliked were detached, stand-alone towers like those in Shanghai, where walking around them established no sense of their height.[14]

A movement-oriented measure of streets on human-scale comes from the Danish urbanist Jan Gehl. Rather than measuring the size of the human body, he explores how moving bodies process the word 'near' – another application of Lussault's theory. 'Depending on the background and light, we can identify people as human rather than animals or bushes at a distance of 300 to 500 metres.' Then, 'only when the distance has been reduced to 100 metres can we see movement and body language in broad outline.' Still we need to move forwards, because there is another, if shorter gap: 'we usually recognize [a particular] person at somewhere between 50 and 70 metres.' Then there is a final stage: 'At a distance of about 22–25 metres, we can accurately read facial expression . . .' Similar calculation can be made for sounds. Shouts for help are audible at 50–70 metres; at half that distance we can understand people speaking loudly in one-way communication, as if standing in an open-air pulpit; cut the number in half again and you can conduct brief, across-the-street conversations. But only from 7 metres and below, 'the more detailed and articulated the conversation can be'. Gehl believes that the critical 'interpersonal threshold' occurs both visually and sonically at around

25 metres, which is the distance at which specific data about another person fill in concretely. How big people are doesn't matter in this way of measuring human scale; it's rather a question of what people see and hear as they move towards one another.[15]

Why aren't the automobile, the train and the aeroplane scale-makers? Because movement is suspended. Little or no human effort has to be exerted to make the machine move; the machine does the work. An interesting study in this regard compares driving a car with manual gears to driving an automatic; the manual-gears driver is less accident-prone because the effort of changing gears attunes the driver more to conditions around him or her, outside the car. With the advent of the driverless car, suspension of engagement in environmental conditions will be complete – which is the dark side of Bill Mitchell's dream. The loss of maker-made scale echoes Peter Merholz's celebration of user-friendly technology: as the effort to make the program work decreases, understanding of how it works also decreases.

From this I deduce that human scale is established not simply by moving, but by moving in a way which is puzzling, as in a maze; which encounters obstacles, as in moving slowly in a crowd; which has to deal with a heavy sensory load, as in lateral vision. The urban planner who would create an unobstructed pedestrian environment is doing the pedestrian no experiential favours. As with 'creativity' inside the Googleplex, described in the previous chapter, so it is outside on the street: people experience human scale in terms of coping with resistances.

As I say, I can't know if my young assistant librarian learned to make her way in a strange place by walking it. But movement's lateral accounting, prehension, positioning and scaling would all be robust ways of orienting herself in a place she didn't know.

III. DIALOGIC PRACTICES – SPEAKING TO STRANGERS

What about verbal orientation? How could she transcend local limits by speaking to strangers? One answer to this question derives from ideas about communication first propounded by the Russian *littér-ateur* Mikhail Bakhtin.

'Dialogics' was the term he coined in the 1930s for the ways in which language is full of 'socio-ideological contradictions between the present and the past, between differing epochs of the past, between different socio-ideological groups in the present, between tendencies, schools, circles . . .'; every voice is framed by and aware of other voices. This is a condition Bakhtin called 'heteroglossia'. Because people are not carbon copies of one another, speech is full of misunderstandings, ambiguities, unmeant suggestions and unspoken desires; in Kant's terms, language is crooked, particularly among strangers who do not share the same local references, the same local knowledge. Heteroglossia marked the rather comic exchanges the assistant-librarian-to-be and I had on the subject of siestas.[16]

Dialogics was a loaded word for someone writing in Stalin's Moscow in the 1930s, where the least sign of ideological nonconformity led straight to the gulag. Dialogics was a dare to this thought-dictatorship in its contrast to dialectics, at least the dialectical reasoning sanctified by the thought-police as dialectical materialism. The official idea of language in society was that via the play between theses and antitheses you arrived at syntheses which unified thoughts and feelings; everyone is on the same page – a page that can be policed. Whereas the dialogical techniques of displacement, disruption or inconclusiveness establish a different kind of speech community – one in which people speak as neighbours in Levinas' sense, never quite on the same page. This speech community cannot be policed.[17]

There are, I think, four dialogical tools which particularly serve urbanites.

Hearing the unsaid People often do not say what they mean, because they talk badly. The other side of this coin is that words can't capture what a person thinks or feels. In literature, Bakhtin addressed these language limits by emphasizing the context in which a character speaks, paying more attention to scene-setting than to dialogue. The reader infers what a character wants to say through the writer's description of him and his world, rather than through his own words. Thanks to contextualizing, although Sancho Panza in *Don Quixote* is frequently inarticulate or obtuse, we can make sense of what he wants to say.

In ordinary life, listening skills do the work of finding meaning in the unsaid. Like anthropologists of the time, the Chicago School wanted to 'hear the unsaid', but was troubled by a sociological neurosis: the representative sample. This neurosis consists in believing that there is something like an authentic voice, or a typical example, of a certain kind of person. This belief conduces to stereotyping – for example, the ignorant Polish peasant, or the Angry White Man. More, the representative sample privileges those people who do speak in the ways others expect of members of a category; the speakers get attention by acting out the stereotype. Robert Park worried that his students weren't listening to people who had a less stereotypical, more complex understanding of their own race or class; these complex thoughts and feelings can cause someone to fall silent. Charlotte Towle thus obliged her interviewers to learn how to be silent themselves, in order to encourage their subjects to struggle for words; the training in the Chicago School of young interviewers involved letting silences hang in the air. Florian Znaniecki recognized that neophytes are made uncomfortable by the silence of a subject, and are tempted to jump in with statements like, 'In other words, Mrs Schwarz, what you mean to say is . . .'. Znaniecki counselled, don't put words in their mouths; to do so is the cardinal sin of sociology.

Since the time of the Chicago School, techniques have evolved for spotlighting meanings which are left inarticulate or contradictory; listening for cognitive dissonances figures in the education of the modern ethnographer. The fact that a subject contradicts him- or herself cannot be taken as a sign he or she is stupid or ignorant; rather, following Bakhtin, it is the context of the speech act that is crooked and contradictory.

Little would be gained by the interviewer saying, 'Mrs Schwarz, you contradict yourself'; that makes the difficulty her problem rather than one of the situation she finds herself in. In depth interviewing, people do in fact worry over these contradictions during the course of a long interview session, exercising focal attention, so that by the end of ninety minutes they have reformatted the problem with which they began.

For instance, many of the working-class subjects Jonathan Cobb and I interviewed for *The Hidden Injuries of Class* began their sessions with anti-black statements which modulated over the course of the interviews into expressions of anger aimed at white people of a higher social class. For our interviewers – mostly white members of the upper-middle class – good listening required an exercise of empathy rather than of identification. The interviewer can only get under the skin of words by conveying willingness to take the speaker seriously – on his or her own terms – rather than conveying 'I know just how you feel'. When racist sentiments are conveyed, and then morph into class sentiments, interviewers need to show respect through a kind of equanimity: 'That's interesting' or 'I hadn't thought of that'; these formulae are the equivalent of the civilized fictions which oil life in a mixed community. The result is often that the subjects in an aggressive interaction will then change what they say.

In sum, there is a sociable as well as a self-disciplining side to the practice of silence: verbal passivity shows respect for the other as a person rather than as a type.

The declarative and the subjunctive voice The second aspect of dialogics has to do with speaking rather than listening. This is the use of the subjunctive voice in order to open up communication. The declarative voice asserting 'I believe X' or 'X is right, Y is wrong' can invite only agreement or disagreement in response. Whereas the subjunctive voice offering 'I would have thought' or 'perhaps' admits a much wider range of responses: doubts and hesitations can be introduced and shared, as can diverging facts or opinions which do not rouse the original speaker to defend him- or herself. Bakhtin writes of such openness as permitting 'languages to be used in ways that are indirect, conditional, distanced'. The philosopher Bernard Williams spoke of the declarative voice as subject to the 'fetish of assertion', an assertiveness which is usually aggressive. But however tinged psychologically, the essential thing about the declarative voice is that it privileges clarity of expression, whereas use of the subjunctive voice instead privileges ambiguity.[18, 19]

The dialogical idea is that the subjunctive voice is a more sociable way to speak than the declarative. People can be more open, exchange more freely, feel less uptight and behave less defensively; they are not fighting their corner. Put in other terms, ambiguity invites collaborative exchange; clarity invites competitive exchange.

Like listening well, effective use of the subjunctive voice requires skill. Every professional negotiator, whether diplomat or union official, learns when and how to create an opening by stepping back from assertion, moving a negotiation forward by speaking more tentatively about what were first presented as clear demands. A kindred skill of negotiating is how most adults sustain intimate relations, rather than simply blurting out desires or opinions. The skill adds to self-restraint a certain cunning. When people say 'perhaps', they may know full well what they think; 'perhaps' issues the invitation to another to speak.

Hearing the unsaid, and using the subjunctive voice, are dialogical ways of communicating in bed, at dinner, in the office. When strangers talk, a third dialogical practice can come into play.

The 'it voice' I've been struck in reading raw interview transcripts produced by the Chicago School by something which many of their researchers didn't seem to remark. Their subjects use two voices: one self-referring, the other more impersonal. 'As an African-American, I found the University of Chicago more accepting than my friends at the University of Illinois . . .' represented the first; 'Why do whites inflict so much suffering on African Americans?' the second. Since the subject is race, the speaker may be asking a rhetorical question to which she knows the answer perfectly well from her own experience – but she does not invoke it. When strangers meet, the 'it voice' can preserve a distance between them, even while they continue to communicate.[20]

In some of the Chicago interviews, this impersonality is maintained over the course of long interview sessions because the subjects want to preserve their privacy. But in others, bringing back everything to one's own small experience seems too limiting to account for the society in which one is living. After one immigrant from a small Polish village told W. I. Thomas that 'I didn't realize I was Polish until I came to Chicago', the subject goes on to explain the differences between Polish villages and the Polish ghetto in Chicago in more general terms. Such speech is a speaker's 'it voice': focused outwards rather than inwards.

The 'it voice' is dialogical because the subject is freed up to range, to observe and to judge, free of the *flâneur*'s propensity to bring everything back to him- or herself. Bakhtin's great American interpreter, Michael Holquist, explored how picaresque heroes like Don Quixote or narrators like Rabelais were free spirits because they were explorers of 'what is' rather than 'who I am'; the energy of these figures came from a release from self.[21]

In analysing the places in which they live, people similarly use both the self-referring and the 'it' voice. 'I' is the pronoun people use when they talk about belonging to a place; 'it' is the pronoun they use in evaluating the strengths and weaknesses of the place in itself. This difference matters because the 'it voice' is the more evaluative and critical one. There's a parallel in thoughts about place to the ways Charlotte Towle earlier noted women talked about marriage: the women she and my mother interviewed moved from discussing their own experience as the spouses of demoralized men to evaluating what either the government or the Communist Party could do about demoralization. When Barack Obama later worked as a community organizer in Chicago, he found that he had to move people beyond recounting a litany of their personal injuries to thinking about the actions they could take; a narrative of personal suffering would not energize them to fight.

Informality Informal conversations like the one I had with Mr Sudhir define a fourth kind of dialogical exchange. You chat without an agenda, such as would be drafted for a meeting; informal exchanges can also be contrasted to gossip, which usually has an agenda – if unspoken – of malice. In an informal chat, as you move from topic to topic, feeling to feeling, you move between levels of meaning, the trivial giving way to the profound, which floats back up to the surface. An informal chat can thus become aimless wandering; what converts it into a dialogical exchange is a certain shape the flow can take. As in the Medellín café, a significant fact will suddenly be spotlit in the midst of the seemingly aimless meandering. The speakers will smell a promising path to pursue, though not quite knowing in advance what they will discover. These exploratory skills keep a discussion going.

Keeping an informal exchange going requires a certain kind of irresponsibility. Rather than thrashing out a subject, as one might in a dialectical debate, the dialogical chat will turn and twist by people picking up on the seeming trivialities which pop up in chat; it's these which can re-channel the conversation. You tell me about your father's cruelty, to which I 'inappropriately' respond by talking about my father's baldness; the inappropriate response in fact frees the exchange from the painful, fixed channel of a confession on ills long meditated upon, so painful you might deliver yourself of a monologue. Responding with comments about my father's baldness lightens the exchange, but more importantly keeps it flowing; I have not forgotten your father's cruelty; indeed, I'm going to look for hints and glints of it as we order a second round of drinks; we will talk more.

To say someone is a good conversationalist, we have in mind this capacity to surf informality. I might remark that few debaters or dialecticians are good at informal conversation; they make their points and, if successful in ramming home those points, others will quit the verbal field. Conversation aborts.

About the flow of informal conversation itself, open-systems analysts usefully contribute a clarification of its turning points, which are technically labelled as non-linear path dependencies, a more digestible phrase if framed in terms of making a thing rather than making conversation. A woodworker sets out to make a large platter; he then discovers knots in his wood, which prompts him to make a bowl rather than a flat platter; he then sees interesting wood grain, which prompts him to carve the bowl with a wavy lip, a lip he has never carved before. At each stage, something occurs which changes the work he set out to do; that is non-linear path dependency. He may modestly minimize his capacity to sniff out possibility by saying that the bowl 'turned out differently than I thought it would at the start . . .' – but he made those changes happen. So too, when you chat with a stranger, your conversation may be just inconsequential bar or club talk. But the two of you – your sexual pheromones unexpectedly flowing – chat with a certain skill, following up some unexpected clues, but not others.

In an open system, there is no destiny – a point also to be considered soberly with regard to love: be honest, you were not destined to meet just this one stranger. Mathematically, it might be possible to retrace clearly via a regression analysis the steps resulting in the carved bowl of the lip or in your embrace, but in forward-mode each of these changes responds to the previous ones in a way that couldn't be foreseen at the start. In place of destiny, which supposes life must turn out in a certain way, in an open system the process shapes the end.

In open-systems theory, this is a good thing. As path dependencies accumulate, the system becomes ever more dynamic, more excited. Bakhtin sought to explain this excited energy in social communications. He imagined this non-linear experience to arise because of intersections between different 'social dialects, characteristic group behaviour, professional jargons, generic languages, languages of generations and age groups, tendentious languages, languages of the authorities, of various circles and of passing fashions'. This is the verbal condition he called 'heteroglossia', and we would call 'a *cité*'.[22]

Heteroglossia can be staged; novelists do it. In a certain kind of Victorian novel it's pretty evident after the first few pages how things will turn out: heroes will inevitably be rewarded, villains will be punished and finally the star-crossed couple will couple. Life speaks of coherence; we are in reassuring hands. In another sort of fiction, the plot twists when events or characters swerve away from what the reader might have expected at the beginning: the villains are gloriously victorious, the loving couple parts. What compels is not merely the surprise, but the ambiguities and difficulties which prove potent, turning the characters away from the expected path. Italo Calvino once remarked that the novelist creating this sort of fiction is actually playing a game with the reader, cunningly shifting the terms of engagement at those moments when everything seems like it will come together. So too, in my chats with Mr Sudhir, it was the unexpected revelation of his domestic probity which kept me chatting with this dealer in stolen iPhones.

The non-linear novel is far more compelling than well-made

fiction; if after reading the first pages I can guess how a novel will turn out, I usually put the book down. In a city, too, heterogeneous voices and actions engage us as well-made expectations do not. One skill in keeping people engaged and interested, in life as in a novel, is to sow unexpected seeds in the course of seemingly aimless, trivial talk – this is the essence of communicating informally.

In sum, I am imagining the assistant librarian making her way by talking to strangers in these four dialogic ways: listening well by attending to what is meant rather than said; using the subjunctive voice to cooperate with rather than confront the other; following up realities that are independent of her own self; following the path of informal exchanges. These dialogic practices would open doors for her.

The city is often pictured as a jungle in which only the aggressive will survive. There is something unrealistic about such a red-in-tooth-and-claw imagery, as Balzac, Flaubert and Stendhal understood long ago. Less combative characters in their novels fare better in the city than the monsters of egotism who are crushed – the novelists taking a pleasure, as we saw in Chapter 2, in their collapse. So, too, off the novelistic page. The dialogic skills I have sketched here are ways of coping with complex realities in which finesse and skill replace naked pushiness. Yet, as well as having that practical value, dialogics is an ethical practice of communication: respectful of others, cooperative rather than competitive, outward- rather than inward-turning. Could it be that an ethics of this sort is a useful, practical, street-smart guide to survival in the city?

IV. RUPTURE MANAGEMENT – THE MIGRANT, A MODEL URBANITE

Migrant strength The protagonist of Teju Cole's remarkable novel *Open City* is a *flâneur* who learns the city in this non-aggressive way. Like many first novels, Cole's is a barely disguised autobiography; just like the author, the narrator is a young Nigerian doctor doing a psychiatric residency in New York. The narrator wanders the city alone, in part to calm down from the stresses of work, but also to try to understand the foreign place. One such wandering occurs at dusk,

after the narrator sees his patient 'M', who is suffering from hallu-
cinations: they have a not too satisfying session; the narrator then
boards a subway train to go home on Manhattan's West Side; the
doors open at his stop, but he does not get off, staying on the train
until it comes to the southern tip of the island. He tries to enter a
locked church, weaves among the ruins left by September 11, goes
into a bar and is propositioned by another man, leaves, and continues
walking. Scene after scene accumulates in this seemingly random
way; his walking knowledge is creating a collage of images.

Dialogical speech also comes into play because the protagonist
deals with patients who are black or white, Puerto Rican or Mexican;
few of his professional encounters are with patients from home. He
therefore needs to penetrate what they think and feel behind the
screen of – for him – foreign words or usages. But the discussions he
has with patients seem fragmentary exchanges, rather than extended,
searching sessions, as would occur in a classical psychoanalysis. As
for all psychiatrists, the narrator/protagonist experiences counter-
transference, hearing in his patients' mental displacements echoes of
his own geographic uprooting. Thus he writes:

> We experience life as a continuity, and only after it falls away, after
> it becomes the past, do we see its discontinuities. The past, if there
> is such a thing, is mostly empty space, great expanses of nothing, in
> which significant persons and events float. Nigeria was like that for
> me: mostly forgotten, except for those few things that I remembered
> with an outsize intensity.[23]

Were this return-to-your-African-roots nostalgia, it would be perhaps a banal sentiment. The novel is powerful because its narrator
realizes that he has become doubly alien, belonging neither there
nor here, then or now. He has become the quintessential rootless
cosmopolitan – that Jewish emblem now covering more generally the
Africans, Asians and Latinos who have crowded into New York. The
novel catches him in the midst of learning how to deal with this
dilemma. The narrator becomes a deep character in exploring the
pains of migration, but displacement does not undo him; his forays
into New York have steadied him, as he learns to deal with complexity, even though his desire for home is not satisfied. Thus his story of

the city acquires depth and weight; he can live here, even if he does not entirely belong here.

I was reminded of three very different figures in the course of this novel. One was Okakura, the student of Heidegger, who differed from his master in saying that you do not need to throw down roots in order to dwell in a place; you need instead to come to terms with absence. The Zen orientation he embodies could be thought of as a master-theory of migration. Less philosophically, Cole's account echoes the migrations of the Russian exile Alexander Herzen in the nineteenth century. A believer in political reform, in 1848 Herzen began an exile which took him from Moscow to Rome to Paris to London; as an old man, worn out and poor in London, he wrote, 'I sit in London where chance has flung me . . . and I stay here [only] because I do not know what to make of myself. An alien race swarms confusedly about me.' Yet this is not entirely a cry of despair (though being Russian, of course he indulged); a few hours after writing these words he goes out to a pub, where he meets an 'interesting, unforeseen' group of working men.[24]

After years of wandering, Herzen comes to conclude that 'home' is a mobile need. That is, the migrant or exile packs the desire for home in his or her suitcase – ever gnawing, it should still not prevent him or her from travelling. Herzen was scathing about Russian exiles who lived in the past in a permanent state of regret, isolated from the places where fortune had flung them. They owed a 'duty to themselves' to make something of their circumstances; they should become aware and alert in the present. Herzen believed that the voyage away and out had made the exile a gift – an awareness of now and here which is lacking in people who have never left home.

The young woman I sponsored in Medellín looked forward to migrating, to leaving home, and she has flourished. Though still harbouring fond memories of home, she is eager for new experience abroad, she has become a skilful *flâneur* and she has wanted to help other members of her family move by establishing herself legally. Perhaps due to her youth, her openness to the present and the future has integrated her; she is an optimistic cosmopolitan. Herzen was forced out of Russia, and he suffered from that involuntary expulsion – a wound it took decades to heal, but eventually he became reconciled to his circumstances. He never legally became British or French, but he sought to avoid the paralysing memory-trap of nostalgia by culti- vating British and French friends. He, a radical burned by complex and dangerous experiences in Russia, none the less shared with the young assistant librarian from Medellín a desire to live in the present. He has integrated in that time sense.

Between the two poles represented by aspiring migrant and in- voluntary exile stands Cole's narrator, who leaves Nigeria freely but comes to feel empty in the new place where he develops profession- ally, or at least feels that something is missing. He is perhaps the model for the Balkan refugees I dealt with in Sweden, even though their circumstances resemble Herzen's. At first, they looked forward to a better, freer, safer life, but in time they constructed a scaffold of regret around their experiences. Practically they had no choice but to adapt by learning Swedish, otherwise lack of language would have confined them to marginal jobs. The adult generation at first wanted to make an effort to mix and dwell in their new home, knowing that otherwise their children's horizons would be limited. Yet integration into Sweden encountered obstacles. Some were not of their own mak- ing; like the PEGIDA marchers in Germany, there was a strong element here that resisted their presence. But such resistance was not enough to explain their construction of regret. In time, a feeling of absence, of something missing, arose in the migrant community, as it did for Cole; the sufferings of the past gained in subjective impor- tance compared to survival in the present; oddly, the younger generation, who had never known homelessness, began to define themselves in terms of a lost home. All of them were included in en- lightened Sweden without becoming integrated. For them, as with Cole and Herzen, it became a matter of living here but not here, of being both absent and present.

The migrant's strength lies in coming to terms with displacement. How might this work as a model for other urbanites?

A philosopher of displacement So far as I know, Gaston Bachelard never actually built a hut, unlike his near contemporary Heidegger, but he imagined one in amazing prose. His book *The Poetics of Space* seems a celebration of the sheltered life, focused on dwelling at peace in a hut. At its end, he declares 'for a dreamer of words, what calm there is in the word "round". How peacefully it makes one's mouth, lips and . . . breath become round . . . *Das Dasein ist rund*. Being is round.' Were this the description of an actual hut, it might be of a Tibetan yurt; the metaphor gets at the enclosure and safety of being inside, feeling sheltered. To this feeling of warmth he contrasts the harshness of the city, citing the theologian Max Picard as saying that 'The streets are like pipes into which men are sucked up'.[25]

Unlike Heidegger in his hut, Bachelard knew that one cannot hide from sucking life; eventually everyone has to leave his or her inner hut, forced to deal with people one does not know, understand or sympathize with. His own intellectual trajectory fleshes out this proposition. Bachelard began adult life as a provincial postman, then put himself through university studying physics, then shifted to the philosophy of science. In middle age he achieved a position in Paris; almost immediately after he arrived, though, he abandoned climbing up the academic ladder, instead writing books with titles like *The Psychoanalysis of Fire* and *The Poetics of Space*. These are works full of sensual descriptions of everyday experiences – a hand scorched by the fire, then salved; a view of the rain seen out of the window after sex. His language arouses, whereas Heidegger's abstracts.

The move to Paris made a bridge between physics and psycho-analysis. In his physics-days Bachelard had emphasized the erratic, non-continuous character of scientific thought. He rejected the com-forting view that knowledge builds up slowly and steadily, as conveyed in the metaphor of knowledge-makers as 'standing on the shoulders of giants'. Instead Bachelard traced in physics certain blockages, stumbles, and the sudden, unforeseen appearance of new ideas. Louis Althusser would later coin the term 'epistemic break' to describe what concerned Bachelard.[26, 27]

Within the psychoanalytic framework, Bachelard was among the first to describe dealing with these ruptures as a form of ego-strength. Rather than following blind desire, the ego seeks for a different power, that of engaging with outside realities; this is the standard Freudian view. The distinctiveness of Bachelard's own view was to see ego-strength as the power to break with existing reality as well as to adapt to it. Like the physicist – or the Media Lab researcher – the ego is actively engaged in making epistemic breaks, in thinking outside the box.

Most psychoanalytical writers of Bachelard's time looked backwards from adulthood into childhood; he looked in the other direction, forwards into adult life. The psychoanalysis Bachelard embraced told him that even in the city we will be searching for hut traces of primal warmth, intimacy and insideness. Against this the adult encounters complexities and unknowns outside. In adulthood, the two combine: the hut is lost, the city gained, absence and presence become inseparable. But, for Bachelard, the stress must be on engaging the present, dealing with epistemic breaks, indeed causing these displacements to occur, painful as they may be.

For Bachelard, learning how to cope with displacement has a social consequence; people become confident that they can live with others who differ, rather than feel so vulnerable that, like Heidegger, they flee. People develop both psychologically and ethically by abandoning the comforts of home; the ego is strengthened.

Here is the connection to the migrant. The voyage to another city makes an epistemic break – whether the voyage is voluntary, as for my young librarian, or involuntary like the Balkan Muslims in Stockholm. The ego is strengthened by making sense of this break, particularly by living in the two dimensions of presence and absence, of now and then. Displacement for Bachelard is not an unalloyed evil; it breeds adult knowledge of mixture and limits. A city filled with people whom we do not know, do not like, or simply do not understand is the breeding ground.

In English, we speak of having an experience, or of becoming experienced. German usefully separates these meanings into two words, *Erlebnis* and *Erfahrung*. Having an experience – *Erlebnis* – is the adventurous word, applying within the German context to the middle-aged Goethe fleeing the cold, rigid Teutonic north for the warm, sensual Latin south, where his senses revived in a new environment. Presence and vividness mark the qualities of *Erlebnis*. It is the realm of the innocently wandering *flâneur*. It seems the everyday enactment of Bachelard's 'epistemic break'. *Erfahrung*, on the other hand, involves sifting through these impressions once a person has accumulated enough of them; 'becoming experienced' is a matter of organizing and ordering the lingering traces of excitement, of creating longer term, stable value. This is the realm of the more skilled *flâneur*, the man or woman capable of engaging strangers dialogically, the person who has to learn to live with the bitter-sweet lessons of displacement. This is more what Bachelard had in mind as 'ego strength'.

There's a dark side to *Erfahrung*. In novels like Gustave Flaubert's *Sentimental Education*, Thomas Mann's *Buddenbrooks* and J. D. Salinger's *Catcher in the Rye*, the experienced father says sternly to his errant, adventurous children that 'life is not just adventure! grow up!' Career, the cares of family, the repayment of student loans will all chasten your ardour for something new and different; the adult world will demand you sacrifice stimulation for the sake of stability. Mann wrote that the vividness of experiment withers under the weight of duty and responsibility. More *Erfahrung* means less *Erlebnis*.

To understand the architecture of open experience, we want to think of the relationship between *Erlebnis* and *Erfahrung* other than as a matter of bourgeois resignation; we want to see their relations as a craftsman would. Over time, the craftsman – let's make her a surgeon – learns different techniques to perform an action like cutting a tendon; she is not limited to doing one thing in only one way. Becoming experienced contrasts with the more junior surgeon's desire to cut a tendon 'correctly', that is, to follow a fixed model of what to do. Without fresh *Erlebnis*, the surgeon will never be prompted to reflect and reorganize what she does. *Erlebnis* entails good epistemic breaks. But this is the only way to improve. In time, with experience, as different skills develop, the models of how to do something multiply. She is open but in control.

As with the craftsman, so it can be with the migrant. In the migrant's case, fresh *Erlebnis* is forced upon him in displacement; to survive he has to become experienced in managing displacement, neither denying its impact nor succumbing to its potential, destructive power. This balance is the migrant's *Erfahrung*. Migrant knowledge is the knowledge all urbanites need, once they leave the security of the familiar and the local. The desire for fresh experience will prompt them to leave, or fresh experience may be forced upon them – but then, like Teju Cole, they will not be able to put the past – elsewhere, a simpler time – out of mind. In this frame of mind, they will enter the larger city. They will need the skills described in this chapter to manage their journey. Just as it doesn't take a genius to acquire good craft skills, so becoming skilled at dwelling is a potential which lies in most people. I am not describing an ideal *cité*, but a *cité* already inside us, waiting.

defects? I will describe a project which attempted to do just this – and failed.

A failed design In 2012, the architect Henry Cobb, along with a team of landscape designers, structural engineers and lighting specialists, made a bid to redesign the lower end of the National Mall in Washington DC. I played Mr Sudhir's role, advising on what the Mall as a synchronous space would feel like. L'Enfant's 1791 plan for Washington, took form around a great open, ceremonial space between the Capitol and the Potomac River. When Andrew Jackson Downing landscaped the Mall in the mid-nineteenth century, he imagined it somewhat in the spirit Olmsted later conceived of Central Park, as a space in which Americans could mingle sociably. Commerce and transport then intruded; during the post-Civil War flush of Washington's growth, a big market arose at the north end of the Mall, next to a busy train station. The planners pushed back; the McMillan Commission at the beginning of the last century expelled the market-holders and returned the Mall to a more beautified state; in time it came to be lined by museums (one of which Henry Cobb helped design).

There were lots of people visiting these museums, but the Mall itself became a relatively sparse space, at least in contrast to the masses of people seemingly everywhere in Central Park. Our site, just below the Capitol, was especially forlorn most weekdays and nights; here, an enormously wide, shallow pool was fronted by a street on which tour buses discharged visitors, the pool backed by shady nooks in which statues of various dignitaries were tucked away. Though we respected the McMillan Commission's desire to keep out commerce, we wanted to bring more life to this part of the Mall by creating a more synchronous space, with many different social activities going on at once.

We addressed three problems. First, how many different activities should be mixed in a synchronous space? One answer to this comes from studies of multitasking. In the early nineteenth century, Sir William Hamilton imagined multitasking as a logical outcome of the fact that people sniff, listen, as well as look all at the same time: all these sensory inputs are summoned to mind at once. Hamilton likened it to holding several marbles in one's hand. Hamilton's follower William

Jevons believed this idea was not sharp enough, and showed that a person can hold – mentally – at most four marbles at the same time. Four different sorts of activities at most occurring at once seemed to conform to the studies inspired by Jevons. In the Mall project, we therefore broke with the classical agora model, one which was in our view too crowded with activities; not all the activities occurring in central Washington should be found here in miniature, as though the public space were a condensed version of the city.

Jevons' rule of thumb on the number of things happening synchronously leads to a second design rule: truly different things should be occurring. In line with the McMillan Commission, we proposed to exclude the kind of trophy-and-talisman commerce which most of the museums lining the Mall conduct inside; we would be friendly, though, to street-food vendors, giving them the space formerly occupied by tour buses. In terms of providing pleasure, the plan entailed picnic areas and a waterfall pool for kids which could be drained to be used for concerts. We also imagined that at times the space could – God forbid – be used for political assemblies. Most of all, we wanted to increase the social-service uses of the space – uses which are usually buried deep inside buildings, far from the citizens who need them. My project consisted of a series of mobile sheds on the stoa model, in which government agencies would conduct advice bureaux for citizens with problems. Different things should happen in the space than the servicing of tourists alone.

One way of framing mixed use of public space as time-sequential is in the after-hours use of a school for the meetings of local political groups or adult clubs. The night is an especially testing time for outdoor public-space design; security fears and worries about promiscuous sex or drug-taking lead many projects to be overlit. Shaded spots like those around the statues behind the Mall pool, while attractive during the day, were seen as dangerous at night; the unexpected turn – so attractive during the day – becomes fearful in the dark. To draw large numbers of people into a park at night, we proposed a system of face-level lighting instead of overhead lighting, and the use of motion sensors to turn lights on when there is activity they need to see; more, we located night-time activities like an outdoor café at the edge of the space, and daytime activities like the kids' pool in its interior, the porous edge sending a signal that the space was not isolated.

These moves exemplify a third aspect of designing synchronicity: it has to issue an invitation to mix, rather than impose mixing. Following Olmsted, in public-space design we need strategies to draw people in. The problem far transcends making the space look pretty: if it is to be truly synchronous, a space must offer people something they cannot easily access elsewhere. This was my thought about locating an old-age social-security office in the Mall: depressing bureaucratic transactions could be softened in this pleasure ground.

Though popular with the public, our plan did not win the approval of our client, a branch of the American Congress. Of course I blame our failure on the client, but in truth we failed because we did not know how to design invitations. The plan issued too many physical invitations, even though its social functions had been edited and slimmed to Jevons' limits. The lack of fencing, the many paths and the carefully lit attractions, especially at night, created confusion about where to enter, and what would happen once you did. The form of the proposed Mall exemplified Simmel's belief that the urbanite, faced with many stimulations, pulls back.

This is the challenge of synchronicity: it breeds a spatial experience both stimulating and disorientating. The form is confusing, whereas the fixed spaces in a diachronic space are not. Therefore, to benefit from the stimulations of an agora while diminishing its confusions, the space needs to be marked in some way which provides orientation – or so I reflected, after we failed.

II. PUNCTUATED – MONUMENTAL AND MUNDANE MARKERS

The holy grail of urban design is to create places which have a particular character. In the Plan Voisin, there is nothing which stands out about any one place in it; this uniform sameness meant that the series of identical towers could, Corbusier hoped, be extended throughout the Marais and indeed infinitely through Paris. The design exemplified that aspect of a closed system in which the parts are homogeneous and additive. The lack of distinctiveness has become reality in the towers of Madame Q's Shanghai, or in the new cities in South Korea whose identical buildings are identified by huge numbers displayed on flags outside so that people can know in which building they live. In systems terms, such an environment is closed because of its interchangeable parts. An open system, by contrast, has parts which cannot be substituted for one another. But imagine a city of five million people with, say, 10,000 centres each of which looks nothing like any other: that variety of forms no designer could devise and no urbanite could make sense of. So how can you make places distinctive in a big city, instead of impossibly unique?

It's possible to give a space character by punctuating it just as one would a piece of writing. In writing, an exclamation point at the end of a sentence adds emphasis; a semicolon breaks up flow, a period stops it. More subtly, quote marks around a word like 'man' invite the reader to pause on a bit of gendered language. So, too, in urban design. Big-bold monuments serve as exclamation points. Walls are periods. Crossroads serve as semicolons, breaking up flow without halting it. These analogies seem fairly straightforward. But what physical forms would work like quote marks, inviting people to pause and reflect?

The exclamation point As soon as his pontificate began in 1585, Sixtus V began to transform Rome. It was late in his life; his reign would last but five years until he died in 1590. As though aware of the shortness of time for his task, the plan for Rome he had long meditated as a cardinal he immediately promulgated as pope. The rationale of Sixtus's remaking of Rome was religious: to link the seven pilgrimage sites of the city. He wanted to connect these sites through straight streets, and to orient pilgrims forward. Thus it was necessary to mark a point ahead, towards which people could move. Sixtus dug into Rome's pagan past for a marker, and came upon the obelisk. Obelisks are tapering three- or four-sided columns set upon a boxy plinth, the tip of the obelisk either sharpened to a point or capped with a small round ball. These would serve as his exclamation points. Obelisks shipped from polytheistic, cat-worshipping Egypt now marked the façades of churches of the Resurrection. They served as invitations for a religious journey.

These exclamation points differed from those of the Christian past. The builders of medieval churches included orientation points by building high spires so that people could know where the churches were; Pope Sixtus V established on the ground how to get to a church, cutting straight streets through Rome's medieval fabric, orienting pilgrims towards the point marked by the tip of the obelisk. This is the same function served by the Washington Memorial obelisk midway between the Capitol and the seated stone figure of Abraham Lincoln at the other end of the Washington Mall; the obelisk orients people inside a ceremonial space.[2]

Were these monuments simply meant to mark a single pilgrimage route, they would be sequential in character, unfolding a ritual path of prayer. Sixtus made a more complex plan: the urbanite in Rome could follow the paths in any direction, wandering at will, crossing different residential districts and markets, mingling with crowds at play rather than at prayer. The obelisks oriented people forward, as well as laying out a spiritual journey inwards.

By the nineteenth century, monumental urbanism seems to have changed the purpose of exclamation points. The major buildings in the city came to be conceived as objects to be looked at, to be viewed like other theatrical spectacles; this was, for instance, the principle guiding the construction of La Madeleine church in Paris, a religious monument whose giant columns in front were exclamation points without a religious purpose; it was pure visual gesture. As were the equestrian statues which came to decorate new public spaces; a factory in Sheffield manufactured many of these for export on an industrial scale, with the local hero's head cast and attached just before the man-on-horseback was shipped out to the colonies. The industrial-era monumental marker ceased to serve either a ritual or an orienting purpose; it became pure decor.

In this, Sixtus's markers might be compared to those in London's Trafalgar Square. The Square is a monument to the great battle of Trafalgar, fought against Napoleon's navy in 1805; victory confirmed the nation's dominance as an imperial power. Designed by John

Nash and then Charles Barry, Trafalgar Square has the huge marker of Nelson's Column in its centre, in homage to Lord Nelson, victor of the battle. There are four plinths edging Trafalgar Square, three devoted to other national heroes. An empty fourth plinth now serves to display sculpture from around the world. Tourists congregate here, but Londoners don't. The markers of national greatness are not a draw to people who live in London; my own observation, after living in London for three decades, is that the natives don't really notice these markers at all.

A maker, that is, has to point to something worth remarking. Big dramatic markers like the obelisk or the man-on-horseback may lose their purpose or their punch.

The semicolon Urbanism offers a more mundane alternative to the exclamation point. This is the crossroads, a physical equivalent of the semicolon: the walking or driving body feels a half-stop of flowing motion which occurs whenever a person turns a corner. This urban semicolon can be created, so the urbanist Manuel de Solà-Morales believes, by contrasting the size of intersecting roads, as New York does with its avenues and streets, the corner itself marking a zone of transition between the two.

In New York the avenue is meant to house larger, taller buildings than the side street, the avenue being more commercial, the street more residential. This was also the principle followed in Shanghai, with small lanes debouching into wider paths. The corner functions as a marker because here the urbanite experiences a shift in focus, a little sensory jolt as he or she adjusts to a change of scale like a shifting of gears. For Solà-Morales, the contrast occurs even at the clipped corners of Cerdà's grid in Barcelona; you can't really anticipate what's around the corner until you make the move.

Solà-Morales and other 'crossroadists' try to build up activities at the corner so that people are attracted to them, differentiating these activities from what's happening on either the street or the avenue. They want to locate the entrance to big buildings at the corner, and put the most dense foot-traffic there, rather than string it out along an avenue; they want to keep big retail away from the smaller streets, instead including in side streets modest retail and small restaurants.

Rather than smoothly blending street into avenue, crossroadists think it important to plan this jolt.[3]

There's an internal parallel to crossroadism in office design. The office plans favoured by Frank Duffy differ from those of the Googleplex in stressing the corners and intersections of offices; he does this by designing something like streets and avenues internally, whereas the Googleplex draws no floor-plate distinctions of activities. Duffy's offices are visually interesting because of these shifts in scale. Good socialist that he is, he also tries to put low-level workers and their work at the corners, rather than hide them away invisibly in the nether reaches of the space.

However realized, the crossroads is an epistemic break in Bachelard's sense, a disjuncture introduced into space. At a corner, more than in the middle length of a street or an avenue, or along an office corridor, we are likely to take our bearings, reckoning where we are.

The quote mark A third kind of spatial punctuation works as a quote mark. Like the corner, the spatial quote mark draws attention specifically to where you are. But whereas a crossroads is a straightforward marker of place, the urban quote mark is not. The practical meaning of this Delphic declaration appears in marking spaces in poor or deprived communities.

In my own practice, I pay a lot of attention to street furniture – to benches, drinking fountains, small trees in concrete pots, and to different forms of sidewalk paving. It has amazed me how little has to be done to brighten up poor people's public space in this way. When working on a tight budget in a poor part of Chicago, for instance, my clients and I used potted shrubs to achieve the same effect along a street that the residents of the Medellín barrio got in their window boxes, varying the species of shrub so that the continuous street wall read as a kind of progression. The government sponsors thought it was a frill.

More than prettifying the city is involved in such simple moves. You might, for instance, place a street bench so that it faces the entrance of a building rather than turns outwards towards the street flow. By siting the bench in front of an ordinary building, the marker declares, 'Here's a place of value because you can rest here' – the designer could convey this by placing the bench in front of nearly any building along the street. A bench placed arbitrarily in front of a building makes no statement other than 'This is a nice space.' It's odd: such an inviting bench in front of such an uninviting building. A poor community can be improved by such arbitrary markers, as with varying the paving in parts of the street, or slathering blank walls with primary-colour paint. These gestures do not mark anything in particular about the environment; rather, they put a mark on it.

Central Park, we recall, was an immense construction meant to give people pleasure by enabling them to escape the city for a confected, highly calculated version of nature. It's stretching a point – but not to the point of breaking – to think of the plastic bench, in its arbitrary placement, as having a kinship with the artifices governing the Park. The Park's playful bridges, underpasses, lakes and bowers are arbitrary impositions, obviously man-made rather than derived from a pre-existing natural landscape. The most widespread natural artifice in cities is the straight line of trees planted at the edges of a sidewalk to demarcate separation of people from traffic; straight lines of isolated, evenly spaced trees are seldom found in natural settings. They are valued, in any setting, just as a form imposed on the street, for ecological as well as aesthetic reasons. We see a line of trees as having increased the value of a street, and we are aware of the very arbitrary way this value has been increased. But this device is not derived from its context; value is imposed.

Put around a word, the quote marks draw your attention to what it means. Grammarians might say the quote marks question the value of the word or phrase within: i.e. don't take that for granted. Yet the quote marks also increase the value of the word inside; as Leon Festinger would put it, the quote marks stimulate focal attention on the arbitrary, the problematic, but also the important: so too in the built environment.

I try to keep my obsessions under control, but indulge me for a few paragraphs. It was in Japan that I understood why I am so fascinated by plastic benches. The landscapers of that society use simple stone markers to devise the most sophisticated kind of arbitrary, problematic, value-making marker.

Save for its use in castle walls, stone has seldom featured as a domestic or commercial building material in classic Japanese architecture, nor indeed in the Chinese architecture which influenced the Japanese. Japan was a country of forests; builders became adept at siting structures made of wood and its paper by-products to deal with the islands' harsh climatic conditions. But rock still mattered, indeed had a sacred value, dating from the worship of rocks in ancient Chinese Shintoism. 'A particularly majestic rock would become a center for contemplation,' notes the garden historian Sunniva Harte, 'and the surrounding area was covered with white stones to denote that it was a religious or spiritual place.'⁴

In the fifth and sixth centuries AD, many thousands of years after the worship of raw rocks began, Shintoism became localized as a worship in constructed shrines, rather than out in the open. Awareness of the sacred character of rocks now merged into an appreciation of their beauty and positioning in and around buildings. The rock morphed into a marker in the built environment.

When Buddhism came to Japan in the Kamakura era (1185–1336), a person viewing these stones was asked to suspend thinking of them as representative of particular symbols. Stone in formal gardens or simply placed outside houses marked something important but indeterminate; it became a floating signifier.

Lifting stone from its animistic references guided the design of the abbot's quarters of Ryōan-ji Temple in Kyoto, whose planner may have been Tessen Soki, a priest who dwelt here in the fifteenth century. The abbot's quarters look out on a rectangular garden of rock and sand, the sand raked and bedded in simple straight lines out of which erupt fifteen rocks, sorted into five groups. The south and west walls facing the building are low, with forest beyond.

There's no mistaking that the abbot's garden of Ryōan-ji Temple is an artifice, carefully created rather than found nature. The bases of the rocks are cut so that they stand at different angles, following the rules of geomancy; the quartz gravel has been strictly selected, it is uniform in size, and chisel marks have been left to show on the erupting stones.

Today, with the garden complete, the place makes a profound impression, or rather two strong impressions. One might be called its studied absences, the sense of elimination and refined erasure. What the garden represents is not the point of being there – in Zen, there is no point; one seeks release from naming, pointing, underlining, intending. But the other impression is of the strong presence of the physical objects in this carefully designed space; one is intensely aware of the stones as things in themselves. Beyond the low wall of the garden, beyond the outside green landscape of trees, highway traffic is audible in the distance, but one's eye remains riveted on the rocks and sand.

The Shinto garden, then, was a place of direct symbols, a garden of representations. The Zen gardener tried to get beyond these representations, to recover the mystery of the natural elements he had so carefully shaped, to efface his own need for them to have an identifiable content. In its arbitrariness, its de-naturalizing, the Zen stone garden aroused a more reflective, self-questioning response. The stones are scare-quote markers.

In sum, an exclamation point – like the obelisk – declares that a place is important. Sadly, as is true of life in general, these declarations can deflate in the course of time, as in Trafalgar Square. A semicolon in space is less demanding; as in a crossroads, it can entail a little jolt in turning a corner, a contrast which crossroadists want to accentuate. The physical quote marks, whether made by placing a plastic bench, planting an artificial line of trees or laying out stones on the ground, marks a form which is at once arbitrary, problematic and value-making.

III. POROUS – THE MEMBRANE

The Nolli map A sponge is porous because it can absorb water – but it still keeps its shape. So too a building is porous when there is an open flow between the inside and outside, yet the structure retains the shape of its functions and form. One of the greatest maps of Rome, made by Giovanni Battista Nolli in 1748, showed how porosity on these terms appeared in the city. The map was based on surveys of the city that Nolli conducted over twelve years. The results were published in two versions: one a series of twelve engravings which together created a large map; the other, a smaller engraving Nolli did with Giovanni Battista Piranesi, the artist of imaginary prisons and real places in Rome.

Before Nolli, most Roman maps were scenic – fanciful pictures of what an artist imagined the city to be like were the artist a bird; buildings were rendered in 3-D, angled as the bird would see them if it flew east towards Rome. Nolli was the first Roman map-makers to orient his image of the city with north at the top, rather than east, because he worked with a magnetic compass to get a common baseline as he painstakingly moved through the city. Nolli's is an ichnographic map, that is, looking straight down in 2-D; it is a figured ground, rendered in contrasting black and white, black for solid building, white for empty space.[5]

These renderings show, in their finer details, the porous relations between solid and void: circles enclosed in squares represent the pillars holding up the Pantheon, contrasting with the delicate T-shaped signs for the pillars in the nearby church of Santa Maria sopra Minerva. The little fountain of the bees then at the corner of Via Sistina and Piazza Barberini is a visible dot, because the wet space is something adults avoid but their children dive into.

The graphics are also social representations. For instance, the Pantheon, that huge, domed ancient Roman temple with light coming only from a hole (the oculus) at the top of the dome, has a fringed white space at the centre because, by Nolli's time, it was used as a church, and was open to the public at all hours. Solid black with sharp edges represents buildings which were private – mostly houses, but also places like certain parts of the Vatican which were forbidden to ordinary Romans. To translate this into modern terms, were Nolli to make a map of Paris in the 1920s, all of the Plan Voisin would have read as a black patch, whereas the Marais, so porous and so compressed, would have been rendered in circles, squares, dots, Ts and shades of grey on white.

Nolli mapped porosity in a city which had thousands of years to ripen. How would Mr Sudhir go about building porosity in less time?

The membrane Stephen Jay Gould draws our attention to an important distinction in natural ecologies between two kinds of edges: boundaries and borders. Borders are porous edges, boundaries are not. The boundary is an edge where things end, a limit beyond which a particular species must not stray or, conversely, which it guards as do prides of lions or packs of wolves by peeing or pooping to tell others to Keep Out! The boundary marks a low-intensity edge. Whereas the border is an edge where different groups interact; for instance, where the shoreline of a lake meets solid land is an active zone of exchange where organisms find and feed off other organisms. Not surprisingly, it is also at the borderline where the work of natural selection is the most intense.

This ecological difference marks human communities too. The closed boundary dominates the modern city. The urban habitat is cut up into segregated parts by streams of traffic and by functional isolation between zones for work, commerce, family and the public realm. 'Octopus city' development in Delhi, as elsewhere, does not spread growth across an area, but rather channels it narrowly. Caracas in Venezuela employs another kind of sealed boundary in the form of high-speed walls of traffic which separate rich and poor. The most popular form of new residential development internationally, as we have observed, is the guarded, gated community inside a boundary wall. One result of its low-intensity edges is that the isolated denizens are not much stimulated by conditions outside; exchanges between different racial, ethnic and class communities are faint.

But left as a black or white contrast, the border/boundary distinction is too crude. It can be refined by zooming in on a living cell. At this level, there is a contrast between a cell wall and a cell membrane. It is an ambiguous distinction at the cellular level, in part because cell linings can sometimes switch function; moreover, a wholly sealed wall would cause the cell to die, as would a totally fluid relation between inside and outside. A cell membrane must at once let matter flow in and out of the cell, but selectively, so that the cell can retain what it needs for nourishment. Porosity exists in dialogue with resistance: a dialogue which sometimes means the cell is open to being inundated, and sometimes is retentive.

This dialogue is what the urbanist should want to initiate, rather than imagining that sheer open space – a pure void – counts as porous. Neither totally sealed nor totally exposed, the dynamic relation

between porosity and resistance is what Nolli rendered in his map
of Rome. It stood in contrast to the Venetian ghetto, as the planners of that space originally intended, shut tight at night against the
surrounding city, its shuttered windows and barred bridges, its surrounding canals guarded by boat throughout the night, creating an
internal boundary within the city.

What is an urban membrane made of? Somewhat paradoxically, it
can be made of stone.

The earliest logic of an urban wall was that it be as thick and tall
and impenetrable as possible for military reasons. The ancient walls
around Beijing, for instance, were about 60 feet thick at the base, 40
feet at the top and 40 feet high (18 metres and 12 metres), made of
rammed earth. The art of military wall-building could be refined
by creating double walls with an empty space between them, as in
Carcassonne, France, which allowed space for manoeuvre separated
from the inner fabric of the city. Another kind of refinement consisted
of a wall with ravelins, which were arrow-shaped platforms jutting
out of a wall, and which allowed javelins, and later cannon, to be
aimed at attackers trying to scale the wall.

For Max Weber a wall was a boundary, an outer limit of the city-
state beyond which lay nothing civic either politically or socially. To
him, the wall itself was a legal idea rather than a physical presence. The
sheer massiveness of ancient walls may have misled him; even a thick
wall can issue an invitation to dwell. On both sides of the Aix-en-
Provence wall were to be found sites for unregulated development in
the city; informal markets selling black-market or untaxed goods
sprang up nestled against the stones; the zone of the wall was where her-
etics, foreign exiles and other misfits tended to gravitate. So too, after
modern artillery rendered the wall a less useful barrier, these military
boundaries often morphed into social spaces. Louis XIV effected this
change in Paris in 1670, converting the ramparts into shady promenades where people could walk. His planners gave the new spaces a
new term: the boulevard. Within a century, many other European
cities followed suit, notably Berlin in 1734. Napoleon I completed the
transformation of the military boundary by demanding that many of
the cities he conquered destroy their walls entirely – this being more a
symbolic humiliation than a military necessity.[6]

All of which is to say that even a solid mass of material, seemingly resistant to any change, can be made porous in a social sense. It's an error to think massive structures are inherently inert, and that the qualities represented in the membrane condition can only appear in lightly built, or temporary, 'pop-up' structures.

Making membranes Today, the planner's challenge is to create membranes. *Percement* is the most direct building technique to turn walls into membranes. The Danish urbanist Jan Gehl has worked out ways of cutting doors and windows into blank walls, unsealing or smashing through them to create new entrances and windows; he has made precise calculations of where and how much to smash in order to bring a street to life. Similarly, in creating a new skyscraper, one big entrance isolating the elements inside, with floors above as separated slices, can be replaced, as in skyscrapers like design firm Gensler's Shanghai Tower in the Pudong section of Shanghai and their interior work for Renzo Piano's New York Times tower in mid-Manhattan, with a more porous vertical design: instead of a central core which services isolated floors, Gensler treats the skyscraper as a true vertical street, fed by many differentiated elevators, and with multi-floor public spaces and radiating corridors.

When people imagine where the life of a community is to be found, they usually look for it in the centre, where planners try to intensify community life. This means neglecting the edge; the community turns inward as a result. Which is an error. I made it several years ago, when I was involved in plans to create a market serving the Hispanic community of Spanish Harlem in New York. This community, one of the poorest in the city, lies above 96th Street on Manhattan's Upper East Side. Just below 96th Street, in an abrupt shift, lay one of the richest communities in the world, running from 96th down to 59th Street, comparable to Mayfair in London or the 7th arrondissement in Paris.

La Marqueta was located in the centre of Spanish Harlem twenty blocks away, in the very centre of the community. We planners regarded 96th Street as a dead edge, where nothing much happened. We chose wrongly. Had we located the market on that street, we might have encouraged activity which brought the rich and the poor into some daily commercial, physical contact. Wiser planners have since learned from our mistake, and on the West Side of Manhattan have sought to locate new community resources at the edges between communities in order to make a more porous edge, to open the gates between different racial and economic communities. Our imagining of the importance of the centre proved isolating; their understanding of the value of the edge and border aims to create neighbours who mix casually.

It's certainly true that edges can serve as tense rather than friendly sites of exchange, as in the parking lots of Boston where buses decanted children of colour into white working-class schools. Casual physical mixing is much less confrontational, as in a rich lady and her maid happening to be in the same place buying milk or booze late at night. Such physical mixing complements the civilities that marked the newsagent's in Clerkenwell; the planner is not forcing explicit articulation of differences on people, but engaging them in a common everyday task. This sort of edge experience is, in terms of the distinction drawn in our discussion of social differences in the city, inclusive rather than integrative.

However, as Mr Sudhir knew well from his own experience, living on the edge is 'edgy', in the sense of 'risky'. These adverbs are more than verbal decor. They describe a third kind of membrane-making.

After the Second World War, Amsterdam was a grim place. The old city had not adapted well to the automobile. It was a cramped city as well; there were few places away from the big canals for people – especially children – to play. Aldo van Eyck determined to do something about this by seizing on found spaces in the city and transforming hundreds of disused or indifferent spaces into urban parks. Unlike Olmsted and Vaux, he used the simplest means at hand in his impoverished city, incorporating blank walls, or too-wide road intersections, to create spaces for children to play and adults to rest. In these spaces, he put different activities – a floral planting, a sandbox, benches – which had no visible demarcations yet remained distinct, their internal relationship porous in the membrane sense.

The radical thing about van Eyck's parks was the urbanist's conception of how children should play: their play-space was not walled off from the street for safety. There are in these parks kerbs, but no iron-link fences. Van Eyck's idea was that the kids should learn the difference between traffic and turf – which children did; the parks in fact had few accidents due to porosity. In the same way, the benches provided for adults had no spatial divide from where the children played; the youngsters were obliged to learn how to place themselves so as not to disrupt elderly people gossiping or snoozing on the benches.

In terms of form, van Eyck created liminal edges, 'liminal' meaning here the experience of a transition even if there is no clear barrier between two states. The liminal passage forms a kind of 'transitional consciousness', as D. W. Winnicott calls it; he first alerted psychologists to the importance of transitional moments which establish the borders between experience for children. The van Eyck park is a prosaic instance of this: to understand how to play, children experience its limits in relation to moving cars or sleeping grandparents; rather than an abrupt either/or, they make a liminal – a membraneous – transition. So, too, in the larger geography of a city, liminal edges can mark the passage from rich to poor places; the Chicago School studied just this liminal condition – without branding it as such – along the east–west streets which fed from the Gold Coast along the lake into the slums of the city further west.

Porous sound The sounds of a city can seem porous in a bad way. The invasive noise of traffic can often be the enemy of sleep; at my age, the deafening clamour of restaurants can ruin going out. If silence is a friend, sonic boundaries would seem better than sonic borders in the built environment.

In fact, the absence of sound would be equally disquieting. The acoustician R. Murray Schafer observes that 'Hearing is a way of touching at a distance.' Technically this means that when an audible sound vibrates at more than 20 hertz it can be felt as a tactile sensation. The sound of footsteps at night or honking horns during the day is an alert to the presence of others; Jane Jacobs' famous dictum that, for safety's sake, buildings should provide 'eyes on the street' should be expanded to 'ears on the street', particularly at night. In Bulgakov's fantasy novel *The Master and Margarita*, the silent arrival of various ghosts, devils and a magic cat inspires terror, because we cannot hear/touch them.[7]

Porous sound, good and bad, can be specified fairly precisely. The experience of sound in a city is shaped by two factors: intensity and intelligibility. Intensity is in part sheer loudness: the footstep-sound of a medium-weight, medium-height man is around 35 decibels at 20 metres on an otherwise silent, night-time street, whereas a rock band playing outside sounds at least 115 decibels. But it is also a matter of frequency: if there are more than four bursts of a sound per second, the ear hears them as one continuous sound. Electrical hum constitutes such a 'flat-line sound', in acoustic jargon; steady traffic noise is another. Whereas at the other, a shotgun blast is an 'impact sound', as is the sudden sound of a unmuffled motorcycle amid the traffic. These sounds are distinct, recognizable, intelligible. The sound of footsteps in an empty street can become an impact sound, as it was for my young protectors in Santo Domingo – a distinct warning noise against the low-level flat-line sound of the barrio asleep. What is usually called 'ambient sound' is technically an averaging of flat-line and impact sounds. Ambient noise at about 35 decibels is optimal for sleep, a group of Russian researchers found, whereas when ambient noise 'is at a level of 50 decibels, there are fairly short intervals of deep sleep, followed on waking by a sense of fatigue'.[8, 9, 10]

In designing a sonic environment, we want to decrease the intensity of flat-line sound to 35 decibels, while keeping the impact sound at a level around 50 decibels, so that a noise gets through to us, but is not shattering. This is good porosity, because sounds are distinct and intelligible but not overwhelming. I'd be happy in a restaurant with that ambient average: I could hear voices at my table, and perhaps I could eavesdrop on another table; these voices would float on a cushion of more indistinct noise.

The Nolli map shows the kinds of places which shape sounds in this porous way, for instance in and around the Pantheon. Despite its cavernous volume, which should magnify echoes, the Pantheon's ambient level is good because of its complex side surfaces, its porticos, its curved top, which is coffered (a ceiling with incised panels rather than a smooth surface). So, too, in the east–west streets running around the Pantheon: the irregular surfaces of their walls, the recessed doorways, the little side alleys – all lower the ambient sound level to about 40 decibels. In a modern building the same sonic effect can appear, as in New York's Chanin Building, a skyscraper built in 1927–9, which achieves a relatively low ambient level at its inside centre simply because of its twists and turns, whereas sound roars through its neighbours whenever doors or windows are opened (if they can be; as in the hotel across the street, most are impermeable, energy-inefficient, sealed glass boxes which keep out the sounds of the city).

The materials that build silence involve crinkling and deflecting. Modern sound-deadening materials, pancaked atop concrete, flat-surface floors, seldom do the job perfectly; older structures tended to work better, just because the composition of the floors themselves was a mixture of many elements – including crushed sea-shells, horse-hair, plaster-coated rags – which created a complex filter.

Echoes (technically, the reverberation time of sounds) diminish and fade in intensity between porous buildings, whereas echoes are quick and sharp between facing glass monoliths; this is because the longer the reverberation time, the weaker the echo becomes. This principle governs interior design as well. The optimal reverberation time in a concert hall – from the stage, off the side and back walls to someone sitting in the middle of the audience – is just under two seconds. In an apartment building we don't want anything like this resonance: stair-wells, for instance, should be angled or twisted so that their echoes have a reverb time of more than 3.5 seconds, and thus the echo becomes quite weak.

You certainly don't want to hear your neighbours' conversations and probably do not want to hear them making love. Still, porous sound in other circumstances can draw people. The urbanist John Bingham-Hall and I are studying sociable sounds in an unlikely site – the pedestrian tunnels underneath the Périphérique in Paris, the highway separating poor, immigrant, newer outskirts from the richer, mixed, older city. People congregate in certain underpasses, to buy daily goods and just hang out, while they avoid other underpasses. We've found that sociable sounds tend to be the sounds of voices, audible distinctly as impact sounds, just above the highway's hum; fur-ther, the intelligible impact sounds project outwards, alerting people to activities within the tunnel. Those underpasses whose sounds attract people to them are shaped in a crinkled fashion, whereas unsociable underpasses are more simply and cleanly made, producing a high-intensity flat-line which drowns out intelligibility within the tunnel, so that only noise is projected outside. The crinkled underpasses of the Périphérique may be as unlikely informal social spaces as the garage roof of Nehru Place, but they explain in part why Nehru Place has worked so well. As in the tunnels, its hawkers of iPhones can be heard distinctly above the hum of moving bodies and traffic.

In the history of cities, the 'cries' of hawkers on the street used to perform the same sociable-sonic function – knife sharpeners, fishmongers, coal haulers, nearly forty distinctive street cries in London – until they were prohibited by the Metropolitan Police Act of 1864. Before that, the town crier announced news or chanted hymns, as recorded by John Milton (in *Il Penseroso*, line 83). Most fundamental, the chiming sound of church bells, which had regulated religious observances, gave way to ringing out the hours from the fourteenth century on, as a way to regulate the labour process by dividing paid work into regular units of time. These clock-bell sounds were louder and of greater intensity than the bells in most parish churches, penetrating all the city; clock-bell porosity was the sound of routinized labour – invasive and inescapable. It was not sociable sound.

In sum, in a closed city the boundary will prevail; an open city will contain more borders. These borders function like cell membranes, with a dynamic tension between porosity and resistance. Membranes can be made at the edges of places, by *percements* of solid walls, by the crinkling of street fabric and by the shaping of intelligible, sociable sounds.

IV. INCOMPLETE – THE SHELL AND THE TYPE FORM

Finally, let's imagine Mr Sudhir at home. Mr Sudhir told me he and his sons were building their family house cinder block by cinder block over the course of time, as their fortunes allowed. In almost every settlement in which migrants have squatted or settled, something similar occurs: poor people become their own architects. Dwellings

may be no more than cinder-block shacks roofed with plastic or corrugated iron; in time, though, if they can, people will add proper
roofs, glass windows, perhaps a second storey; the 'architecture' is a
long-unfolding labour. At any one moment, though, the self-built
project is an incomplete form.

Urbanism has much to learn from the ways very poor people are
obliged to work with incomplete forms. Can a form be made incomplete on purpose, by design, rather than by necessity, as it is for Mr
Sudhir's family? What would be gained?

The shell One answer lies in Iquique, Chile, a city in the desert
about 1,500 kilometres north of Santiago, where about a hundred
families had originally squatted in a site called the Quinta Monroy.
The original migrants were the Aymara, an ethnic group spanning
the Chilean-Peruvian-Bolivian high plains. Quinta Monroy was a
talisman of the future: out of small places like this, immense settlements of tens or hundreds of thousands of people are mushrooming
in Latin America.

Here the Chilean architect Alejandro Aravena launched a project
to build incomplete forms. His idea was to design half a good house
which the inhabitants could fill in with their own labour, rather than
provide a finished dwelling built to a lower standard. In the Iquique
version of incomplete form, half the first and second storeys of buildings are walled in, and provisioned with proper electricity and
plumbing. This infrastructure is located on the gable end of the house
rather than on the party wall with as yet unfinished space; this detail
allows the maximum flexibility in filling in the space. A further refinement is to build the entrance stairs outside the house, so that, if
desired, first and second storeys can be independent dwellings: either
storey can be rented out or used by different generations in a family.

Aravena's project treated Quinta Monroy as a test bed for social
housing. Urbanistically, the individual houses are grouped together
into rectangles forming the sides of a shared communal square, a
Chilean's poor version of the London terrace squares in Bloomsbury.
Like Cerdà, Aravena intends them to scale up, so that they become an
additive grid. Unlike Jane Jacobs, he has no fear of scaling up, even
though he has started small; the appalling conditions of the poor in

his country demand a large-scale solution. But again, unlike Lewis Mumford's pre-made garden city, this solution should involve the poor themselves as makers of their own environment. This is the social logic behind this incomplete form, again translating very concretely into the infrastructure of party walls and the location of staircases.

The shell is the building type of projects like Iquique. The shell has appeared in varied guises, not only as an answer to the needs of the poor: for instance, the eighteenth-century Georgian terrace; it was shaped like a shoebox, its sides fronting alike the squares and streets of the city. In structural terms, the terraces were yesterday's version of today's lofts, the floor-plates supported by only a few posts and internal structural walls of brick or stone kept to a minimum. The Georgian shoebox was a particularly good kind of shell, since its dimensions were small enough so that every room front and back in the house had direct access to natural light and ventilation. In this, it contrasted with Baron Haussmann's dwellings in Paris, larger in overall size, wrapped around dank, dark central staircases, with poor access to light and air in many of their inner rooms. Over the centuries the Georgian shell has evolved in function, even when relatively constant in form, as in Woburn Walk, designed by Thomas Cubitt in the 1820s, which now contains upper-storey offices, as well as domestic flats. Open spaces can similarly function like shells. During the First World War, a grand square like Berkeley Square was cleared of its flowers and filled with wounded soldiers; during the Second, the metal railings around the square were taken down to be melted into shells; then, after the war, the function evolved again, to marry open nature and protected access.[11]

In principle, today should be the age of the Shell Triumphant. Thanks to poured concrete and mass-manufactured steel I-beams, we can construct buildings with huge floor-plates only minimally cluttered by posts or other structural obstructions. The trading floors of investment firms embody the Shell Triumphant, with row upon row of desks in a space in which everybody can see everyone else – if only they were to look up from their hypnotizing screens. More artfully, thin shell structures can float now above the ground. The structural principles for floating shells came from the Russian engineer Vladimir Shukhov, who made a huge, self-supporting curved-roof shed in Vyksa in 1897; freed of any interior supports, it could be put to any use. The geodesic dome is Vyksa's heir, the domes being constructed by a lattice of interlocking triangles covered by a protective skin. Buckminster Fuller thought such a dome, both super-light and super-strong, could be magnified almost to infinity; in his zanier moments he hoped to cover entire cities with geodesic domes. More modest in size, but still huge, geodesic domes like the Fukuoka Dome in Japan permit a variety of uses – as does the Millennium Dome (though not strictly geodesic) which Richard Rogers created in London in 1999.

Shells create forms whose possibilities are not exhausted in any particular configuration imposed at the start. The shell also creates porosity within a building, since structurally there are few fixed barriers. Its making invites more making. As in building, so in communication, words are shells of meaning. Words incompletely express what people mean to say.

But when should this open-ended process stop? When is the building finished, the communication concluded?

The unfinished and the unfinishable Pure process can be destructive. Many of the alterations of the Georgian terrace shoebox have over time degraded what was originally a rather severely beautiful form: neon-lit shops and signage at street level erase a once modest address to the street; above stairs, the rooms are chopped up into cubbyhole spaces, their windows truncated by air-conditioners. So too are many loft spaces in New York deformed, and to the horror of purists in Xintiandi, Shanghai, even the restored lofts of the shikumen, recently so spacious and so snob-worthy, are all succumbing to a new, poorer generation of young choppers and truncators.

Basic rules of form have to protect against this shapeless drift, just as pure process in the *cité* could entail an endless, wandering Twitter-stream of communication, the *cité* condemned to momentary stimulations. There is a dilemma here. If drift is the enemy, change still has to be possible, otherwise people are merely acting out prescribed roles in fixed places; they need the freedom and the means to alter static form.

In the fine arts, this dilemma appears in those fatal words, 'It's done.' Fatal because 'done' can equate with 'dead'. Rodin registered the problem of termination on the surfaces of his cast sculptures. These skins are full of rough clay-knife marks and bits of unfinished detail in order to engage the viewing eye in the material substance of the pieces, so his one-time studio assistant Rainer Maria Rilke wrote. The process of creation seems ongoing, yet the sculptor learned when to stop, by calculating how many slits the clay surface could bear. Any classical musician who works from a score cannot know clearly when to stop. Were he or she to think, 'At last! The Hammerklavier Sonata is just as it should be!' why would the musician ever perform the piece again? A performer wants to keep playing, to hear the Hammerklavier always anew and so keep the music (and the musician) alive. In this sense, performance is an unfinishable art.

Urbanism of the open sort tries to resolve this problem through the creation of type-forms.

The type-form A type-form is a piece of urban DNA which takes on different shapes in different circumstances. A type-form could be likened to the theme in theme-and-variations music. Themes in music open up as the composer exploits little breaks harmonically or melodically, even in the most seemingly seamless music; in Handel's 'Harmonious Blacksmith' variations, for instance, a little chromatic slippage at the end of the initial tune allows Handel the freedom to romp. In the same way, type-forms open up urban design; the themes are not so integrated, totalized, 'harmonious' as to leave no room for variation, yet the changes rung on the urban theme follow a certain logic.

Consider the construction of the prosaic outdoor step. The 'theme' is set in the human body, in how high the leg is lifted comfortably as it climbs a step; the step's height is called a 'riser'. As a general rule of thumb, risers are lower in outside construction than inside (the risers are about 110 mm outside, 150 mm inside); steps to sit on, as in Rome's Spanish Steps, are about 150 mm high. Normally, in a walking staircase-step, the horizontal length of its tread is twice that of its riser. A step outside has to be laid tilting very slightly downwards so that it sheds water, and so that, in cold climates, ice pockets do not form.[12]

Within these constraints, many variations are possible – in the width of the stairs, what the stairs are made of, or where they are placed – because the raised leg does not work like an escalator, stepping always, inflexibly, predictably. In the Washington Mall project, we used many variations of width and configured sitting steps next to walking in contrasting ways. The Washington Mall had been traditionally lit from above; the steps we proposed were wired and lit from within, in a line of LCD lights at the seam between each riser and tread. This prosaic design certainly does not provide an urban experience equivalent to the 'Hammerklavier', but it is structured in the same way: there is a basic set of relationships which admit variations in form. The basic relationships are defined – harmonically in the music, physiologically in the urban body; the maker/musician creates variations within these constraints.

Type-forms can be verbal as well as physical. Gaston Bachelard writes that 'the poetic image is essentially variational', which means that the tropes of metaphor, metonymy and rhyme are variations on a structural theme. Roland Barthes also speaks of an 'image-repertoire' on which poets draw. The work of improvising and ringing changes on a foundational image is for him more demanding work for the poet than creating an entirely new image.[13, 14]

In the realm of buildings, the type-form is open to substitutions as well as variations. A king-brace roof (the two sides of the roof tied together by a triangular brace) addresses the fundamental problem of shear, which is the tendency of weight above to push away the sides of a building; you can make a king brace of wood, metal or plastic. Whereas a flushing toilet is not so flexible a type-form, because you can't easily substitute wood or paper for its vitreous walls.[15]

The type-form has a loose fit between form and function, but still the two are contingent. In the realm of urban engineering, this loose fit is enabled by redundant systems of plumbing or electrical outlets. Provisioning more than you need for immediate use means you can adapt the building to new conditions. This is particularly important in efforts to transform old office buildings into apartments, for instance, as is now happening in New York's Wall Street and Shanghai's Bund; the buildings which can be most easily transformed were over-built in the first place, with plenty of pipes, corridors and non-structural party walls making possible the installation of new domestic bathrooms, kitchens and the like. Overloaded infrastructure, that is, serves to loosen up use, whereas building only what is needed originally can render the building technologically obsolete in short order. As in Foster's docking stations, the tighter the fit the less the flexibility.

Thus the type-form differs from its cousin, the shell. The shell is empty; the type-form is, as it were, the snail inside. There is a content within which both limits and encourages change. A type-form differs also from a prototype. The type-form sets the terms for making a family of possible objects – objects yet to be made – while the prototype already exists in built form, as a specific demonstration of what can be done. Part of the problem with Bill Mitchell's Media Lab experiments for driverless cars was that he thought in terms of type-forms rather than prototypes; he could explain – sort of – the relationship of the hardware to the human body, but he couldn't show an actual example of what he meant. Still, thinking in terms of type-form rather than prototype loosened up his imagination. The prototype represents a turning point in winnowing these possibilities, closing down alternatives.

Much urban development is flogged to the public as improvement of an existing state of affairs, but the type-form cautions against thinking that variations are quality-driven. The variations on a theme do not necessarily improve the theme itself. To take a titanic musical analogy: in the course of time Stradivarius cut his cellos slightly differently, experimenting with various varnishes (in ways we still don't understand exactly), but later Strads are not better than earlier ones; they are just different.

In the everyday world, variation is more often driven by the need to sell new products than motivated by *Homo faber*'s desire for quality – a truth apparent to anyone using computer programs whose 'updates' actually degrade in successive iterations. It's mindless change in this commercial form which the urbanist Gordon Cullen fought against, and why he chose long-term uses of space as establishing the guidelines for design. But this reasonable critique of type-forming runs up against the conservatism familiar to anyone in academia – the fear of doing something different swathed in bilge about lack of precedents, let well enough alone, etc. Between these two poles, how can an urban type-form be quality-driven?

Barcelona type-forms its grid A hundred and fifty years after Cerdà laid down the grid plan for Barcelona, it needed a rethink. The city had become choked with cars both moving and parked; the pollution they created was not as life-threatening as that in Beijing or Delhi, but still was harmful. Moreover, the clogging of Cerdà's streets with cars had squeezed sociability into the chamfered corners of the grid blocks. Most of all, green space in Barcelona has shrunk. In Cerdà's time there was lots of it; today, the 6.6 square metres of green space per inhabitant in the city compare to 27 in London and 87.5 in Amsterdam (the rule of thumb established by the World Health Organization puts 9 square metres per capita as a minimum).[16]

'Taking back the streets' has an economic undertow in Barcelona due to the threat posed by mass tourism to the city. The sheer number of tourists increases dramatically each year; these temporary locals pass indifferently through the neighbourhoods towards the big tourist spots in the city – Las Ramblas, the Cathedral, the beaches. Like day tourists in Venice, another tourist-smothered city, Barcelona's visitors take more than they give, using city services but contributing little through taxes to the services they use. Tourist economies in general do not generate much in the way of non-tourist spin-offs, nor generate much in the way of high-skilled labour for residents of a city.

From the mayor to the ordinary Barcelonan there has thus arisen a strong desire to use public space differently. Treating the Cerdian block as a type-form rather than a fixed form can enable this. The plan is as follows: imagine a piece of Cerdian fabric, now composed of nine city blocks through which people and traffic flow across three horizontal and three vertical streets; in place of this there will be one superblock, a *superilles*; around its perimeter traffic will flow, and within the superblock the three horizontal and vertical streets will be pedestrianized. The logic of doing this is not just the amenity of car-free existence; rather, the concentration of sociable and economic activity at the chamfered corner is meant to spread out, because people can easily get to places throughout the superblock.

Meant to begin in Cerdà's home neighbourhood of Eixample, this remaking is sometimes sold as Jane-Jacobs-comes-to-Barcelona – but misleadingly; there's nothing bottom-up about this plan. In order for the superblocks to work, they have to be coordinated on a large scale: the traffic expelled from within the *superille* has to be able to circulate around each perimeter, and pass into the larger city. An Eixample *superille* will be sized about 400 × 400 metres, containing between 5,000 and 6,000 people. This larger scale is necessary to make the transport system work; it keeps the number of buses servicing the *superille* to a minimum while also putting access to a bus within about a five-minute walk for any resident. The hope is that over time, by scaling up, the *superilles* will recover green space; though not spoken aloud, the plans aim at creating new Barcelonan public space separated from the tourist maelstrom around public monuments.

These plans exemplify an important general issue: type-forms can upgrade the character of a place in a positive way by scaling *up* their form. Just as in seeing and analysing, so in making things bigger they might become more variegated and more complex; after all, that's how evolution from small to large organisms has worked. In the built environment, though, scaling up runs contrary to the belief that small places have more character than big ones – a belief which is grounded solidly on the fact that crude sameness and neutral character mark most large-scale building today. In some cases, as in the Barcelona *superilles*, bigger is better quality.

V. MULTIPLE – SEED-PLANNING

Mr Sudhir may now seem on the verge of creating the open city. But he can't do this if he uses the word 'the'. There is no one model for an open city. Shells and type-forms, borders and markers, incompletely made spaces – all take a variety of shapes on the musical model of theme-and-variation. The high tech of the smart city is also open when it coordinates shifting complexities rather than reduces them to a single standard of efficiency. What is true of the *ville* is true of the *cité*. Different kinds of experiences do not mesh socially; a complex *cité* is more like a mixture than a compound. Thus he could plan 'an' open city, while his neighbour selling chapatis, by using the same formal tools, could compose a quite different place.

This sensible proposition is the key to scaling up in an open way. You repeat a generic form like a street market in different places and circumstances around the city, and different kinds of street markets then evolve. Medellín offers a striking example of this kind of planning. The planners commissioned libraries for several poor districts of the city, specifying maximum costs and minimum construction standards; but they left it to individual communities and architects to work out what the individual libraries would look like. The result is what very different structures are used in very different ways: some are open all hours, some shut at night; some cater for children, others for adults; some look like traditional libraries, others, such as Giancarlo Mazzanti's black blocks, nothing like.

This technique I will baptize as 'seed-planning'. Were you a farmer you would understand instantly what this kind of planning is about, but unfortunately you have spent too much time in cafés. On the family farm, your rural self would have noticed that the same seed sown in different circumstances of water, wind and soil produces different colonies of plants, some dense with leaves but with few flowers or fruits, other colonies with relatively few plants, but each a vigorous grower. An application of sheep dip will have one consequence for the growth of colonies while cow manure . . . you don't actually have to leave the café terrace to get the point. The seeds serve as typeforms whose manifestations – plants – change character in different circumstances.

Cities aren't farmed today. Instead they are master-planned. The fully grown plant is treated as the plan. Perhaps some of its details might be changed – a storey or two clipped off a tall building here, a ground floor set back an extra metre there, in order to adapt to different conditions, but these prunings come too late; only an initially unrealized, incomplete form – a seed – will have the time to grow into its surroundings. The master plan divides a city up into a closed system where each place and function relates logically to other places – which again ignores the farming reality that different colonies of the same seeds will compete for water, mutate over time or die out by contact with one another: a farm has a dynamic rather than a static ecology. In urban planning, when things do what they are not supposed to do – for example, when people neglect one bus-stop and overcrowd a nearby one a hundred metres away – the master-planner, with his maps of population/transit distribution so precise, so reasonable, may think the master plan has failed, whereas if he thought like a farmer he would know that this is how colonization works: like the weather, there is something unforeseen and not entirely controllable at work.

The smaller analogue to this disruption exists in choreographing the movements within a building. Expensive consultant space-planners lay out efficient pathways in Google Maps fashion so as to avoid congestion and keep people moving; the plans are then contravened by 'desire lines', which are the ways people use buildings. Employees may search for a route which takes them near their boss ('notice me, I'm working late!') or close to a dishy employee whom the *flâneur* is trying to date – neither of which desires is in the master-planning brief. Instead of masterminding the whole, seed-planning seeks to create 'pocket of order' in open-systems terms. The essence of seed-planning is minimum specification of how form relates to function; this leaves room for maximum variation and innovation.

Baron Haussmann – and after him Albert Speer, and after him Robert Moses – made wilful master plans, disregarding people's desires and needs. But the vice of top-down master-planning is not the same as trying to see the city on a big scale. Another kind of big-scale thinking arose as a reaction against the place-wrecking power of the free market. It is how Mumford and other Fabians thought about countervailing master plans: as in the garden city, these were meant to provide everyone with access to good housing, jobs and public services. In time, as the urban-law scholar Gerald Frug has pointed out, such aspirations have faded from conscious debate and deliberation. The reason for this fading vision among progressives is partly a matter of how 'big' relates to 'good'. Master-planning of Mumford's well-intentioned sort assumes people want to live a stable, balanced life. The simplification of the city follows from making this assumption, and the result is not good. A stable, balanced life is a life losing energy – and so is a stable, balanced city.

A specific barrier to flexibility-seeking, complexifying seed-planning is the conviction that places should have a clear visual identity. In planning circles, this belief is owed in large part to Kevin Lynch, the resident intellectual among urbanists at MIT a generation before the Media Lab came into being. Lynch argued for the value of assembling the forms of the city in fixed, clear images. His argument was based on a particular piece of research. *The Image of the City* emerged from interviews with residents of Boston about how they related to the built environment; he concluded that people think in fixed and clear snapshots about what 'home' looks like or other places in the city which matter to them. Lynch showed how people made mind-maps of the entire city by connecting the mental photos of its scenes to one another. His approach stressed legibility as a positive social value: the more defined a place is, the more people can feel 'This is my neighbourhood', or 'I belong here.'[17]

The background for this argument was the eighteenth-century landscape gardener's belief that each bit of land has a distinct local character of soils, micro-climates and the like which the gardener should bring out in the way he or she sculpted the land and planted it – its *genius loci*. The cult of using only native plants came out of this belief in the distinctive character of local places. In rural Britain, this made sense because the landscapes of the British Isles are so varied in topography and climate; 20 kilometres can mark the difference between two entirely different *genii loci*. Again, this is rural knowledge, akin to the knowledge the farmer has about the same seeds sprouting in different colonies. But Lynch drew on the *genius loci* to narrow the scope of urban design.

As his work progressed, its terms became more abstract. Geometry replaced photographic representations. Lynch came to believe that human habitats are built from four basic geometric shapes: the line, the circle, the fractal and the orthogonal. How people inhabit these forms became less important than how the elements are arranged, in five primal sites in the city: paths, districts, edges, nodes and landmarks. He clung to the conviction with which he initially began, arguing that urban design should aim at achieving a clear pattern, a legible image, an identity using these geometries – just the opposite of entertaining the 'difficulties, ambiguities, and complexities' that Robert Venturi valued.[18]

From the social point of view, there is a big objection. 'That's what an African-American community looks like' easily morphs into 'That's where the blacks belong.' Even in more benign environments, say a neighbourhood filled with Polish people, how will the urbanist clarify its visual identity? You might give the local Catholic church a street-side face-lift; protect the rents on the local Warsaw-in-London club; license food stalls selling kielbasa and other heart-attack Polish delicacies. But some immigrant Welsh also live there, even some British-born Jews. Clarifying images of a community's identity will render the presence of these minority groups invisible. What is a danger in the *ville* is also a danger psychologically: the conviction that one has a master self-image, a dominant identity, as black, Latino, gay or British, shrinks the multi-layered richness of the self.

A *ville* using open elements which are then seed-planned will come to look, instead, like a collage. This analogy is rich. When Colin Rowe and Fred Koetter wrote their book *Collage City* they drew on a non-artistic form of collaging, the flip-chart which layers one set of data about a place or condition on top of another. The guru for this procedure was Edward Tufte, a graphic designer who pioneered the imaginative display of statistical data. Rowe and Koetter applied the flip-chart technique by starting with a familiar street map; the next layer might show housing densities, then day-time uses, then night-time ones. The problem here is that the graphical image becomes hard to make sense of as layers are added – just the opposite problem from the simple clarities of Lynch's geometries or the bull's-eye target in which Park and Burgess had represented the city. In general, flip-charts work well only if one image fits neatly in form and colour over the forms below it – and just such clarity is not how Rowe and Koetter thought cities worked. They were frustrated by their own method.[19, 20]

Georges Braque could have provided another model for how to visualize a complex, open-form, seeded city. The honour of 'inventing' collage is often attributed to Braque and Picasso, though in fact the pasting on a flat surface of various ribbons, newspaper scraps, old dance cards, drawings, rabbit tails, etc., goes back to the domestic memory-screens popular with families in the nineteenth century. In 1912 Braque and Picasso transformed this cosy home art into high art. Braque did so first by cutting out pieces of simulated oak-grain wallpaper and glueing drawings in charcoal onto them. The collage principle here is of adjacency rather than layering, as in the flip-chart. Because it emphasizes edges and highlights contrasts, this kind of art 'reads' – we can discern something distinctive going on, just as is possible in well-made porous sound. The three-dimensional collages made by Joseph Cornell take this a further step, representing ambiguity clearly. He filled wooden boxes with, for instance, stuffed small birds sitting on the same shelf as aspirin bottles and knitting needles. A stuffed sparrow seems to be reading the warning label on a bottle of Bayer aspirin. The boxes are haunting just because these adjacencies could mean something – or nothing.

Philosophically, the contrast between collage forms and the razor-sharp image appeared in a friendly exchange of letters a century ago between John Dewey and Benedetto Croce, a believer in ideal forms. For Dewey, people exchanging and interacting produces forms of the collage sort, marking verbal edges and adjacencies, misunderstandings and shared understandings; the language of writers like Dewey's contemporaries James Joyce and Gertrude Stein are literary collages. This complexity is why (as we saw in Chapter 6 on the friction-free ethos) it's so important to Dewey that people work with resistance, learning from it rather than repressing it. Whereas for Croce, a form has a stand-alone essence, no matter what its uses or settings. Adjacency is interesting but not important to Croce; he thinks collage to be 'a fear of form'. Lynch's four geometric shapes and five primal sites would appeal to him as illuminating the essence of a city rather than as a simplification.[21, 22]

In sum, an open *ville* is marked by five forms which allow the *cité* to become complex. Public space promotes synchronous activities. It privileges the border over the boundary, aiming to make the relations between parts of the city porous. It marks the city in modest ways, using simple materials and placing markers arbitrarily in order to highlight nondescript places. It makes use of type-forms in its building to create an urban version of theme and variations in music. Finally, through seed-planning the themes themselves – where to place schools, housing, shops or parks – are allowed to develop independently throughout the city, yielding a complex image of the urban whole. An open *ville* will avoid committing the sins of repetition and static form; it will create the material conditions in which people might thicken and deepen their experience of collective life.

Mr Sudhir is neither a modern artist nor a philosopher. His interest in collage would be, I think, that of someone trying to make sense of where to go once he is forced out of Nehru Place, as he is likely to be. He would be in search of a location for his business which connected to the rest of the city, bringing him customers from all over, but connecting irregularly, leaving him free to pursue his business without being subject to central controls. The city which would serve him in this struggle will be structured by the five open forms.

9

The Bond of Making

In bed, the curt phrase 'if only' expresses a frustrated or rejected lover's dream: the affair could have been so wonderful, but isn't likely to happen; now the lover is resigned, and pure longing has a sweetness all of its own. Outside the bedroom, the two words 'if only' name personal aspirations which are not fulfilled in school or at work, and here there is no sweetness. Regret saps the energy people need to endure.

Such thoughts were in my mind when I decided to set up a modest, part-time planning practice. I did not want to consign my ideas to the limbo of 'if only'. I did not want to live in a passive relation to reality. When put into practice, my convictions, I knew, would be tempered and would change – I would fail, often, but I would not regret it. And so it has proved.

I have worked at the poles of planning, serving as a consultant to small communities and to an international organization. Such experience is not representative of the vast majority of planners, the full-time professionals who work for city governments. Moreover, I am the first to admit that the planning practices described in the following pages have a retrospective clarity they lacked when I first felt the sting of Jane Jacobs' taunt, 'So what would you do?' It took time to find ways to engage the gap between the built and the lived, the *ville* and the *cité*.

I. CO-PRODUCE – WORKING WITH OPEN FORMS

Co-production, not consultation After Jane Jacobs, few planners would brazenly declare to the public, as Robert Moses did,

'Submit; I know what's best.' In place of that brazen assertion, there are subtler ways to wield the whip. A community 'consultation', for instance, typically involves a planning department explaining how and where it wants to build a new road; members of the public, from cycle champions to people living near the road, then howl in protest; the planning authority takes these objections 'under advisement' after a 'fruitful exchange of views'; then the planning authority proceeds to do pretty much what it meant to do in the first place. A little flourish in this planning process, akin to other diplomatic negotiations, consists of planting in the proposals at the outset certain details the planner is perfectly willing to see dropped, giving the illusion that a real negotiation has happened. (A trick common to some London plans is to propose purposely high street-lamp wattages which are then lowered as a result of consultation.)

On the wrong side of the smart-city divide between prescribing and coordinating, at public consultation meetings the planner is the star and the people the spectators. In a remarkable book on expertise, *Acting in an Uncertain World*, Michel Callon observes that the cult of 'the expert' increases when the guru dismisses as irrelevant or trivial problems of which he/she is not the visible authority. Practicalities like the FAR (floor area ratio) described in Delhi, or the technicalities of code variances, thus come swathed in a mystifying aura. Even if the expert does not dominate the meeting in this overbearing way, the spatial organization of public consultations stifles exchange.[1]

There is usually a document, which almost no one in the room has read, accompanied viva voce by a slide presentation, the images clicking over too fast to dwell on. The physical setting can work against engagement; a raised rostrum facing rows of chairs transforms the public into spectators, as in the ancient pynx. So, too, the carefully made models displaying the proposal in all its perfection come with a look-but-do-not-touch message. The result is to dematerialize the proposals themselves; the public cannot get engaged in how the proposals would feel, physically, or would lodge in people's experience over time.

The consultation format is a very bad way to handle conflict. Outrage – shouting down the man at the podium in his suit and tie, armed with his laser pointer, his graphs, his stats – is the logical if extreme way in these circumstances to speak truth to power. But in small-scale planning work, the figure at the podium is not always The Man as developer, politician or expert-Svengali. Many of those figures at the podium are mid-level technicians, and many of those specialists are uncomfortable in the role the outraged public has assigned them: Poodle to Power. Forced into an adversarial position with the public, such benighted planners fall back on stating what the rules and regulations are – don't blame me, I didn't make them. This defence is another way to deflate the consultation itself. The rules are the rules; the technician is glad to explain them, but really is in no position to judge them. Either in 'poodle to power' or 'don't blame me' mode, the planner him- or herself gets nothing from the exchange; the closing mantra, 'We will take your views under advisement', is usually spoken with relief that the event is over. The public is left to nurse its outrage.

Co-production by contrast aims at making engagement matter to both sides, by having the technically trained maker and the life-experienced dweller generate the plans in the first place; open urban forms such as I've described in the previous chapter can serve as orienting points for doing so. That's the theory. How might it be put into practice?

Three techniques of co-production I have sought to stimulate co-production by deploying certain materials in meetings in a visceral way, using styrofoam models, clear plastic display overlays and portfolios of parts which people could touch and assemble. I look for different settings to break with the passive-theatre format; this is particularly necessary for the planning work done by UNDP and UN-Habitat, which seeks to engage poor people directly in situ rather than in offices or conference centres. My favoured venues have been churches, not out of any religious inclination, but rather because these are large sheltered spaces in which models, flip-charts and portfolios can be laid out, and left relatively securely. The 'desks' I favour are trestle tables on which 4 by 8 sheets of plywood can be laid; during meetings people stand, walking around the physical objects they are creating.

I am a big fan of styrofoam. It's easy to cut and carve, which means that people themselves can do the work of producing a model. The 'expert' will show the component parts which people might carve, usually bringing a bag of these parts to serve as type-forms. The point of this model-building is not to produce one but several models of the same building. We would show people how components could be combined in several ways, using a kind of styrofoam glue which is quick-drying and water-solvent, so that it is easy to create, alter or break up a form. The subjunctive voice thus can morph into visual form, in which possibilities and what-if? scenarios take the place of policy declarations.

The component elements here are an urbanist's particular contribution. At the simplest level, people without design experience tend to think in rectilinear blocks – which are also the easiest to cut. But if you chamfer the corner of a block, as Cerdà did, you need enough blocks to see how the chamfered blocks create an ensemble. The 'expertise' just involves specifying how many corner-shaved blocks will be needed to create a grid. A more taxing technical aspect is size: the bigger the size of the components the better. The model which is viscerally felt is one in which people can imagine they are walking through it on the ground plane, peering at and pondering big blocks on a table. A smallish model tends to invite bird's-eye viewing – but we are not birds.

In this regard, it was quite striking to me to look once again at Corbusier's Plan Voisin in two model sizes. The small version looks reasonable; the magnified model makes clear its sterility. So the planner has to calculate how big the carving scale should be, given the project at hand, to enable people to have that illusion of walking through the model. An even more demanding expertise in using styrofoam blocks lies in showing how the modelled structure is likely to wear – the effect of time. Often people are not aware of what is most likely in a structure to be vulnerable. Thus in some of the models in a planning competition UNESCO ran in Cairo, the planners made gashes and crushes in the styrofoam, based on various computer projections – deformations which would not be intuitively obvious to the ordinary urbanite.

At the level of everyday planning, tables full of alternative styrofoam models break the habit of imagining there is a one-to-one fit between form and function. More incisively, they prompt people to think about the nature of a type-form. A Chicago project which explored how to configure a new primary school had to determine what was the most important space: the classroom, the assembly hall or the playground? A Googleplex might jumble together all these spaces and functions, but if you are a child in a poor school, the isolation and security of a classroom space in which to study might prove more important than a fusion which is distracting. In that case, the blocks representing rooms build up the structure rather than fill in a pre-set envelope.

In architecture schools, making models becomes an exercise in rendering complex two-dimensional visual ideas into palpable three-dimensional forms. The appearance of CAD (computer-aided design) has not obliterated the need for model-making, since in physically constructing a built object you know it more intimately than you do when the computer constructs it for you. Outside of an architecture class, a community will think of using models in a somewhat similar way. The model makes you feel the image, because the prehension described in Chapter 7 is activated; moreover, being able to walk around the model activates the scale-making activities which occur, again as described in that chapter, when the body is mobile.[2]

For a parks project in Shanghai, Madame Q and I bought big blocks of styrofoam, hoping to have local residents cut and sculpt the material into a variety of terrace shapes, benches, children's play-furniture and the like. The shapes themselves were crude by architecture-school standards, which is the point: such models are a rough representation of reality, its very roughness inviting discussion about what the actual reality should be. Moreover, the fact that styrofoam models can be cut big adds to their communal value. In Shanghai, when test-driving our proposal, Madame Q found that being able to pick up and move around a building a quarter the size of her own body increased people's engagement with the form, just as playing chess outside with life-size figures is a more tactile experience of chess than playing it inside hunched over a table, or playing online.

Whether table or ground size, the portable styrofoam model aids in untying the form–function knot. In our Shanghai experiment, we had five different park benches put together on two different terraces, then asked people if the various combinations could be used by both established residents and people without official papers (at the time, you needed a 'passport' to live in Shanghai). Just because it was bizarre – what does a park bench have to do with legal residence? – the discussion side-stepped more channelled and controlled kinds of discourse.

Plastic overlays are familiar objects in every sales pitch, usually arranged as flip-charts to tell a story culminating in 'Buy!' In a co-production, these plastic sheets have to be crafted in a different way. Here's the procedure: on the pegs of a blackboard sitting on an easel there are loosely attached large sheets of clear plastic on which are stencilled particular aspects of a site: its outer form, its traffic circulation within, its pedestrian patterns. Over each sheet of existing reality, a new sheet of proposed changes can be laid.

One of our projects doing this began as an academic exercise with student co-producers and then migrated into the community with a very different set of clients. Guido Robazza, Antoine Paccoud and I made plastic overlays to analyse how to build a housing shelter on the Lower East Side in New York. The programme for the shelter included rooms for the homeless, the elderly and adolescent orphans – potentially a toxic mix. The distributions of these three groups could be sorted out in various ways and each plastic sheet showed a particular way: overlaid on each other, the designer could study similarities and differences. The architecture students wanted to synthesize an overall image; the people who would actually live there had a different spatial desire. Adolescent orphans, not surprisingly, need parents; thus they wanted to be as close as possible to the elderly as surrogate grandparents. The curse of old age is isolation, so there was an answering impulse, but it was weaker. The meetings at which different levels of contact were displayed on the flip-charts were thus more socially oriented than working out functional space-allocation. A particular virtue of the plastic sheet is that in such circumstances it enables people to make discoveries about porosity. In overlaying two different ways to combine the elderly and the adolescent on the same floor of a shelter, we found corners where something like a membrane could be made, providing some space for interaction, while also offering a buffer.

I've described this project deceptively by making it seem simple technically. As Fred Koetter and Colin Rowe found in making the collages for *Collage City*, overlaying data is a complex process, and often produces an unilluminating collage. A technical difficulty is that the numbers are usually collected from different sources, using non-congruent categories; you need to break inside big data sets to use their materials. In the shelter project, we had to spend much time on creating a shared data 'bed' from which different comparisons could be derived, harmonizing unlike data sets from architects, the city, a charity, and surveys conducted among the elderly and the adolescents about the spaces they wanted to live in.

Today you can create overlays on a computer with great sophistication, but the big plastic sheets (we used 100 cm by 140 cm sheets, nearly human scale) in their very physical size make the changes more visceral to a group of sixty to a hundred people. Anyone can manipulate the sheets, going back and forth between different images. The material unwieldiness of the sheets encouraged men in a church in New York's Spanish Harlem to take over making the presentations: 'Professor, let me . . .' Though I was physically robust then, I was quite willing to be consigned to the role of weakling intellectual.

It's important in this kind of analysis that the sheets be detachable, rather than bound in the flip-chart format used in sales pitches. This is so that the story they tell can then be reconfigured and rearranged: if you see the density sheet, made of single-coloured dots, mapped over a figured-ground sheet (which, like the Nolli maps described in the previous chapter, show buildings in black and open space in white), you tell one kind of story; overlay the density sheet on a map of the wealth of people in the buildings – the sheet made of different coloured dots – and you tell quite another.

I've come to think that the overlay procedure most suits situations in which a community has to loosen the form–function knot, as in the closed proposition that a school building should only house teaching. You can easily play with the places where different activities can occur within the envelope of a school building simply by changing overlays, then discussing what they look like.

A third way to co-produce a plan lies in utilizing a portfolio of parts. I have all my life been addicted to catalogues, from those showing building supplies to window treatments to the frou-frou of architectural ornaments. (Undoubtedly, there is a Freudian explanation, focusing on toy-deprivation in my third and fourth years.) This addiction I have imported into the labour of co-production.

The catalogue of parts is related to styrofoam design, but is not its twin; rather, a fleshing out and specification of styrofoam's rough forms. The architect Rem Koolhaas devoted a recent Venice Biennale to a sophisticated catalogue of parts, but poor communities cannot usually afford to assemble, as in a showroom, fifteen different windows to choose from, so this imaginative work has to be done at a visceral remove. The production values of these portfolios are therefore more important. We spend money on the booklets, as for a commercial catalogue; in Cairo, people displayed them on their tables as an addition to their household decor. Because of my own catalogue fetish, I was in fact an expert on the varieties of metal domestic doors and plastic freeze-break window frames offered to the public, and learned to present these prosaic objects in a flattering graphic guise.

In the open way of design, people should be free to choose whatever materials and components appeal to them. But because their knowledge of what's possible is limited, they tend to fall back on what's familiar and traditional. In the Netherlands in the 1960s, when planners worked with localities to build new housing, the residents didn't want new; though poorer economically than the trendies in Xintiandi, these ordinary citizens also wanted the assurance of familiarity. And in Aravena's Iquique projects, the modernist building envelopes created by the architect are gradually filled in with Spanish colonial windows. In self-build projects, people often have no idea of what's possible – why should they? They are not subscribers to architectural journals. There's something unreal about asking people instantly to invent something new, as could an expert engineer or architect.

So too in the catalogues we assembled. Since we worked most with poor communities, the portfolios featured construction materials available to the poor for self-build. However these tend to be of low quality. We selected the best components for each budget; surprisingly, there are some cheap but innovative materials on the market. When people had money to spend above the minimum, they went, as in more wealthy communities, for the tried-and-tested rather than for innovative or interesting shapes. The asymmetry between making a project of good design quality and inhabitants' desire has to be resolved in some way.

Expert exit I thought out one way to deal with this asymmetry from the work of Chicago community organizer Saul Alinsky. Alinsky's organizers were not 'facilitators' – that dreadful word disguises control as advice. His people got involved; they argued, got angry, stood corrected, and made no bones about the fact that they had more knowledge and wider experience than the people they worked with. Community organizing like his seems to break with the Chicago School's method of letting people interpret for themselves, the politics of passive empathy. But the two were not entirely different. Alinsky's way of community organizing sensitized his followers to the moment when it was time to go, leaving the community to make its own decisions.

I tried to orient my planning work to that moment when it was time for me and my teams to get out of the way. Having given our own views of good and bad in various alternative designs, I would tell the community that at a certain point we would be leaving them to decide what to do. This procedure is what makes the planning open-ended. When an authority leaves the scene, what then happens? I'll give two very different examples.

In Cabrini–Green, a poor part of Chicago (where I grew up), our leaving was empowering, because the authorities seldom trusted people to decide what to do; the community drew on our left-behind materials to make its own decisions about a new kindergarten, and the decision-making itself was branded 'Cabrini Pride'. Once we'd left, the physical objects we had left behind us were perceived in a different way – or so we learned eventually. Clipped or squashed styrofoam now became a presence, a reality, an actor on its own rather than a medium for exchanges between us and our clients. 'I stared at the flip-chart,' one woman told me, 'thinking about how much you smoked when you were explaining it. Now no you, no smoke, just it . . .' I asked her why that mattered. 'I saw things on the flip-chart I hadn't noticed when you were around.'

A much graver experience of expert exit came to me in Beirut after the end of its civil war, for which I need to provide some background.

The Lebanese Civil War lasted fifteen years, from 1975 to 1990, though violent conflict has continued to reverberate in the country. Originally a battle between the Maronite Christian elite of the country against a coalition of Muslim groups allied with the Palestine Liberation Organization, the conflict kaleidoscoped when the warring factions shifted, and was complicated further by the incursion of outside belligerents, mainly Israel and Syria. A quarter of a million people died during this period, hundreds of thousands were displaced internally, and further hundreds of thousands fled abroad. The UN entered the civil war through an interim body, UNIFIL, which sought to assist international peace-keeping after Israel's invasions of Lebanon in 1978 and 1982. (Israel withdrew its forces finally in 2000, though it continues to be an air-power threat; a significant push-back against the Syrian presence occurred in 2006.) Other UN agencies played a small but useful role after 1990 in providing technical assistance for the reconstruction of Beirut.

The civil war involved much neighbourhood to neighbourhood combat within Beirut, mortars and machine-guns remaking the physical and social fabric of the city. Stairwells, for instance, became relatively safer zones in buildings than rooms with glass windows; these service shafts became the public spaces within buildings where families ate and slept during barrages. The 'Green Line' showed the consequences of long-term conflict up close: here two adjacent neighbourhoods, one Christian, the other Muslim fought over the boundary separating them for so long that tall grasses and even trees sprang up in the rubble. As a university student who had gone there before the civil war, I was inspired by Beirut as a cosmopolitan place whose many different groups managed to cohabit; returning three decades later, the scale of physical ruin dispelled those memories. Having learned at an MIT conference about post-civil war planning in

Beirut, I returned not to engage in planning myself but rather to observe how the reconstruction was working.[3]

In South Beirut one reconstruction team insisted that at least some members of the parties at war be present in discussions about how to clear rubble and then rebuild. At first the factions seethed and the meetings got nowhere; gradually, though, their attention turned to different ways to reconstruct the damage by focusing more on the physical situation and less on each other. When discussion focused on what to do about rubble, or how to string electricity lines, a sullen truce held between the warring factions.

Expert exit appeared in this context. 'I am sorry to have left you,' a UN planner remarked, returning a week after his mother fell ill. 'We managed to get on,' a South Beiruti replied. The participants, now focused on the length of electricity wire they needed in a particular neighbourhood rather than on their mutual grievances, did exactly that. Exit inspired no warm reconciliations; the weight of difference was too great. But the disappearance of my colleague did not lead to a breakdown of the planning process; instead, his exit meant the participants had to take ownership of the reconstruction problem concretely, by setting deadlines for specific parts of a rubble-clearance project, or calculating where to buy the wire for temporary electricity lines.

In Chapters 5, I described how in London potential conflict was managed by superficial rituals of courtesy. Here, by contrast, was a graver way of dealing with difference: focus on the physical fabric rather than on each other. This way of working collaboratively was contrary to the reconstruction of the rest of the city under the sway of a Saudi construction firm, which practised relentless top-down planning. This ethos of co-production contrasts also to the ethos guiding Sergio Fajardo in Medellín; there, architect-designed libraries gave people buildings worth taking pride in, once the good designer has done his or her work. Looking back, I would say of this and similar moments I observed in Beirut that they suspended discussions about 'who' in the social sense – who belongs in a place, who doesn't – by focusing more impersonally on 'what' in the physical sense.

For all these reasons, in working with communities I have tried to avoid the trap of branding them, of giving them identities so that they seem special places for special people. The worth of co-production is that it speaks in the plural, creating different versions of open cities, rather than in the singular. The three practices I have described aim at this openness, by providing alternative models for place rather than clarity of place.

All three practices relate to the ethical value of the 'commons'. Originally, the English word 'commons' referred to a field that farmers shared for pasturing animals; the Enclosure Acts of various countries in the seventeenth and eighteenth centuries privatized these spaces, so that animals could graze only on their owner's land. As a physical space, the agricultural commons evidenced features of porosity, as discussed in the previous chapter; mini-herds grazed adjacent to or among one another, the edges between them being animal borders, whereas enclosure stimulated the making of stone boundaries. The process of enclosure often created family food shortages, because small plots of private land restricted the number of cattle or sheep a single yeoman farmer could maintain. Property thus took precedence over productivity.

Left-leaning common sense has sought to reverse this formula, by arguing that shared resources augment productivity. In the nineteenth century, the Abbé de Lamennais argued for this view from a Christian viewpoint, believing that the cloister gardens were more economically efficient than vegetable plots maintained by single individuals or families; shared labour among a large group meant continuous labour night and day, week in and week out, labour which was dedicated to and spurred on by a principle higher than oneself. From an entirely secular point of view, Karl Marx argued for something akin; so did Émile Durkheim, in his description of 'organic solidarity', as also did Durkheim's nephew, the anthropologist Marcel Mauss, who founded modern studies of cooperation. These arguments became concretely demonstrable in the cooperative banks, burial societies and mutual insurance companies created at the time.

Today, in the systems realm, open-source software represents a pooling of resources in what is often called the 'digital commons'. The celebration of the commons is now generally not about service to a higher principle, as it was for Lamennais; rather, it concerns mutual benefit. Still, there is an idealist tinge about 'commoning' which names the impulse to share goods and services, and names also various groups who seek to organize that sharing.

Co-production has a slightly different ethical focus. It's a more sandpaper experience.

Co-producing with a machine The technological *ville* can be divided into prescriptive or coordinative smart cities (see Chapter 6). The prescriptive smart city is not a co-producer of urban form with the citizen: both the forms and functions of places are set in advance, and the citizen uses them, following the seductive but mind-numbing rule of doing what is most user-friendly. It is a closed *ville*. The co-ordinative smart city is a co-productive one, its real-time data enabling people to think not only about how to use the city, but also, as in Lyons or Curitiba, how to model different building forms and street plans. Alternative forms provide the model of a modern open *ville*.

How do you hold a conversation with a machine? Today, we are in fact speaking with machines nearly every minute of our waking lives. Often these discussions close with the programmed print or voice telling us what to do: the 'Command' key is aptly named on the keyboard – it is neither a dialogic discussion nor a co-production.

The procedures I've described can be directly transferred from paper or styrofoam to screen; thanks to certain computer-aided design programs, it has been possible for a decade to build the equivalent of styrofoam models onscreen, and to walk through them; the advent of 3-D printing now means that actual styrofoam models can be cut for people to peruse. As in all screen-work, there is a certain loss of tactile engagement, but an enormous social gain: you don't need to be physically present at a planning meeting to participate in it. Yet the transfer is not perfect. This is due in part to the nature of the digital machines people use. These machines come in two forms: replicants and robots. We users hold different kinds of conversations with them.

A replicant is a machine that mimics human functions, only works better, like a heart pulsar, or the mechanical arms used in auto plants. Though they never tire, replicants are something we can make sense of because they are doing what we do. In interacting with a replicant, like a voice-activated, voice-answering device, we communicate as with another person.

A proper robot is not based on the human body, but has an independent form based on other logics. Take the driverless car Bill Mitchell was designing. The automobile could function as a replicant if it offered a steering wheel and brakes, even though the human driver would, hopefully, never have to use them; still, the passenger need not feel passively in the hands of the machine. If the driverless car functioned as a robot, without steering wheels and brakes, the experience would be like riding in a train or aeroplane – a passive one – the passenger taking its operations on trust. Almost all smart technology faces the same choice. In Google Maps, for instance, suppressing the map image, following the written verbal directions alone, will take you to the same place as restoring the map, with its moving dot (you) following the recommended path. The first, mapless way is robotic; the second, moving dot on screen, is replicantic. Assemblies of computers which coordinate big-data processing are replicantic in modelling their conduits on the neural activity of the brain, but robotic in distributing information without needing to mimic brain-cell chemistry.

It might seem that replicants rather than robots are the machine partners we should want in co-production. But not at that critical moment of exit. It's easier to take over a problem from a robot than a replicant. This is just because the robot is less like us, and its powers do not invite comparison to our own. In the factory workplace, studies have shown that robots tend to be regarded as tools of limited scope, though infinite power, to perform a particular function, while replicants are seen as threats, as super-humans replacing human beings on the assembly line. Most robots are not user-friendly in the sense that they seem like ourselves, and so we can identify with their actions, whereas replicants invite that comparison – to our disadvantage. Invidious comparisons open up in the tech world as in the personalized class realm described in Chapter 5.[4]

In design work, the robot function appears in images onscreen which shows the hidden structure beneath the building's skin, whereas 3-D printing is a more replicant procedure, replacing the human hand cutting styrofoam with a mechanical cutter which does the job like – but much better than – a hand. Because of that invidious comparison I've shied away from using too much 3-D printing in co-production work. As in other aspects of high tech, the robot becomes useful in a sense the Google salesmen of user-friendly do not intend: friendly as a resource, rather than a replacement. People need to use their own reason with regard to the environment, rather than passively follow cockpit commands; a robot makes this process easier than a replicant. We need to think about machines as user-strange rather than user-friendly presences. Just as in the *cité* we should be open to strangers, but can have only a limited dependence on them, so should it be with the ways we relate to high tech.

In sum, co-production counters in a straightforward way the belief that there's only one right way to do something, and rejects the equally closed idea that we should imitate best practices as defined by experts, whether human or digital. But the machine signals something less straightforward: cooperation in a complex environment requires keeping a certain distance from those with whom you cooperate. Though we may want to be on our guard with machines, this may seem perverse humanly. The secret of working with others requires detachment of a kind – detachment which differs from Simmel's mask.

II. COOPERATIVE
BUT NOT CLOSE – SOCIALITY

It might seem that as people get to know each other better, they will inevitably draw closer; the stranger will disappear and the neighbour, friend or lover will appear. This is to misunderstand the complex layering of social life, in which we have in time to respect that which is unknowable, inaccessible, in the other. By contrast, 'union' and solidarity can violate the distinctiveness of the other, a violation which Gustave Le Bon depicted as the acid effect of urban crowds, which dissolve people into an unthinking mass.

How then do we continue to associate with others from whom none the less we keep our distance? From John Locke on, one answer to this question has been utilitarian: you need to be with others to do what you cannot accomplish alone. Grit your teeth and join. But you do not need to linger over a beer with people in a bar; indeed, by a utilitarian calculus you are wasting time. This calculus of utility misses the sociable impulse which animates cooperation with people who are not, and will not become, intimate.

A workshop For as long as I have been writing, I have been observing a bakery in Boston. Over the nearly fifty years I have tracked it, the bakery has changed hands only three times. Originally a family business, it was sold by its Greek immigrant founders to a larger bakery concern about thirty years ago, the new owners bringing in automated equipment and transforming the business from an artisanal shop to an industrial plant. Then about a decade ago, the big concern divested itself of this holding, and the bakery returned to family ownership, this time Latino. Now employing about forty people, the bakery has seized a niche market for itself by appealing to Boston's young elite as an organic operation; it could brand itself 'Bakers to Google'.[5, 6]

During its middle period, the absentee owners automated the plant by bringing in machines designed as replicants which did the complete set of tasks involved in baking; employees tending the machines did not know how to bake. The bread was good, but there was no reason for customers to buy it from this bakery rather than anywhere else, since the product was standardized. When the Latino owners bought the business, the bakers retrained in the craft of making speciality breads and regained control over the machines, particularly the ovens, which were now regulated by the baker's eye rather than a pre-set oven temperature.

The bakery first drew me because, a half century ago, its owners were stalwarts in the campaign to resist racial integration of Boston's schools, also hiring no African Americans, who were seen by the Greeks as carrying the virus of failure. By the time the bakery was sold to the big food firm, barring people from employment on racial grounds had become illegal; this meant a swift change of personnel inside the plant, bringing in a mixture of Portuguese, Mexicans and African Americans who were paid minimum wages, had little attachment to the plant, and who moved elsewhere as soon as they could find slightly better-paid jobs. The bakery's third chapter saw it return to an aspiring immigrant family, hiring a diverse crew of Latinos and African Americans, plus taking back some second-generation relatives of the original owners.

These people have stayed, and have proved cooperative on the shop floor, which has boosted the firm's productivity and so its profitability. In contrast to the diplomatic courtesies in Clerkenwell's mixed community, here cooperation involves much more intense exchanges between workers about their work – for instance, when the mixing machines are stopped to judge dough consistency, or when workers peer through the thick glass doors of the ovens to judge doneness. These judgement calls prompt much debate, though it's compressed in time because of the baking cycle. Cultural differences don't seem to count much at these moments. Good liberal that I am, I was distressed when one of the Greek bakers referred to a batch of baguettes as 'Cuban' coloured, i.e. too dark, but no one other than me paid any attention to the adjective. In the words of the urbanist Ash Amin, a workplace like this becomes 'indifferent to difference'.

However, working cooperatively in this way does not draw people closer. Keeping one's distance becomes evident at a bar, near the bakery entrance, where workers socialize. Once a dimly lit haunt, furnished with metal card tables covered by checkered plastic cloth, the bar is now showing early signs of the gentrification virus, with uncurtained windows and wooden tables stained with a matt finish. Work is occasionally referred to after work – like employees anywhere and everywhere, the bakers pay sharp attention to signs of employer stupidity; much of their other banter, though, consists of sports talk which escapes me. But I do pick up how they signal distance. Intent together inside the bakery, relaxed in the bar, they never ask people of another ethnicity home.

The fact that the bakery is in a big city may explain why. Visionary workshop designs stressing solidarity have generally been sited outside the city. Claude-Nicolas Ledoux's eighteenth-century saltworks at Arc-et-Senans, for instance, was a self-contained community where workers lived and refined salt in the Forest of Chaux in the countryside of eastern France; as an ensemble it was something like a monastery without religion; so, too, the phalansteries Charles Fourier devised in the nineteenth century were workshops purposely removed from the city – closed-in, self-contained, total communities. In the complex society of the city, people have differentiated, partial relations with one another. You can work well with another person without being like him – or indeed liking him.

The cooperative workshop also contrasts with the mixed neighbourhood. Under threat of unleashing communal poison, a mixed neighbourhood can turn people away from directly addressing their differences. In the workshop, difference assumes another aspect: the fact of difference is not a productive fact; were people to dwell on how like or unlike they are, they could not work well together; who is working would take precedence over what is to be done. The Googleplex also offers a contrast to the craft bakery. Sushi bar, ping-pong table and gym are all meant to stimulate productivity by bringing sociable pleasure into the workplace. Whereas the bakers, when they seek pleasure, look for it outside.

For all these reasons, the bakery today sends a philosophical signal: it exemplifies sociality.

Sociality In the utilitarian way of thinking, for people to act effectively together they need to share a common purpose or goal. In a meeting, you need to reach a consensus before you act. In an earlier book, *Together*, I tried to show that cooperation need not be tied to consensus. There are many forms of cooperation in which people cannot share with others – as in a diplomatic negotiation, where you are dealing with people whose interests cannot be reconciled to yours.[7]

What, then, glues people together? Locke's answer, as noted earlier, is that you need them to do things you cannot do alone. This is *synoikismos*, described by Aristotle in terms of collective defence and trade.

What this utilitarian answer leaves out is the subjective dimension of cooperation. Think of soldiers who continue to fight even when a battle becomes hopeless. The utilitarian way of fighting would dictate that you desert your comrades if the end-result of fighting together is doomed. The bakery shows a less extreme subjective bond: a contained sociability which allows people to engage with one another, disposing them to work well together, even though that experience does not bond them ever more intimately. They take pride in the work, which breeds respect for other workers.

'Sociality' names feeling a kind of limited fraternity with others based on sharing an impersonal task. That limited fraternity arises when people are doing something together rather than being together. In planning, sociality plays a crucial role. Signs of its presence appeared in our meetings if people listened increasingly attentively to others rather than sticking doggedly to their initial views. Sociality strengthened when planners left the room, as in Cabrini–Green or South Beirut; people are left with a task, no longer supported by an expert. Attention shifts to the thing being constructed.

The open-planning approach is distinctive because the trigger for sociality is a problematic object – as in the four versions of a school or health clinic, built of styrofoam, resting on a table. These tangible things, even in their very crude and rough state, invite people to become involved hands-on in thinking out what should be done. Interestingly, the act of deciding which model to choose may not banish the uncertainties people had harboured before. I could see this doubt remain in my own practice when, after meetings, people would continue contemplating the styrofoam models on the table, or start flipping through the plastic charts yet again. If the time for cooperation had closed, engagement with the objects produced had not.

In the *cité*, sociality is an emotional counterpoint of impersonality – *pace* Le Bon, who thought that violent solidarity rules the crowd. Sociality does not appear in Georg Simmel's account of metropolitan life, because he was considering people being in public, moving along a street, having no productive relation to others through whom they move. Sociality appears when strangers are doing something productive, together. The glass of beer after work, followed by farewells at the bus or Tube stop, sends a signal of caring about the others – whereas the pleasures on offer in the Googleplex advertise being with others, sharing pleasure and comfort. The bakers' bosses are, I would say, less manipulative. Writ large, sociality is both a modest and an honest social bond.

As with all aspects of life, a certain kind of politics is involved in the experience of sociality. As appeared in Chapter 6, Alexis de Tocqueville used the word 'democracy' in two senses. The first concerned majority rule, which he feared because the majority, mob-like, could inflict its will tyrannically on the minority, the 51 per cent oppressing the 49 per cent. The second sense of democracy he equated with 'individualism'. Here he was thinking of a society in which people had become detached from one another, absorbed in their own affairs; he feared this sort of individualism – so far removed from individual strivings of the rugged sort – because it 'noiselessly unwound the springs of action'. A society in which people share pretty much the same tastes and beliefs, in which life is simplified and made as easy, as user-friendly, as possible, is a society losing energy of a sort: cooperation between those people who differ withers. Tocqueville believed that voluntary organizations were one answer to this threat, enticing people to get involved, to participate rather than to withdraw. Voluntary organizations as he thought of them are sites of sociality.

The three practices I've described follow this Tocquevillian logic of participation. But the expert's voluntary exit gives a particular twist to the process, obliging people to reformat the work. If left alone to itself, an organization's decision-making can be simplified by voting; the result is democratic but in the sense Tocqueville first wrote about: the will of the majority has prevailed. Dialogic processes, and socialite bonds, are ended by democratic action; tyranny of the majority looms. The voice of the minority no longer counts.

In the planning practices I've described, it does. A good deal of ambivalence remains even after a decision has been reached – just because it's evident building can proceed in different ways. There is no closure, no one right way.

Moreover, an unjust decision can be better resisted. Long ago Hegel, in his description of the master–slave relationship, explained one way in which this resistance can work. 'You are hurting me!' is an injured person's cry which focuses on what the master is doing; the orbit of oppression, its language as well as its actions, is defined by the master; indeed, the word 'suffering' in ancient Greek is a near cousin to the word 'passive'. In Hegel's view, the sufferer stops being a slave only when his or her feelings are no longer inscribed within this orbit. The political sociologist James Scott has studied, for instance, how racially enslaved groups in the American South developed a communicative language among themselves which seemed to their masters gibberish; in speaking to each other in ways the masters could not understand, they were no longer mentally enslaved.

As I was finishing this chapter, a terrible tragedy occurred in London which showed Hegel's classic proposition in a different light. In the early morning of 14 June 2017 fire consumed Grenfell Tower, a social-housing high-rise set on the edge of the fashionable Kensington area in West London. Seventy-nine people died. The blaze did its work quickly because new exterior cladding conducted the flames rapidly from a fourth-floor interior all around the exterior of the building, up and down its twenty-four storeys. The cladding, consisting of an aluminium composite sandwiching a poylethylene core (a product called Reynobond PE), looks bright and clean and proclaims 'upgrade', but in fact it is dangerously inflammable. It is a little cheaper than an alternative, which cost just £2 a square metre more, that has a genuine fire-retardent core. (Reynobond is banned for use in tall buildings in the USA and Germany.) The British planners went for the 'cost effective' option.[8]

After the event, the authorities and the victims began speaking a different language – which became a problem. Both the political authorities and the official planners explained how the decisions which led to the renovation were made, and who made them, without quite being able to say that they went for the cheapest option because the tower housed mostly poor people. The victims, shocked and confused by the fire, wanted recognition of their sufferings. Trauma is inarticulate. It is necessary in a dialogical way to sense what people are feeling, rather than to address the cloud of words surrounding trauma; but the Kensington authorities lacked emotional intelligence. The recognition gap widened almost immediately. A public meeting was shut down when the residents noisily, confusedly, appeared at it; when the Prime Minister came to visit the disaster scene, she spoke to firemen but not to residents. An official enquiry was launched; its head, a former accountant who admitted he knew little about housing the poor, said he wanted a focused, *ergo* limited, enquiry. This declaration only widened the gap between officials and victims – the latter couldn't channel the loss of their homes into bullet points. The breach between the master's language and their own has in the end served the master.

I am certain that the way of co-production I have sketched in this chapter could have prevented the Grenfell Tower tragedy occurring in the first place. No properly informed resident given the opportunity to choose between Reynobond PE and a slightly more expensive cladding would ever have opted for the cheaper version – but residents were not given the chance to make that choice. The planners could, it is true, have mentioned in the public consultations that the product they preferred was banned for use in the US and Germany, but this inconvenient fact was not brought up.

In general, by exploring alternatives at the very beginning of building, the process of co-production can expose dangers and difficulties; deliberation about alternatives elicits rational assessment; the exit of the expert at the moment of decision-making empowers those who are going to live in the project. The public is trusted rather than treated. Experts find their proper role as advisors. The procedures I've laid out are one way to co-produce; they are based on face-to-face engagement but could also work, as I've tried to show, online at a larger scale, using high tech as a tool. Rather than Hegel's exit from the master–slave relation, we need an open, interactive way of building the environment. The result may be ambiguous, and leave people dissatisfied; still, this is a more democratic, and more truthful, kind of building than the closed, top-down, economized approach which produced this terrible fire.

PART FOUR

Ethics for the City

10

Time's Shadows

Shelley's poem 'Ozymandias' begins:

> I met a traveller from an antique land,
> Who said – 'Two vast and trunkless legs of stone
> Stand in the desert . . .

A few lines below he declares:

> And on the pedestal, these words appear:
> "My name is Ozymandias, King of Kings,
> Look on my Works ye Mighty, and despair!"
> No thing beside remains . . .'

The poem conveys the obvious but neglected truth that time effaces the works of Man. The final part of our enquiry takes 'Ozymandias' into the city. Shelley gives a bitter twist to the builder's buzzword 'sustainable'. How then should men and women think about what they build? And how they live?

While I was convalescing, a friend brought me *The Swerve*, a book in which Stephen Greenblatt describes the recovery in the Renaissance of an ancient poem, Lucretius' *On the Nature of Things*. The long poem counsels those about to die to lose their fear of death, for there is nothing which remains after death, no transcendent spirit; life just begins, happens and stops. This is Shelley's outlook taken to its logical extreme. My friend, you may think, was no friend in recommending Lucretius as bedside reading. However, Lucretius says that we should be reconciled to this state because, in life, nothing is preordained or predictable. The path of events seldom follows a straight line of cause and effect; instead, there are detours, wobbles and dead ends. These he calls 'swerves' (*clinamens*). Atoms move 'at absolutely unpredictable times and places deflected slightly from their straight course, making indeterminate if minute movements (*nec plus quam minimum*), causing collisions and conjunctions, setting physical materials on an unpredictable path'. Lucretius was a philosopher of open-ended time.[1,2]

The ancient world incarnated these powers of chance in the goddess Fortuna. She presided over discovery and invention, a goddess of new wines, new cuts for ships' sails and novel shapes for buildings; she could, however, turn the sweet-tasting elixir into a poison or cause a new temple to collapse. She morphed in late antiquity into a metaphor – the Wheel of Fortune – the metaphor conveying in part that chance rules human creation, just as Lucretius' *clinamens* rule physics.

The Enlightenment emphasized Fortuna's smile. In 1754 the aesthete Horace Walpole wrote to his friend Horace Mann that he had coined a new word, 'serendipity'. This new word, derived from a Persian source, meant a 'happy accident', which Walpole expressed eloquently as men 'making discoveries, by accidents and sagacity, of things they were not in quest of'. His is a positive version of open time; his confidence in finding what he did not expect was founded on a conviction that Nature is essentially benign.[3]

Today, Fortuna no longer smiles resolutely; as the climate changes, she threatens the built environment. Contained in that 'change' – a misleadingly flat word – is the unfolding of chance in disorientating, disruptive events; these powers of Fortuna become evident in sudden floods or erratic temperature spikes. Can the city build its way out of such crises? Attempts to do so reveal more broadly, as I will try to show, the unstable character of any built environment.

I. NATURE STRIKES THE CITY – LONG- AND SHORT-TERM THREATS

Time's two shadows As the lights dimmed across Lower Manhattan when Hurricane Sandy struck in the autumn of 2012, an expert announced on the radio that there was really nothing to worry about.

The security wall protecting Manhattan's electric power station at the east end of 14th Street next to the East River was, he said, twelve feet high, more than enough to keep the generators dry within. 'More than enough' was based on statistical averaging from past water rise. Power died as the river rose fourteen feet, breaching the wall. The expert then resurfaced, this time from an emergency-powered radio station, to announce that Hurricane Sandy was a once-in-a-century event, though we had had another once-in-a-century storm only a year before (one which thankfully veered away from the city).

These false claims occurred because the expert thought within the relatively closed orbit of averaging. Though its long-term consequences are certain, climate change is an erratic phenomenon year-on-year – as with those two once-in-a-century storms occurring only a year apart. Similarly, while it's certain that the Gulf Stream will alter its course, due in part to meltdown of ice at the world's poles and the rise in sea levels, the new course of the Gulf Stream is hard to predict. About warming itself, as the NASA Earth Observatory project in the United States has shown, episodic storms will become more intense, as a result of the steady heating of the water mass over which they form, but again, the exact intensity is hard to predict. Though there's absolutely no scientific doubt about climate change occurring, indeterminacy rules the unfolding of its events.[4]

Climate change casts a long-term shadow of inevitability as well as Fortuna's short-term, unpredictable events; both require a rethink about how cities are built.

The long-term shadow most immediately apparent comes from pollution – evident wherever people gag at each intake of breath. The worst killer, though, is not one sensed so overtly; it is fine-particulate air pollution (measured as PM2.5) which over the course of time degrades the lungs and causes cancers of many sorts. In 2013, China's big-city PM2.5 index was on average twelve times that of London, and fourteen times that of New York; at times the PM2.5 can rise in Beijing to 525, whereas the upper healthy number is about 20. Coal-burning plants generating electricity are largely responsible. To deal with such a predictable villain, the Chinese are making huge investments in other energy sources for their cities.[5] Shelley is irrelevant to this effort.

Some other long-term urban climate threats do not suggest such straightforward responses. For instance, a target of 2 degrees of permissible global warming has been set for the next decades by the Intergovernmental Panel on Climate Change (IPCC); but the target looks certain to be missed. To meet the 2-degree target, cement – which is quite polluting to fabricate – should no longer serve as a ubiquitous building material, but cheap replacement materials are not currently to hand. To save on the energy used in air-conditioning, windows in buildings should open, yet it's impossibly dangerous to have open windows on the sixtieth floor of a building. The sealed glass box might be reduced in height in order to enable natural air flow from outside, but in a kind of phallic competition, cities are building ever taller towers. Low or passive energy building figures in advertising hype far more often than actually appear on the ground; the UN-Habitat estimate is that only about 15 per cent of the new building in emerging cities is energy-efficient in any meaningful sense.[6, 7]

Sometimes the erratic storms and temperature spikes of unfolding climatic change are described as chaotic, but the systems-analyst Neil Johnson disputes the use of that word. A complex system 'tends to move between different types of arrangements in such a way that pockets of order are created', whereas 'chaos' means 'the system's output varies so erratically that it seems random'. This distinction challenges a phenomenon dear to some chaos aficionados: the flapping wings of the butterfly which, by a series of events, cause a thunderstorm halfway around the globe. In fact this story isn't one of sheer chaos, rather a chain of path dependencies by which, in small steps, along a crooked but explainable path, the insect wing stirs a breeze which stirs other, increasingly bigger breezes, ending in the storm. Such path dependency operates in the climate realm as well, so that a chain of air temperature changes in the middle of an ocean can, via a series of events, produce varied watery surges at its edges.[8]

We are always counselled to think long term, but the long-term challenges of climate change are so enormous that they can arouse Stoicism of the bad sort, i.e. try nothing because nothing can be done. However, in dealing with short-term, erratic events, it might be more possible to do something effective and will-instilling. Which means rethinking water.

Malign water There are few large cities which are totally land-locked. From ancient times to the present, waterways have supported the economy and determined the shape of big cities like Shanghai, London and New York. Managing water has long served as a focus for cooperative work. In the medieval Netherlands, for example, communal efforts to wrest land from the sea by digging ditches, sluices and dykes bonded people; a historian of Amsterdam, Geert Mak, remarks that these joint efforts caused 'a curious coagulation of power relations, a culture of consensus and compromise which softened and eventually concealed even the fiercest generational conflicts.' However, the dykes and docks themselves held little aesthetic interest for pre-modern designers; managing water was just the utilitarian subject of the city.[9]

In the course of modern times, the watery edges of cities began to change in meaning, becoming aesthetic sites. As early as 1802, the *European Magazine* described the original West India Docks in London, of which Canary Wharf now forms a part: 'Nothing can be conceived more beautiful than the Dock. The water is of the necessary depth; its surface, [thanks to the locks] smooth as a mirror, presents to the eye a haven secure from storms.' This view expressed a joining together of commerce and aesthetics. But the join came apart in the centres of cities as ports required ever more space: container ports are now so land-hungry that they are usually located far from the centres of population; trucks and aeroplanes have taken over the functions of service boats. In the urban centre, a purely aesthetic experience of water was signalled in Olmsted's Central Park; in the reservoir of the Park, great sheets of water becoming something just to view. Daniel Burnham realized this aesthetic primacy in the design he made for Chicago's lakefront in 1909; he expelled any hint of practical usage, lining the edge between water and land with parks, promenades and other low-density uses. 'The viewing of water', he wrote, 'is a solitary act, the regard of nothingness; in viewing water man turns his back, literally, on the conditions which support his life.'[10]

Watery aesthetics have had a practical knock-on effect, by creating a source of unequal value in cities. New water-edge projects in Mumbai propose, for instance, to evict a mass of small-scale businesses and pavement-dwellers from the waterfront; the justification offered by the developers is in part visual, that of 'cleaning up' the view by reducing the density of people and complexity of uses. The offer of visual pleasure at the cost of mixed social and economic use afflicts similar proposals in Buenos Aires and London – all children in form of Burnham's Plan and all leading to social exclusion in the name of visual pleasure.

In the era of climate change, there is another shift of the kaleidoscope: water has become a destructive as well as a functional and a scenic material. The malign threat posed by water to cities is threefold. Places built at the edge of seas, like New York or Rio or Mumbai, risk episodic flooding; lack of water is going to be a problem for cities inland, since established aquifers are drying up; new rainfall patterns are shifting water to places where few people live. Flooding results when there is too much run-off; drought when there is too little groundwater retention. Climate change exacerbates both flooding and drought – traumatically. Ice melt, rising seas and changing flows within them translate above ground and over land as irregular patterns of too much or too little rain.

Malign water threats derive from some basics of the hydrological cycle. Evaporation from the oceans is in general about 9 per cent more than water which returns as rainfall over the seas; this 9 per cent produces rain which can fall over land, and is the principal source of water for rivers flowing through the land. How much of this water in the land will be retained in the ground, rather than run off? There's a difference between paved places with sewer systems beneath versus undeveloped land: one estimate reckons that in completely hard-surfaced, sewered environments, 85 per cent of rainfall will run off, and only 15 per cent will get into the ground in the first place.[11]

Most water ecologies, it should be said, are not homeostatically balanced as is a heartbeat, which should be rhythmically steady. Even without chance *clinamens*, the equilibrium of water ecologies shifts. That's what happens in the evolution of lakes, for instance, as they move from an oligotrophic to a eutrophic condition – the first weed-and-algae scarce, fish-rich and deep; the second clotted with plants, starved of fish and gradually silting up at the bottom. This process transforms, over a long stretch of time, lakes into land. Stabilizing the balance point between weed and fish, by introducing just the right plants and fish fry, is a human intervention that works against this natural shift over time. Unlike such efforts at stabilization, which aim to preserve water mass, man-made atmospheric warming speeds up the oligotrophic to eutrophic shift, and so changes wetlands to dry land.

In sum, a lack of water is the long-term threat of global climate change, as aquifers dry up underground, and the hydrological cycle alters above ground. Too much water becomes a malign force in the short term, due to erratic storms and water run-offs. How might building the city differently address these destructive, watery powers? It's a huge question; here are two answers in the wake of Hurricane Sandy.

Two berms In general, there are two separate strategies to address climate change: mitigation and adaptation. The first tries to reduce the sources of trauma, as in constructing berms (high barriers) to repulse storm surges. The second works with the trauma, as in wetlands, which slow down water surges, and continually reshape themselves as buffers. Mitigation and adaptation strategies should be complementary but are often at odds. In the case of the New York power station after Hurricane Sandy, debate centred on whether to fortify and barricade the plant where it stands against the edge of the East River, or to accept that this mitigating defence is hopeless, recognize the fact that overwhelming storms are likely to occur frequently, and move the power station inland. The debates crystallized in proposals to build two different kinds of berms, in which sand, earth and rubble can be piled up in different ways to deal with storm surges. One kind of berm – the mitigating berm – sought to break the power of storm surges when the waves of water first struck. The other kind of berm – the adaptive berm – tried to work with the uncertain ebb and flow of water after the attack.

The proponents of mitigation think that, ideally, the strong city maintains its balance and equilibrium when challenged; in the power-station discussion, for instance, mitigation proponents argued that the storm-surge walls protecting machinery should be built so high that a storm surge could never wash over them, making the power station an impregnable fortress. Another variant of mitigating the effects of the waves would be high-pressure pumps and drains laid around the electrical machinery; yet another – the most expensive – would build up a complete second and even third back-up system in the event the first line of defence failed. Behind these perfectly plausible notions is the idea of establishing some sort of infrastructural steady-state; the word 'resilience' describes here the aim that the system would quickly spring back to its usual functioning.

Critics of mitigation strategies claim that this is not thinking outside the box. Instead, strategies have to be more adaptive, in the sense of working with disruptions, rather than trying to defend against them and keep the city on an even keel. The adaptive proposal for the power station says abandon the shoreline site, and move the plant inland to higher ground. In shifting the site, the power station would have to become smaller in scale, because the high land of Manhattan is so densely built that several plants would have to do the work of one at the edge. The idea of adaptation in proposals like these means that the built form would have to change in the face of erratic events.

The divergence between mitigation and adaptation strategies became evident when, in the wake of Hurricane Sandy, my colleagues Henk Ovink and Eric Klinenberg were commissioned by the government and the Rockefeller Foundation to come up with proposals for climate-change projects in New York. (Ovink is currently 'minister of water' for the Netherlands; Klinenberg an expert on the sociology of disasters.) Rebuild by Design was meant to counter the scaremongering which warned that millions of people will have to abandon coastal cities like New York in the coming century, or the sci-fi pessimism, beloved of Hollywood movies, that we are at the end of civilization.[12]

The mitigation approach is best represented by the 'Dryline' berm proposed for the southern rim of Manhattan by the firm of Bjarke Ingels, elsewhere encountered in these pages as the designers of a Googleplex insulating that 'creative innovation hub' from the city. The Dryline, invoking the High Line pleasure park made out of a disused elevated railway track, would be essentially a ten-mile long berm, a built-up edge along the southern Manhattan tip, made of infilled sand and earth created just beyond the existing waterfront, on top of which and behind which there are constructed pleasure gardens, urban trails and the like. The Dryline thus promises pleasure in its place-making at the same time as the berm serves as a defence against storm surges. The problem, the climate scientist Klaus Jacob points out, is that the Dryline has a fixed height (currently 15 feet) and, as sea levels rise, storm surges will breach it.

As with the radio broadcaster, the designers are trapped in a fixed, closed calculation. And as with the streets around the Googleplex, it's not really possible to shut out the surrounding environment, in the long term. If it offers an illusion of sustainable safety, however, the great merit of this project is to demote water from its malign sovereignty over the city in a climate *clinamen*. Moreover, the actual planning of the parks is good, with lots of nice detail over the entire ten-mile stretch of the berm, even if many of these would be wiped out once the berm was overtopped.[13]

A Rebuild by Design project which emphasizes adaptation is the 'Living Breakwaters' berm being constructed around Staten Island, just across from the Dryline, particularly its south shore area of Tottenville. Living Breakwaters constructs a series of berms reaching out into the waters, designed to provide 'a layered system of protection'. These berms are made to erode and remake themselves over the course of time, since the hydrology of berms constructed as deep-trenched structures means that tidal action will gradually renew them; the dunes between the breakwaters are planned to slowly erode in the process of less traumatic sea-rise. This project aims to sustain oyster beds in Tottenville, an outcome which is productive rather than playful, as in the selling point of the Dryline. The two kinds of berm differ in the appeal they make to the public. Living Breakwaters brings a productive benefit invisible to the eye; the urban dweller needs to understand it intellectually in order to appreciate it. The Dryline assures visibly; its ethos is user-friendly.

Hard-edged parks of the sort Burnham built, which replaced wetlands with concrete, unfortunately diminish natural water management via either kind of berm. If a more flexible way of thinking about land, berm-building is in turn more than a soil-shaping project. It raises questions about what should be planted to make wetlands work; for instance, certain non-native reeds, relatively insensitive to phenol-tainted water, are required to invite Nature back in, by dispelling the taint and establishing shelter for fish. Since the surrounding ecology is so different from a primeval condition, doing nothing and letting things return to their natural state accomplishes little.

There lurks a large ethical issue in debates about mitigation and adaptation. Climate change is largely man-made. Man therefore should try to think about his or her place in nature in more modest terms, working with nature rather than trying to dominate it.

The dark sublime From antiquity on, the wildness of mountains made them seem uninhabitable, beyond the powers of domestication, whereas civilization could flourish in valleys, or on flat terrain close to the sea. At the end of the eighteenth century, Marjorie Hope Nicolson writes, in contrast to the 'pattern, regularity, symmetry, restraint, proportion' imposed by man horizontally on the natural world, in cities, high mountain ranges symbolized 'diversity, variety, irregularity, most of all . . . indefiniteness and vastness'. Thus Byron could write:

> Above me are the Alps,
> The palaces of nature, whose vast walls
> Have pinnacled in clouds their snowy scalps,
> And throned eternity in icy halls
> Of cold sublimity, where forms and falls
> The avalanche – the thunderbolt of snow!
> All that expands the spirit, yet appals,
> Gather around these summits . . .

This was a dark, destructive vision of the sublime: Nature dwarfing Man's makings. Water has now taken the place of mountains as a malign sublime. Mountains are unmoving, immobile, whereas malign water strikes erratically in hurricanes or goes on strike during droughts, the eternal versus the erratic.[14, 15]

The awe of Nature was a great theme of the Romantic era, embodied in the writings of Senancour and in the landscape painting of the era: Americans will think of the Hudson River School, Europeans of Caspar David Friedrich. In these landscapes *Homo faber* is absent, nature is perceived in all its untouched immensity. Friedrich coupled this awesome view with the equal sentiment of fear – his lone human figures seeming perched on the edge of falling into the abyss of a valley or a river torrent. It's a way of seeing Nature unlike the Enlightenment's, wherein Walpole and his like felt easy in natural surroundings, and again unlike the earlier nature paintings of Claude Lorrain – canvases in which monumental pieces of architecture are inserted comfortably to reinforce and accent the shape of valleys, fields or rivers. Claude sees *Homo faber*'s works as a continuity with landscape; Friedrich does not – he dramatizes the absence of man-made comforts in order to make the viewer feel, subjectively, his or her own smallness.

Malign water represents a further evolution of the dark sublime, beyond that of the Romantics in which the hand of Man is absent. Now darkness has appeared because of what *Homo faber* makes, many ecologists now believing Nature to be striking back. Were he alive today, undoubtedly Martin Heidegger would say 'I told you so!' about man-made climate traumas. 'You had a false idea about nature, you thought you could bend it to your will.' His own withdrawal from the city came, apart from its Nazi ideology, from the desire to live less aggressively, to be more at peace with nature.

That desire has a long pedigree, stretching back, as we saw in Chapter 2, to Virgil's flight from Rome. Rousseau is Walpole's near contemporary in the eighteenth century; Rousseau's hymns to living simply in the fresh air, to breast-feeding infants into their second year, to wearing home-spun clothes appealed to his contemporaries. Like him, they contrasted these natural ways of dwelling to the artifices of the city. In the industrial era, it seemed to Marx that polluting factories, coupled with abandoned fields, were part of the great transformation of modern society; like proletarian labour, Nature was exploited. As early as in the *Grundrisse*, he wrote that, 'Nature becomes . . . purely an object for men, something merely useful, and is no longer recognized as a power working for itself . . . men subject nature to the requirements of their needs, either as an item of consumption or as a means of production.'[16, 17]

It's worth noting that only people of a certain class could make friends with Nature in a friendly way. If you were a woman who dressed à la Rousseau in simple muslin shifts at home, then you required fires blazing constantly to keep warm. Your natural near-nakedness also required a well-insulated house; the poor bundled up because their hovels were badly built. A modern parallel to muslin is organic muesli, which is simple, delicious and pricey. In the built environment, green ecologies equate, in the smart cities of Masdar and Songdo, with costly construction. The challenge is how to create a modest but unprivileged relation to Nature. Which requires building that relation.

In coping with the climatic crisis, the variant of Hamlet's question which would run 'to build or not to build . . .' has a clear answer: build. The environment has to be built differently. The ethical way to build in cities accepts the primacy of adaptation. Sheer mitigation is an immodest strategy. Malign water now has a power over us we cannot reverse; as is true in other areas of experience, we need to work with forces hostile to us. But these nostrums cut further. Mitigation and adaptation are basic modes of all building. These two ways of responding to erratic climate change hold up a mirror to all the work necessary to make a *ville*.

II. RUPTURE AND ACCRETION – 'NORMAL' URBAN TIME

Building the *ville* occurs in two frames of time. In the first, time's arrow moves steadily forwards; buildings and spaces are added slowly to the environment. Things added to the built environment are often small: a single house made or renovated, a vest-pocket park. In the second, time's arrow moves forward by big, bold declarations which rupture what existed in the environment before. It is the time of the megaproject, whether that be Bazalgette's sewers, Haussmann's streets, Cerdà's blocks or Olmsted's park. The first time is adaptive in character, accounting the context of what's already been made. This is Jane Jacobs' domain of 'slow growth'. The second can seem a malign time, violating or erasing context, as did Corbusier's Plan

Voisin, and as do many smart cities which vaunt breaking traditional urban forms. 'Now' becomes the adversary of 'before'.

The domain of the slowly growing, the adapting, the accreting, tugs at us sentimentally, but rupture is inevitable in the modern built environment if only because modern buildings expire more rapidly than many buildings from earlier periods. We now figure the lifespan of commercial high-rises at thirty-five to forty years, whereas the Georgian terraces which have lasted for hundreds of years could last further hundreds. The reasons do not lie in poor building construction, but rather in rigid specification, a consequence of core investing favouring investments in structures built absolutely fit for purpose. As uses change, habitation evolves, the buildings outlive their useful existence. This rupture typifies Shanghai's roads to nowhere on which I travelled with Madame Q. Something exactly similar is happening in many areas of London's South Bank. The new buildings will have a much shorter shelf-life than the old, because they have a rigid form/function in a rapidly evolving city. This chameleon character of the modern urban landscape reinforces the sentimental aura of the old.

The contraries of accretion and rupture stimulate debate today in urban development throughout the world. Projects which rupture the existing urban fabric tend to be power boasts, particularly the symbolic public structures which politicians favour – Olympic stadiums, art museums, aquariums (which were fashionable big-ticket items a few years ago). An aquarium is not of much value to a school struggling to find money for books; the appeal of growth through accretion is thus strengthened because it can seem by contrast to be bottom-up development in cities ruled top-down.

But in the *cité*, if you are an Asian immigrant trying to send your child to a good school in a distant neighbourhood and are told, 'You will have to be patient; people's attitudes change slowly', you might think of rupture, socially, as an agent of justice. So in too the *ville*. The sheer size of the modern megacity suggests the need for radical new big urban forms. Mexico City, for instance, has probably 25 million inhabitants, spread out over a huge terrain. Most of them are poor and they can't find work locally; they have commutes of two or three hours. They need a better answer to navigating a city the size of the Netherlands than the incremental transport solutions so far offered them which have failed. They need something big to change in the city.

This debate about the dimensions of rupture and accretion is thus too complicated to be reduced to top-down versus bottom-up. One way to advance the understanding of urban time is to relate it to the time of climate change. Can big ruptures be likened to a storm striking the city? In Jane Jacobs' frame of reference they should be. As in the highway Robert Moses wanted to run through Washington Square in New York, they are 'cataclysmic' projects; this is also how Benjamin figures progress, as a man-made storm sowing destruction. Rupture = trauma.

As in dealing with climate change, where we want to practise both adaptation and mitigation, it makes better sense to think of accretion over time and rupture by design as ways of *ville*-making which can run in parallel. Indeed, they need to do so: the building of a new railroad station for Mexico City residents or the replacement of coal plants by solar-energy generators in Beijing aren't projects which can ripen slowly in the fullness of time, but local adaptations to them may take a long time to work out.

Battery Park City A good place to contemplate the balance between rupture and accretion is Battery Park City, a new neighbourhood at the southern tip of Manhattan which took the brunt of Hurricane Sandy. Battery Park City was constructed mainly in the 1980s and 1990s on landfill to create a more mixed neighbourhood than the office towers of Wall Street to the east. The idea was to build a *ville* which looked like the rest of residential Manhattan, echoing the grid first laid down in the city in 1811. Stanton Eckstut, the principal planner of this neighbourhood, put the credo of his work directly: 'Most buildings must be background architecture, though some can achieve "stardom". But the first priority is the well-designed street.' In this, his credo was set directly against Le Corbusier's Plan Voisin. His impulse to imitate the existing street pattern has led to other, similar planning moves, for instance to re-create the Manhattan street wall, or to mimic the variety of low-rise town-house façades on the Upper East and West Side side streets. The landscaping

of Battery Park City, led by the landscape architect M. Paul Fried-
berg, re-creates a New York which many New Yorkers wish had
been: nice tree plantings not stunted by decades of dog urine; concrete tubs of pretty flowers which no one has stolen. The overall plan
has a five-point list of principles: '1. thinking small; 2. using what
exists; 3. integrating; 4. using streets to create place; 5. establishing
design guidelines.'

Against these guidelines, critics say that Battery Park City seems a
simulation of prettified time, the past idealized, just as Xintiandi is
today in Shanghai. Its diversity is instant diversity, accomplished all
at once by design. The streets which Rector Place imitates achieved
their diversity of façade, on the contrary, because they filled in slowly,
over the course of several generations, each generation adding its own
tastes in design to the street. Moreover, variations in internal building forms and the relation of the low centres of blocks to their tall
vertical edges came about as a result of diversity in economic fortune
and usage over the course of those generations; the streets look complex because they reflect the accumulation of differences in the ways
people lived on them.

What is the time-logic behind this critique? Accreting elements
constitute a theme and variations, a type-form, created by the intersection of building and dwelling. Take the most mundane urban
object, the stoop. Raised stoops are entrance steps prescribed by New
York's building code which reformed housing in poor parts of the
city in the 1890s. These wide steps were designed simply to get people
in and out of crowded housing; however, the people who lived in the
tenements gradually colonized these stoops as sociable spaces, especially during New York's vicious summer heat, by putting down
blankets on the steps in order to sit, or using the treads as tabletops
for food and drink. It wasn't a matter of a new use disabling an old
form, but of making it a more complex form, not restricted to one
use, and so (in terms of systems) more open.

Accretion in Battery Park City is a peculiar kind of type-form
building. The planners applied the results of theme-and-variations
development wholesale to a new place; that is, they didn't do the
variation work themselves, but appropriated it from others. That may
seem like cheating, but this instant community built on landfill has

aged well. Battery Park City has retained its essentially middle-class character, whereas the areas around it – Tribeca and Wall Street – have fallen relentlessly to the rich. Moreover, neighbours inhabit this neighbourhood; there is a wide variety of communally organized groups which do everything from cleaning up tourist trash to participating in events housed in ground-level meeting rooms in the towers of the community.

Still, there's a problem with this appropriation, one evident in the playground spaces reserved for children. Infants cavorting in the carefully raked sandboxes are happy enough, but the community ballfields at North End Avenue between Murray and Warren Streets are often deserted. The reason is deeper than the dwindling population of teens in the city. The nice places provided to hang out here contrast to basketball courts like those at the corner of 6th Avenue and 3rd Street, places kids reach by subway from all over the city. Iron-mesh fences frame these courts for basketball, with only a few straggly trees. Trucks and honking taxis struggling up 6th Avenue create a deafening volume of sound which combines with the portable radios tuned to Latin or to rapping beats. Everything in these crowded playgrounds is hard surface. But teens, including those from Battery Park City, gravitate to them, because here they have done their own appropriation; it was not done for them.

Inside Eckstut's community, there is one big rupture: a huge office tower complex called Brookfield Place, designed by César Pelli, with an indoor tropical garden at its base and a marina for yachts outside. The tower breaks with the neighbourhood ethos: the tropical plants would die if exposed to New York City's air, and the owners of the yachts are not locals. Hideous though the building is, one good thing about the Pelli tower is that it does not seek to hide the fact that it is a rupture of the surrounding context. From the start of the project, the rupture was preordained, since its financing came internationally from people who were – core-investor fashion – buying space rather than a place.

In a resonant phrase, Émile Durkheim said that 'man does not recognize himself' when plunged into new forms of collective actions. The generation before Durkheim, this phrase applied dramatically to the American soldiers who first practised mechanized warfare against civilians, a practice which emerged in the American Civil War; their own actions bewildered them. Durkheim thought the soldiers' bewilderment applied more generally: a rupture disorients consciousness of self and others. For a contrary school of thought, ruptures are a call to action. Radical labour organizers have taken the strike, for instance, as a moment of political awakening rather than just a bargaining-chip technique; the breakdown clarifies what's wrong with the system.[18]

Open-systems thinking looks at a rupture as changing an entire system – waking the system up, as it were, by creating tipping points. A small change triggers bigger ones, as with the proverbial butterfly and the storm. In a closed system, small events accumulate and accrete, but do not tip; rather, they add up step by step in a smoothly linear fashion. If growth occurs, it is because there is just more of something rather than a sudden jump-start through breaking the existing pattern.

Planners in New York hoped that Battery Park City would be an urban tipping point, provoking much bigger changes in Lower Manhattan, transforming Wall Street from a financial machine to an area mixing housing, schools, offices, art galleries and small shops. Slow, additive growth of the Jacobs' sort, spreading down from Tribeca to Wall Street, didn't seem to jump-start the change from office to residential the planners wanted; a big, dramatic project was necessary – even if that project sought to look as if it were just the same as the rest of the city. But Battery Park City did not 'tip', because of the eight-lane West Side Highway which lined it on one side. This proved a real boundary rather than a barrier, cutting off the project from seeping porously into its surroundings.

Pelli's office tower complex both ruptures its residential and recreational surroundings and is an arbitrary marker of value – just like the plastic bench, though infinitely more costly. It declares, 'Here is something for you, if you are looking for a wood-panelled office with a view of the Statue of Liberty no matter its immediate context.' If you happen to be a local resident, or you like good buildings, Pelli's tower complex is a negative marker, because New York is filled with commercial towers just like it, which have travelled straight out of an architect's filing cabinet into the ground. None the less, there is something to be said for this arbitrary rupture of the Battery Park Dream.

This arbitrary imposition contrasts to waterfront projects like Heron Quays in London's Docklands, where we seem to be looking at a part of the city from another time. The simulation of a very large structure, as though it had always been there, is a way to hide exactly the scale of intrusion upon the urban fabric. By creating the illusion of a building from a different era, the very presence of the structure is made legitimate. Judgement is clouded over by the sense of a *fait* long *accompli*, about which one can do nothing. Whereas here, by virtue of this sore urban thumb, you cannot but help becoming aware of the imposition, the assertion of a different value. As I've ruefully come to realize, that's just the work my plastic benches are trying to do at the other end of the economic and social scale, by declaring in front of decayed buildings that there's something of value here, something not in context.

In this regard, Corbusier bequeathed the wrong image of rupture. His idea of rupturing the past was to erase it, to flatten it and build over it, so that the urban dweller would lose any sense of what was there before. A good rupture is not an erasure – in art or in life. The modern painter Cy Twombly quotes the seventeenth-century painter Nicolas Poussin both in the titles of some of his works and in fragments of imagery, only to throw into relief his own dripping, splattered lines. So, too, the good rupture could be a building which, jarringly, does not fit into a traditional neighbourhood, or a park which, like the High Line, does not look like the normal pleasure-ground, or a public space like the playground over the sewage plant. This is the point of rupture by design: it can create consciousness of place by throwing its context into relief.

Contextual planning is seductive because it respects the environment which has grown up in time, that time-cross of dwelling and making which Corbusian grade-flat-and-build does not. Do not change that Georgian lintel, do not cut down that tree, be discreet if you add a new window, be sure it blends in: respect. Like all seductions, though, planning 'in context' may deceive; this is not what modern context is about. The streetscape context common to Chicago and Shanghai consists of McDonald's, Starbucks, Apple, the HSBC cash machine; or, more expensively, Gucci and the BMW showroom. The context of sameness extends to infrastructure. Were the towers of Shanghai and Chicago stripped naked, their steel skeletons would appear pretty much identical in structure (indeed, big engineering firms in both cities have likely bought their steel from the same manufacturers, as they have almost all other building components). Standardization without character is the 'context' of the modern *ville*.

Just here we want to assess the relation of adaptation and rupture in a climate crisis to this relation in ordinary building. The ethical balance is different. Adaptation to climate change recognizes Man's limits to building himself out of the crisis. In ordinary kinds of building, adaptation may be a submission to man-made power.

Thinking in context, practising adaptive planning, means you introduce changes slowly so that they don't disrupt the existing order of things, so that they are gradually absorbed and integrated with what came before. Such gradualism is a way to privilege friction-free change. Its alterations are conservative in character: you can't build something which sticks out, you are prudent, you don't cause trouble. Needs are not urgent: the black child seeking admission to a white school will have to wait. There is no crisis.

There is nothing better about the past just because it has already happened. So, too, there is nothing better about the new just because it is unlike the past. Arty architects tend to make a fetish of rupture, as citizens of the same kingdom in which art galleries get rich selling 'transgressive' art, in which technology start-ups promise to 'revolutionize' the industry, in which investment banks look to make money through financial instruments no one has ever thought of before. But still, without the rupture of everyday building, both *ville* and *cité* wither.

As we have seen, in the realm of climate change, time casts a different kind of shadow in the long term than it does in its jagged, unfolding short term. In the ordinary realm of building, time exists in two similar dimensions: the long term of accreting form, and the forms which rupture fabric or building typologies in the present. What difference exactly do these shadows make to the question of the quality of the built environment?

To answer, it might be useful to think about the role time plays in craftsmanship. Craft skills develop slowly; that is, they accrete. The calculations I did for *The Craftsman* led to the now-familiar '10,000 hour rule' – the length of time it takes to master the complex skills to play pro tennis or the cello, or become a good surgeon. Moreover, each of the skills that make up a craft practice is contextual; the good surgeon's snipping techniques have to relate to the careful digging out of flesh and the many other kinds of skilled gestures he or she will have to deploy in the course of an operation.

Yet for the craftsman to improve his or her skills, a rupture has to occur, a skills-storm is needed. If something is out of place, if something cannot be assimilated in the realm of the already-known, the rupture can provoke carpenter or surgeon to rethink what the practitioner already knows. In the world of craftsmanship, these ruptures are tipping points of a particular and valuable kind: the craftsman's skills get better for having faced the unexpected: old skills then expand, or new ones are added to old. I am not describing an ideal state, but rather the means by which most of the craftsmen I've studied get better at their work: they need at crucial points to undo what previously they've taken for granted. In the same way, Festinger found that rupturing a routine – and so creating a cognitive dissonance – provoked and stimulated animals in his laboratory; at the other end of the spectrum, John Dewey argued that artists develop through encountering resistance.

In the built environment, rupture does not inevitably improve the quality of building. It can provoke, it can awaken awareness of the surroundings, of contrasting environments – as Pelli's tower does – but the consequence is not inherently better building. In none of the cities which we have surveyed, from Shanghai to Chicago, has the fact that a building or plan is new form, or that it rips a tear in an existing fabric, in itself improved the quality of the built environment. An idealist philosopher like Benedetto Croce – Dewey's friendly antagonist – would say, of course, that the quality of a thing is independent of the time in which it exists. But if you are a practically minded person, you may find that assertion baffling. Isn't building a craft? Then why shouldn't it obey the rules of craft skill, becoming better through the interplay of accretion and rupture in time?

These ethical hemmings and hawings and comparisons come down to a sharp point: as in craftsmanship, a good-quality environment is one which can be repaired.

III. REPAIR — THE TEST OF QUALITY

Rescuing a cliché The words 'resilience' and 'sustainability' are clichés which dominate urbanism today. Everyone is for them, whatever they mean: the United Nations, the Rockefeller Foundation, the builders of Masdar, indeed most builders, tout the pair to legitimate urban developments good, bad or indifferent. The partners in this marriage of clichés are not, however, quite identical. A note sustained in music has the quality of suspending time. So too in building, 'sustainable' can mean enduring, permanent, durable. Whereas 'resilient' means a recovery from forces or pressures which occur in time. A resilient metal can absorb stresses so that it does not break or become permanently deformed; it springs back. In craftwork, a resilient object can be repaired; so can a resilient environment. It can in time spring back.

Cities are constantly in need of repair – a fact which is not news to any urbanite navigating torn-up streets, suffering from electricity brown-outs, or boarding antiquated public transport. As a practical matter, repairs of defective construction cost more than doing the work right in the first place. Penny-pinching, delayed maintenance makes transport harder to repair, as with commuter railroads in New York and London. So too a looser fit between form and function would have prevented the huge new investments Shanghai now needs to make to fix its roads to nowhere. In a closed system, when something goes wrong in one element, the whole system may stop functioning or collapse, as in top-down management when mistakes presented as commands poison the whole corporate body.

In general, an open city is more reparable than a closed city. It is looser in operation, its power relations are more interactive than directive, it is thus capable of adapting and retooling when things go wrong or come to the end of their useful life. That's the principle. In practice, how should an open city go about making repairs, how can it become resilient?

The urbanist has particular things to learn from the craftsman about how to make a repair. In approaching a broken vase, a craftsman can follow three different strategies: restoration, remediation or reconfiguration. These three strategies are just those a city can use if under attack from climate change or ruptured from within.[19]

Forms of repair In restoring a vase, the craftsman seeks to make the object look just like new. He or she uses every bit of broken porcelain possible, fills in with materials made to the original formula, uses a transparent binder. In restoring a painting, this kind of repair is more complicated, because the picture restorer has to decide, say, for an early Renaissance landscape, what state to restore – its moment of initial completion, or a time, perhaps two centuries later, when the landscape became famous. But in both, the labours of the craftsman are meant to appear invisible, and time suspended.

The vase could secondly be repaired by remediation. In this kind of work, the craftsman would use a modern porcelain formula instead of imitating the original, and use a binding glue to hold the object together which is stronger than the original but shows itself on the pot's surface. The same kind of remediation happens in repairing a broken machine by substituting a new and improved memory chip for the original, so that the device runs faster. But still, in a remediation, the object does what it was originally meant to do: the vase holds the same amount of water for flowers; the machine runs the same programs. Now the hand of the craftsman is evident in the remediated object, and the remedy is better made, in some respects, than the original.

A third kind of repair consists of reconfiguration. Here, the fact that something has broken serves as an occasion to make the object different from before, in both form and function. The craftsman faced with a cracked vase decides that he or she can use the shattered bits to make a platter instead of a vase, embedding these in a caustic binder which seals the sharp edges, so that the old-new object can hold fruit or meat, thus recomposing it in function as well as form. Up to modern times, thrifty ceramicists did this all the time, so that few precious materials were thrown away. Reconfiguration works similarly in the thrifty use of machines – an old automobile is stripped of its glass and steel, which are melted down, then used for windows and structural beams in a building. In reconfiguration, the craftsman becomes an inventor of form, rather than the servant of forms conceived by others. The original object serves as materials for work flowing forwards in time, its material becoming Lucretian, like his material configurations possessing no predestined form or fate.

These three forms of repair span the gamut from closed to open form. Restoration is a closed kind of repair: the model rules in materials, form and function; in remediation, the materials are set free but there is still a tight tie between form and function; in reconfiguration, that tie is loosened, even though the materials remain those of the original.

Urban analogues to restoration, remediation and reconfiguration take us closer to understanding resilience. The simulations for sale in Shanghai of a Victorian village or Bauhaus town are restorations in which the hand of the modern maker is meant to be invisible. Remedial work like that of Mumford's garden city uses a variety of materials, old and new, farms and factories, but the join between form and function is tight. Reconfiguration of a city employs the open forms described in Chapter 8: the type-form enables the process of variation, the *ville* becomes more complex via creating synchronicities, less determinate thanks to incomplete form, more socially interactive due to its porous edges, punctuated by will: the tie between form and function loosens for all these reasons, and the city becomes free to evolve. It opens up.

Repair cast in these terms has political resonances. The social analogue to restoring the broken vase to its original state is restoring a culture to its origins – or, rather, the desire to return to an Edenic time when people seemed to live in a pure and authentic way. Serb nationalists, for instance, believed their culture existed in a pure state in the thirteenth century; modern Serb 'restorers' wage war against their Muslim neighbours, with whom they had lived for seven centuries, in order to recover that purity. Restoration of national purity is resilience of a closed sort.

Remediation has a more centrist, mixed character, as in traditional

American beliefs in the balance of powers in a government; the machine of state can continue to work, even if the human materials of which it is made change. The American constitutional framers believed that so long as the three branches of government differed, each could remedy the defects of the other two; the system would thus maintain its equilibrium. (Correspondingly, they believed that having the same faction rule all three branches, as is true at the moment, is a recipe for dictatorship.) Analytically, 'sustainable' and 'resilient' part company in this sort of remediation. You don't want the one party or faction to be sustainable in the sense of enduring and time-proof; you do want the system to be resilient, springing back from inadequacies or incapacities in any one part.

Finally, revolution is one political version of reconfiguration: the vase of state is broken, so make something different. In reality, radical political changes make use of existing bureaucrats, soldiers and physical resources, reconfiguring these in a new binding medium, just like the fragments of a shattered, reconfigured vase. As in the Russian Revolution: the old ways of soldiering did not change under the Bolsheviks, there were still hierarchies of command – indeed, these became more rigid, the troops having less autonomy in the field than in imperial times. More openly, a political reconfiguration is not an erasure of the power that came before; rather, it is a rethink of how its elements fit or don't fit together.

All of which is pertinent to thinking about how to repair a city suffering from climate change. The berm proposed by Bjarke Ingels promises sustainability; that is, despite flooding or wind, it is meant to endure. The berms being made by Living Breakwaters promise resilience by drawing on reconfiguration as a mode of repair. They work with change rather than against it.

Lucretius is a good counsellor today in thinking about climate change, particularly about climate change as it affects cities. He recommends we do not fight against that turbulence of time, but rather accept it, live with it and work with it. So too the conflicts between rupture and accretion of form; these 'collisions and conjunctions [set] physical materials on an unpredictable path'. Lucretius is not the sort of Stoic who says be passive, do nothing, succumb to Shelleyan despair – in fact, few ancient Stoics ever recommended inert

submission to fate. In ancient Greek, the word *krisis* meant a decision, required when things come to a head and can be no longer
avoided. Lucretius' Latin shaded that Greek word by saying that we
have to decide calmly what to do when faced with a crisis; the Stoic
scorned the crisis mentality which is driven by hysteria or terror. That
ancient spirit is what the techniques of resilience should aim to recover in the city. The most valuable among them is the craft of
reconfiguration.

Conclusion: One Among Many

Kantstrasse Kantstrasse, a long, wide and straight street, begins in West Berlin's commercial district, then cuts through a more genteel area around Savignyplatz, then becomes a centre for the Asian community in the city, and morphs finally into the main street for a section of Berlin's old working class. I began to study Kantstrasse as a result of my stroke. Physical stamina erodes instantly when the brain blows a fuse, and this energy can be recovered only through steady exercise. Along Kantstrasse I built up my body by taking long walks; in these rambles, the street seemed to condense the ethics of the city.

The monumental buildings and public spaces which marked imperial, Nazi and then communist Berlin do not appear here. A wonderfully pompous, pre-First World War theatre, the Theater des Westens, does anchor the street at its commercial start, and there is one self-conscious architectural 'statement' nearby – the Berlin Stock Exchange on Fasanenstrasse – which eerily resembles a McDonald's sign stretched out in three dimensions. Other than these, its housing, shops and streetscape are unremarkable.

Kantstrasse is rather neglected by Berlin's immense population of young trendies who flock to the centre and the east. Yet the street is lively, interesting and full of character along almost its entire length. One or two places in Kantstrasse are vividly communal, such as the Paris Bar, a hang-out for elderly bourgeois bohemians like me, but more typical of the street is the nearby Schwarzes Café, an all-night spot where a younger clientele gathers, few of whom seem to know one another.

As in other big cities, there are many solitary people living in and near Kantstrasse; one benchmark estimate of people living alone in cities of over two million population hovers in the 25–30 per cent range. This is largely because adults are surviving longer into old age, and also because of the withering of that once-urgent necessity to marry and have children as soon as one becomes adult. Places along Kantstrasse cater for solitaries – convenience shops offer takeout mini-meals for one person and sell single bananas and onions for the solitary chef. But though many lone people populate the street, it does not convey a desolate air, since individuals are out and about commercially during the day, and more socially at night.[1]

Locals do engage with strangers on the street, but also keep their distance. In the last three years, for instance, an excellent music shop has been replaced by a more upmarket business. I found, upon enquiring within, that the manager, herself an amateur bassoon player, observed that her firm had priced out the musicians – 'the rent is outrageous!' However, 'that was then', she announced as she left me for a paying customer. A Vietnamese greengrocer, after remarking on how welcome Anglo-Saxons like me now are in his home country, laughed when he sold me what he called 'Kraut-unfriendly' hot chillies. My sociological antennae quivered: I asked if he felt he was living in a hostile place. A shrug put an end to my questions.

The disengagement on Kantstrasse became more tangible after my stroke. Vertigo is a common consequence of strokes, especially after strenuous exercise. In my Kantstrasse walks I had often to steady myself by putting my back to the walls of buildings or to the plate glass of shopfronts. This has elicited glances from other people strolling along, but a look has usually sufficed and the lookers have left me alone. In one way I was glad of this; I did not want to be made a fuss over, singled out as infirm. But even so, since an elderly man flattening himself against a wall is not a daily sight in Kantstrasse, I wondered why they did not react beyond a look.

The obvious reason would be that Kantstrasse represents the urban condition which Simmel described: mixed in its peoples and in its activities, stimulating because of the mix, it is still not a warm and responsive community. In Kantstrasse, people wear Simmel's mask, don't get involved, close off emotionally. That explanation might have seemed too easy to Immanuel Kant, for whom Kantstrasse is named. To him, this realm of strangers might appear more open, in a cosmopolitan way.

Kant In his essay of 1784, Kant asserted that a cosmopolitan should not deeply identify with any one place or people. As we have seen, in the sixteenth century such a cosmopolitan was personified by the diplomat able to skate from place and place, culture to culture. Kant expanded the figure of the cosmopolitan to represent the 'universal citizen', an emblem of humanity transcending local customs and traditions. Four years after the appearance of Kant's essay, his acolyte Christoph Martin Wieland explained his master's assertion by saying that, 'Cosmopolitans . . . regard all the peoples of the earth as so many branches of a single family . . . [composed of] rational beings.' But Kant himself did not believe the cosmopolitan condition was so sweet.[2]

Kant imagines cosmopolitanism as the response to a basic human tension: 'Man has an inclination to associate with others,' he writes, '. . . [b]ut he also has a strong propensity to isolate himself from others . . .' Kant calls this tension 'unsocial sociability', by which he means the 'propensity to enter into society, [but] bound together with a mutual opposition which constantly threatens to break up the society'. It is this tension that makes human experience crooked; people both need to get and fear getting involved with others. To survive 'unsocial sociability' it's necessary to establish mutual distances, to deal dispassionately and impersonally with people.[3]

The social critic Ash Amin describes the Kantian cosmopolitan as a person who has become 'indifferent to difference', with the practical consequence that he or she can practise toleration. Toleration was the cardinal virtue for Karl Popper in defining open societies, as it was for Isaiah Berlin; toleration is required since there exists no one truth but rather conflicting and equally valid truths. Toleration depends, we might say, on indifference to truth – at least, truth as a life-and-death matter. Kant is not a cosmopolitan of this liberal sort. He declares, 'Man . . . requires a master, who will break his will and force him to obey a will that is universally valid . . .' He isn't thinking of a person, a Führer, who will do so, but rather of a set of principles which draw people out of themselves, obliging them to think in general rather than personal terms.[4, 5]

If Kant's case seems extreme, reflect that the figure of the cosmopolitan who is indifferent to difference lies at the heart of Christianity. 'The city of God is not concerned with differences of custom, law, or institution,' St Augustine wrote. This sacred cosmopolitanism transcends the local and the particular in order to embrace a higher truth; all four Gospels describe Jesus as a wanderer, as a man belonging nowhere, His truth valid everywhere.[6]

In secular terms the Kantian cosmopolitan citizen has a certain kind of justice on his or her side. How do we speak truth to power? Not by crying out 'you hurt me', but rather by declaring 'what you do is wrong'. So too, in a famous passage in the *Phenomenology of Spirit*, Hegel argued for the same impersonal shift: a slave frees himself or herself mentally from the master's yoke by depersonalizing the terms of the conflict, demanding that the master justify his behaviour in principle, rationally. As appeared in Grenfell Tower, impersonality can disarm justice, but still the stranger constitutes the dominant figure of the city, his or her indifference both a behavioural fact and an ethical conundrum.[7]

A Kantian cité? Kant sets the terms of a great drama playing out in cities. Kant's image of the disengaged cosmopolitan could describe the global citizens and globalizing forces transforming cities now. The core investors of Chapter 3 who dominate modern urban investment easily figure now as Kantian subjects, moving capital around the globe detached from place, rising above feelings for or attachments to the places in which they invest. But so, too, are poorer migrants Kantian subjects, like the adaptable young woman librarian from Medellín, surviving only because they can look beyond the limits of local custom and tradition.

Indifference of the Tocquevillian sort is a vice in the *cité*, manifested in the racial and class silos of gated communities; this inward withdrawal can be translated into built form, as in the Googleplex. The superficial courtesies practised by people in the wake of conflicts in London's Clerkenwell were also pushing others away; the truth about how Jews and Muslims felt about one another was hidden from view.

To Ferdinand Tönnies, the warmth of community seems an anti-dote to indifference. In his way of thinking, people warm to one another the more intimate they become. This view is falsified when-ever a couple decide to divorce. It sits oddly, also, in terms of informal urban relations. Intimacy is a danger to people like Mr Sudhir. His survival does not depend on getting to know his customers or his neighbours better; in fact, because he is hawking stolen merchandise, the more anonymous he is the better. In Nehru Place, informal terri-tory is transitory: shopkeepers appear and disappear; the start-up offices lining the open market are vacated every few months. These material conditions affect Mr Sudhir's desire for intimacy: his per-sonal disclosures to me were an intermission – pregnant to me but casual to him. I suspect he had forgotten me an hour after serving me tea.

However, indifference can take on another, more positive aspect. In Kantstrasse, the fact that I remained upright meant that people need not get involved, since no action was required of them. So too in Medellín, street-smarts sifted physical sensations which required action from those which did not. In the synchronous space of the ancient agora, people edited activities which clamoured at the same time for their attention, focusing on those that needed a response, like gesturing to a god's shrine; treating other demands, like a merchant's cry 'Buy my olives', as noise they could filter out. The Kantstrasse glance, I came to understand, reflected a distinction between doing and being. The stranger need not do anything in regard to another stranger.

That distinction contrasts the active and the passive. Electroni-cally, the user-friendly program does not demand much more of the user than to follow the rules, whereas an open-source program often obliges the user to make the programs he uses. While the prescriptive smart city demands little from its inhabitants, the coordinative smart city demands much. Social relations among makers, such as the bak-ers in Boston, has proved in many ways more satisfying than the social life with neighbours among whom they dwell in a low-key way. So, too, 'passifying' the public occurs in public 'consultations', whereas co-productions ask the public to play a more active role. All the open forms discussed in this book invite active engagement, because none is stable or self-sufficing.

If the open *cité* is a place of doing rather than being, what it does not do is arouse sympathy for others. Adam Smith, in *The Theory of Moral Sentiments*, provided one of the first physiological explanations of how sympathy works. When you see a man fall in the street you run to help him because you can imagine the pain as your own kneecap shattering. In Kantstrasse, passers-by following Adam Smith would have imagined themselves leaning against a wall in distress, and so asked me if they could help.[8]

The golden rule transforms this physiological response into an ethical command. The Islamic Hadith, for example, report the Prophet saying to a follower, 'As you would have people do to you, do to them; and what you dislike to be done to you, don't do to them.' Treating the other as yourself implies reciprocity, as in the Confucian *Analects* (an ethical rather than a theological guide): Zi Gong (a disciple of Confucius) asked: 'Is there any one word that could guide a person throughout life?' The Master replied: 'How about "*shu*" [reciprocity]: *never impose on others what you would not choose for yourself*?'[9, 10]

These precepts depend on the strength of identification with another. A former American president, in declaring 'I feel your pain', presented himself as totally open to others. To lend a sympathetic ear to each and every voter is of course necessary to win votes, but there is something deeply wrong with this declaration. First of all, there is a kind of moral imperialism built into the president's mantra; to be able to identify with anyone means that nothing they experience is beyond my grasp, my power to feel, my appropriation. The corollary would be, if I can't identify with another's experience, then I may cease to care for him or her. I am indifferent to the stranger who remains strange, who is essentially, unbridgeably other. This perversity is built into the golden rule.

In Sweden, I thought about how identification with the Other based on uprooting might apply to refugees. Jewish tradition stresses the common bond of humanity, as did Kant's disciple Wieland, but for a more tragic reason – as in Leviticus 19:34: 'The stranger who resides with you shall be to you as one of your citizens; you shall love him as yourself; for you were strangers in the land of Egypt.' In Sweden, it was evident, even in the first flush of optimism after their wanderings had ended, that identification between Bosnians and Swedes would not come easily; the strangers would have to make a strenuous effort to learn Swedish for instance, and the Swedes would have to accept veiled girls in class. As befits an enlightened society, Swedes did not then and, despite the pendulum's swings back and forth in the last three decades, still do not want to shun foreigners. But for them, as for other countries that have been generous to refugees, identification with alien ethical values is not a matter of being totally open in the sense of receptive – just as for many refugees full openness to the hosts is not possible. Neither can identify.

A contrast to the golden rule appears in the essay of Georg Simmel serving as the companion piece to 'The Metropolis and Mental Life'. In 'The Stranger' Simmel wrote that strangers hold up mirrors to established communities and ways of life. Sometimes, as with the PEGIDA marchers, images of the stranger define exactly how a people does not want to see itself, as in the portrait in Oscar Wilde's *The Picture of Dorian Grey*. Sometimes, though, as at the Munich train station, people forget about themselves and respond to the stranger's need: the refugees are hungry, period. They don't make you feel hungry.[11]

The Kantian rationale for a *cité* is that identification should not rule it; in the same measure, people ought to become 'indifferent to difference'. Unchained from anthropology, they can then open up to those unlike themselves living in the same place. To Alexander Herzen and Teju Cole, Kant's counsel might be, do not regret your uprooting. Do things now, for their own sake.

Cosmopolitan pain I saw this counsel up close in the life of Hannah Arendt, who taught me. In her book *The Human Condition*, conceived in the 1950s, she imagines the public sphere as a place where people can discuss and debate freely and equally because they are cut loose from their particular, private circumstances. In later writings she argued against identity-based politics, particularly those based on race. But her version of the public realm, unlike Kant's, depends on place: an agora in ancient Athens, a piazza of medieval Siena, a coffee shop on New York's Upper West Side – any site where different groups can talk face to face.

Arendt would have made a good open-systems theorist. To her, encounters in the dense urban centre produce no sweeping or stable truths. What she called 'natality' was an effort of remaking life with others, of rebirthing if you follow her word, as a never-ending process of communication and interaction. 'Natality' produces pockets of order in time, as the mathematician Neil Johnson would have it; it requires dialogic exchanges, as Bakhtin described them; and in learning how to collaborate over time, 'natality' is something people get better at, becoming competent urbanites.

But still, as I now realize, all of this theory came at an immense cost to her. That appears in the contrast between Arendt and Jane Jacobs, who lived in New York at the same time but so far as I know had no contact with one another. Jacobs, so committed in her defence of local community in New York, was none the less willing to leave it during the Vietnam War out of revulsion at the national polity and for the sake of her family. As a person forced into immigration rather than choosing it, Arendt faced a different dilemma: she felt contempt for America in many ways, but was determined to stick it out; 'you can't walk backwards,' she once said to me, apropos of Klee's Angel. Yet, whereas Jacobs made a good new life for herself in Canada, locally engaged as always, certain signs of being absent, perhaps distressed, sometimes escaped Arendt. These appeared at the moments when she caught herself up short, withdrawing into silence after lapsing back into German.

Her belief that life has continually to be remade echoes Bachelard's figure of quitting the security of the hut – whose *Dasein* is like a child's cradle – for the difficulties of the city. So, too, the work of building a city entails ruptures and breaks. This is the realm of doing – of reconfiguration.

Open As a *ville*, Kantstrasse is open in form. It is used synchronously during the day as grocers, kitchen suppliers, medical clinics and restaurants are mixed up in the buildings lining the street. These buildings are incomplete in form in the sense that they can be, and are, constantly reconfigured at ground level. Adaptation appears also in the use made of the spaces under the railroad tracks in Savigny-platz; these arches now house a bookshop, an OK restaurant and cheap-clothing shops. Porosity appears in the side streets abutting the elevated railroad tracks to the south as Kantstrasse stretches into more working-class territory. The built forms here are irregular behind their street façades; above the ground level, Asian and German inhabitants share housing. The Kurfürstendamm, which runs parallel to Kantstrasse, and which is much showier, with movie theatres, luxury-goods shops and famous hotels, draws the tourists, even though these charms are now faded. The shadings between people along Kantstrasse are gradual and messy rather than abrupt, occurring mid-block rather than neatly at the corners.

If open in form, Kantstrasse did not come into being openly, as a co-production between urbanist and urbanite. In part, this has to do with the Second World War. Allied bombing damaged some of the urban fabric here, requiring quick repair or instant new building; the slow, deliberative process of co-production was not an option. During the decades following, in which Berlin was a divided city, the authorities, anxious to showcase free Berlin, kept a tight control over its development. For these historic reasons, the street is not entirely a perfect model of the open *ville*.

However, like Haussmann's Paris, it is a place which has taken on a life of its own, independent of its makers' intentions. No Berlin urbanist in the 1960s, for instance, foresaw the advent of Asians in the street, yet the place has been able to absorb and accommodate them. Put abstractly, the forms themselves acquire an agency of their own in time; they are not limited to the intentions of their original makers. Like the *cité*, the forms of this *ville* are open in time.

The porous membranes between communities, the type-forms varying from place to place, the seed-planning which distributes them: all are more than local in application, yet the character of such forms is not overwhelming and monumental. The open *ville* is full of character due to its markings, its irregularities, its incomplete structures. Streets like Haussmann's boulevards have acquired this Kantian 'crookedness', even though Haussmann intended them to be monumental and imposing. War did the same in Kantstrasse. These streets have acquired, as it were, a self-effacing mein at a large scale.

It wasn't inevitable that Haussmann's boulevards became the boulevards of today, nor that Delhi would enable informality, nor that Kantstrasse would become so hospitable to diversity. Planners can, though, aid this process: we can propose forms, and if necessary we can confront people who are not living in an open way. But urbanism's problem has been more a self-destructive emphasis on control and order, as in the Charter of Athens of the last century, a wilfulness which stands in the way of form's own evolution. The ethical connection between urbanist and urbanite lies in practising a certain kind of modesty: living one among many, engaged by a world which does not mirror oneself. Living one among many enables, in Robert Venturi's words, 'richness of meaning rather than clarity of meaning'. That is the ethics of an open city.

Notes

1 INTRODUCTION: CROOKED, OPEN, MODEST

1. Jacques Le Goff, *La Civilisation de L'occident médiéval* (Paris: Flammarion, 1997).
2. Immanuel Kant, *Idea for a Universal History from a Cosmopolitan Point of View* (1784). The best English translation remains Lewis White Beck in *Kant: On History* (New York: Bobbs-Merrill, 1963). 'Crooked timber' appears in Thesis 6.
3. Jerome Groopman, 'Cancer: A Time for Skeptics', *The New York Review of Books*, 10 March 2016.
4. Francis Crick, *What Mad Pursuit: A Personal View of Scientific Discovery* (London: Penguin Books, 1990).
5. Melanie Mitchell, *Complexity: A Guided Tour* (New York: Oxford University Press, 2009), p. 13.
6. Steven Strogatz, *Sync* (London: Allen Lane, 2003), pp. 181–2.
7. Flo Conway and Jim Siegelman, *Dark Hero of the Information Age: In Search of Norbert Wiener, the Father of Cybernetics* (New York: Basic Books, 2005).
8. Robert Venturi, *Complexity and Contradiction in Architecture* (New York: Museum of Modern Art, 1966), p. 16.
9. William Mitchell, *City of Bits* (Cambridge, Mass.: MIT Press, 1996), p. 7
10. Aristotle, *The Politics*, translated by T. A. Sinclair (1962); revised translation by Trevor J. Saunders (1981) (London: Penguin Books, 1992).
11. William James, 'Pragmatism, Action and Will', in *Pragmatism: The Classic Writings*, ed. H. S. Thayer (Cambridge, Mass.: Hackett, 1982), p. 181.
12. Yochai Benkler, 'Degrees of Freedom, Dimensions of Power', *Daedalus* 145, no. 1 (2016): 20, 23. See also Shoshana Zuboff, 'Big Other: Surveillance Capitalism and the Prospects of Information Civilization', *Journal of Information Technology* 30, no. 1 (2015): 75–89, and Tim

Wu, *The Master Switch: The Rise and Fall of Information Empires* (New York: Knopf, 2010).

13. The Burckhardt phrase appears in English in Ernst Cassirer, 'Force and Freedom: Remarks on the English Edition of Jacob Burckhardt's "Reflections on History"', *The American Scholar* 13, no. 4 (1944): 409–10.

14. Giovanni Pico della Mirandola, 'Oration on the Dignity of Man', in *The Renaissance Philosophy of Man*, ed. Ernst Cassirer, Paul Oskar Kristeller and John Herman Randall, Jr (Chicago: University of Chicago Press, 1948), p. 225.

15. Michel de Montaigne, 'Same Design: Differing Outcomes', in *The Complete Essays*, trans. M. A. Screech (London: Penguin, 2003), pp. 140–49.

16. Bernard Rudofsky, *Architecture Without Architects: A Short Introduction to Non-Pedigreed Architecture* (Albuquerque: University of New Mexico Press, 1999). Ironically the original book consisted of the catalogue of an exhibition Rudofsky put on at that bastion of art-style, the Museum of Modern Art in New York, in 1964.

17. Gordon Cullen, *Townscape* (London: The Architectural Press, 1961), pp. 175–81.

18. Richard Sennett, *The Craftsman* (New Haven: Yale University Press, 2008), pp. 197–9.

19. Richard Sennett, *Together: The Rituals, Pleasures and Politics of Cooperation* (New Haven: Yale University Press/London: Allen Lane, 2012).

2 UNSTABLE FOUNDATIONS

1. Ildefons Cerdà, *Teoría de la construcción de las Ciudades (Theory of City Construction)* (1859) (Barcelona: Ajuntament de Barcelona, 1991).

2. This is a story I sought to tell, in fictional form, in my novel *Palais-Royal* (New York: Knopf, 1986). For the more general picture, see Roy Porter, *Disease, Medicine and Society in England, 1550–1860*, 2nd edn (Cambridge: Cambridge University Press, 1995), pp. 17–26.

3. David L. Pike, *Subterranean Cities: The World beneath Paris and London, 1800–1945* (Ithaca: Cornell University Press, 2005), p. 234.

4. Friedrich Engels, *The Condition of the Working-Class in England in 1844*, trans. Florence Kelley Wischnewetzky (London: Allen & Unwin, 1892), p. viii.

5. Peter Hall, *Cities in Civilization* (London: Weidenfeld and Nicolson, 1998), pp. 691–93.

6. Karl Marx and Friedrick Engels, *The Communist Manifesto*, http://www.gutenberg.org/ebooks/61.

7. Charles Baudelaire, 'The Painter of Modern Life', in *Baudelaire: Selected Writings on Art and Artists*, trans. P. E. Charvet (Cambridge: Cambridge University Press, 1981), pp. 403, 402.

8. Zygmunt Bauman, *Liquid Modernity* (Cambridge: Polity Press, 2000).

9. Cf. David H. Pinkney, *Napoleon III and the Rebuilding of Paris* (Princeton: Princeton University Press, 1972) and Charles E. Beveridge, *Frederick Law Olmsted: Designing the American Landscape* (New York: Rizzoli International Publications, 1995).

10. Antoine Paccoud, 'A Politics of Regulation: Haussmann's Planning Practice and Badiou's Philosophy', PhD thesis, London School of Economics and Political Science (LSE), 2012.

11. See Richard Sennett, *The Fall of Public Man* (1977) (New York: W. W. Norton, 2017).

12. K. C. Kurt Chris Dohse, 'Effects of Field of View and Stereo Graphics on Memory in Immersive Command and Control', MSc thesis, Iowa State University, 2007, Retrospective Theses and Dissertations 14673.

13. Degas quoted in Roberto Calasso, *La Folie Baudelaire* (London: Allen Lane, 2012), p. 171.

14. Joan Busquets, *Barcelona: The Urban Evolution of a Compact City* (Rovereto: Nicolodi, 2005), p. 129.

15. Joseph Rykwert, *The Idea of a Town: The Anthropology of Urban Form in Rome, Italy and the Ancient World* (Cambridge, Mass.: MIT Press, 1988).

16. Ildefonso Cerdà, *Teoría general de la urbanización* (*General Theory of Urbanization*) (1867) (Barcelona: Instituto de Estudios Fiscales, 1968–71).

17. Lewis Mumford, *The City in History* (New York: Harcourt, Brace & World, 1961), p. 421. See also Peter Marcuse, 'The Grid as City Plan: New York City and Laissez-Faire Planning in the Nineteenth Century', *Planning Perspectives* 2, no. 3 (1987): 287–310.

18. Eric Firley and Caroline Stahl, *The Urban Housing Handbook* (London: Wiley, 2009), p. 295.

19. Arturo Soria y Puig (ed.), *Cerdà: The Five Bases of the General Theory of Urbanization* (Madrid: Electa, 1999).

20. Anne Power, *Estates on the Edge: The Social Consequences of Mass Housing in Northern Europe* (New York: St Martin's Press, 1997).

21. Frederick Law Olmsted, 'Public Parks and the Enlargement of Towns', in *Frederick Law Olmste:, Essential Texts*, ed. Robert Twombly (New York: W. W. Norton, 2010), pp. 225ff.

22. Maps at www.insecula.com/CentralPark.

23. Michael Pollak, 'What is Jamaica, Queens, Named After?', *The New York Times*, 3 July 2014.

24. For informality, see Charles E. Beveridge and David Schuyler (eds), *The Papers of Frederick Law Olmsted*, Vol. 3: *Creating Central Park, 1857–1861* (Baltimore: Johns Hopkins University Press, 1983).

25. See the photographs assembled by Marcia Reiss in *Central Park Then and Now* (San Diego, CA: Thunder Bay Press, 2010).

26. Olmsted, 'A Consideration of the Justifying Value of a Public Park', in *Frederick Law Olmsted: Essential Texts*, ed. Robert Twombly (New York: W. W. Norton, 2010), pp. 283ff.

27. Piet Oudolf and Noel Kingsbury, *Planting Design: Gardens in Time and Space* (Portland, Oregon: Timber Press, 2005), pp. 36ff. A typology derived from J. Philip Grime, *Plant Strategies, Vegetation Processes, and Ecosystem Properties* (Chichester: Wiley, 2001).

28. Gustave Le Bon, *The Crowd: A Study of the Popular Mind* (1895), trans. Jaap van Ginneken (Kitchener, Ontario: Batoche Books, 2001), pp. 14–17.

29. Sigmund Freud, *Group Psychology and the Analysis of the Ego* (1921) (New York: W. W. Norton, 1975).

30. Elias Canetti, *Crowds and Power* (New York: Viking Press, 1962).

31. José Ortega y Gasset, *The Revolt of the Masses* (1930) (New York: W. W. Norton, 1964).

32. Georg Simmel, 'The Metropolis and Mental Life', in Georg Simmel, *On Individuality and Social Forms: Selected Writings*, ed. Donald N. Levine (Chicago: Chicago University Press, 1971), pp. 324–39.

33. I am now quoting from my own translation, in Georg Simmel, 'The Metropolis and Mental Life', in *Classic Essays on the Culture of Cities*, ed. Richard Sennett (New York: Appleton-Century-Crofts, 1969), p. 48.

34. Ibid.

35. Ibid.

36. Ibid., p. 47.

37. Greg Castillo, 'Gorki Street and the Design of the Stalin Revolution', in *Streets: Critical Perspectives on Public Space*, ed. Zeynep Çelik, Diane Favro and Richard Ingersoll (Berkeley: University of California Press, 1994), pp. 57–70.

38. James Winter, *London's Teeming Streets, 1830–1914* (New York: Routledge, 1993), p. 100.

39. Cf. the work done by the Space Syntax Laboratory at the Bartlett School of Architecture, University College London. The Lab's work on density is explained in Nick Stockton, 'There's a Science to Foot Traffic, and It Can Help Us Design Better Cities', *Wired Magazine*, 27 January 2014, www.wired.com/2014/01/space-syntax-china/.

40. Spiro Kostof, *The City Assembled: The Elements of Urban Form through History* (Boston: Little, Brown, 1992), p. 214.

41. William H. Whyte, *The Social Life of Small Urban Spaces*, DVD/video, Direct Cinema Ltd, Santa Monica, California, 1988.

42. Henry Shaftoe, *Convivial Urban Spaces: Creating Effective Public Spaces* (London: Routledge, 2008), pp. 88–91.

43. Marianne Weber, *Max Weber: A Biography*, trans. Harry Zohn (New York: John Wiley & Sons, Inc., 1975).

44. Jonathan Steinberg, *Bismarck: A Life* (Oxford: Oxford University Press, 2011), p. 86.

45. Stefan Zweig, *The World of Yesterday* (1942), trans. Anthea Bell (London: Pushkin Press, 2009), Chapter VIII, 'Brightness and Shadows over Europe'.

46. The original reference is Max Weber, *Wirtschaft und Gesellschaft* (Tübingen: J. C. B. Mohr (P. Siebeck), 1922), p. 00; the essay was first published in 1921, and was probably written in 1917. My translation.

47. Max Weber, *Economy and Society: An Outline of Interpretive Sociology*, ed. Guenther Roth and Claus Wittich, Vol. 1 (New York: Bedminster Press, 1968), p. 4.

3 *CITÉ* AND *VILLE* DIVORCE

1. William I. Thomas and Florian Znaniecki, *The Polish Peasant in Europe and America* (New York: Knopf, 1927).

2. Harvey W. Zorbaugh, *The Gold Coast and the Slum* (Chicago: University of Chicago Press, 1929).

3. Martin Bulmer, *The Chicago School of Sociology: Institutionalization, Diversity, and the Rise of Sociological Research* (Chicago: University of Chicago Press, 1986), pp. 59–60.

4. See Richard Sennett, *Families against the City* (Cambridge, Mass.: Harvard University Press, 1970).

5. My mother did fieldwork on this subject for Charlotte Towle, *Common Human Needs* (Washington, DC: Federal Security Agency, 1945), *passim*.

6. Robert Park, 'The City: Suggestions for the Investigation of Human Behavior in the Urban Environment', in *Classic Essays on the Culture*

of Cities, ed. Richard Sennett (New York: Appleton-Century-Crofts, 1969), pp. 91–130, at p. 91.

7. Louis Wirth, 'Urbanism as a Way of Life', *American Journal of Sociology* 44, no. 1 (1938): 20.

8. Michael Dennis, *Court & Garden: From the French Hôtel to the City of Modern Architecture* (Cambridge, Mass.: MIT Press, 1986), p. 213.

9. Le Corbusier, *When the Cathedrals Were White*, trans. Francis E. Hyslop, Jr (New York: Reynal & Hitchcock, 1947), p. 47.

10. A good general account is Eric Mumford, *The CIAM Discourse on Urbanism, 1928–1960* (Cambridge, Mass.: MIT Press, 2000).

11. Le Corbusier, *The Athens Charter*, trans. Anthony Eardley (New York: Grossman Publishers, 1973), p. 65 (dwelling, no. 29), p. 70 (recreation, no. 37), p. 76 (work, no. 46), pp. 84–5 (transport, nos. 62 and 64).

12. James Holston, *The Modernist City: An Anthropological Critique of Brasília* (Chicago: Chicago University Press, 1989), p. 77.

13. Corbusier, *The Athens Charter*, p. 88 (no. 70).

14. José Luis Sert, *Can Our Cities Survive?: An ABC of Urban Problems, Their Analysis, Their Solutions. Based on the Proposals Formulated by the C.I.A.M., International Congresses for Modern Architecture* ... (Cambridge, Mass.: Harvard University Press, 1944).

15. Jonathan Barnett, 'The Way We Were, the Way We Are: The Theory and Practice of Designing Cities since 1956', *Harvard Design Magazine*, no. 24, 'The Origins and Evolution of "Urban Design", 1956–2006', 2006.

16. Alex Krieger, '*HDM* Symposium: Can Design Improve Life in Cities? Closing Comments or Where and How Does Urban Design Happen?', in ibid.

17. Barnett, 'The Way We Were, the Way We Are.

18. Aristotle, *Politics*, Book, Chapters 11–12, http://www.gutenberg.org/files/6762/6762-h/6762-h.htm#link2HCH0090.

19. Richard Sennett, 'An Urban Anarchist: Jane Jacobs', *The New York Review of Books*, 1 January 1970.

20. Lewis Mumford, *Technics and Civilization* (Chicago: University of Chicago Press, 1934), pp. 344–58.

21. These are the standards used by the American Association of State Highway and Transportation Officials, adopted by Chinese civil engineers. See http://www.aboutcivil.org/typical-cross-section-of-highways.html.

4 KLEE'S ANGEL LEAVES EUROPE

1. Rana Dasgupta, *Capital: The Eruption of Delhi* (London: Canongate Books, 2015), p. 362.
2. Helge Mooshammer, Peter Mörtenböck, Teddy Cruz and Fonna Forman (eds), *Informal Market Worlds Reader: The Architecture of Economic Pressure* (Rotterdam: Naio10 Publishers, 2015).
3. Eric Firley and Caroline Stahl, *The Urban Housing Handbook* (London: Wiley, 2009).
4. Teresa P. R. Caldeira, 'Peripheral Urbanization: Autoconstruction, Transversal Logics, and Politics in Cities of the Global South', *Environment and Planning D: Society and Space*, 35, no. 1 (2017): 3–20.
5. D. Asher Ghertner, *Rule by Aesthetics: World-Class City Making in Delhi* (New York: Oxford University Press, 2015), p. 9.
6. The current best general guide to these changes is the UN's 2014 revision of *World Urbanization Prospects*, found electronically at https://esa.un.org/unpd/wup/publications/files/wup2014-highlights.Pdf.
7. Saskia Sassen, *Expulsions* (Cambridge, Mass.: Harvard University Press, 2014).
8. Density figures for Delhi come from the Registrar General and Census Commissioner's Office: http://www.censusindia.gov.in/2011-Common/CensusData2011.html; for France, from https://www.insee.fr.
9. Jean Gottmann, *Megalopolis: The Urbanized Northeastern Seaboard of the United States* (New York: Twentieth Century Fund, 1961).
10. Cf. Steef Buijs, Wendy Tan and Devisari Tunas (eds), *Megacities: Exploring a Sustainable Future* (Rotterdam: Naio10 Publishers, 2010).
11. Cf. Saskia Sassen, *The Global City* (Princeton: Princeton University Press, 1998).
12. William H. Janeway, *Doing Capitalism in the Innovation Economy: Markets, Speculation and the State* (Cambridge: Cambridge University Press, 2017), Chapter 4, *passim*.
13. Saskia Sassen, *Cities in a World Economy*, 4th edn (Los Angeles: Sage Publications, 2012).
14. Liu Thai Ker, 'Urbanizing Singapore', in *Megacities*, ed. Buijs, Tan and Tunas, pp. 246–7. Singapore stands out as an exception to this rule.
15. Ravi Teja Sharma, 'Floor Area Ratio, Ground Coverage Increased in Delhi; Move to Benefit Buyers', *The Economic Times* (India), 27 November 2014.
16. Martín Rama, Tara Béteille, Yue Li, Pradeep K. Mitra and John Lincoln Newman, *Addressing Inequality in South Asia* (Washington, DC: World Bank Group, 2015).

17. Hai-Anh H. Dang and Peter F. Lanjouw, 'Poverty Dynamics in India between 2004 and 2012: Insights from Longitudinal Analysis Using Synthetic Panel Data', Policy Research Working Paper 7270, World Bank Group (2015).

18. See a public panel that followed a screening of the film at the Haus der Kulturen der Welt at http://hkw.de/en/app/mediathek/video/26489.

19. About the Bund and its relation to the purely Chinese, see Harriet Sergeant, Shanghai (London: Jonathan Cape, 1991).

20. As a general primer on urban China, see Thomas J. Campanella, The Concrete Dragon: China's Urban Revolution and What It Means for the World (New York: Princeton Architectural Press, 2008).

21. My thanks to Bob Liu Roberts for alerting me to Xu Mingqian, 'Development of Old Neighborhoods in Central Shanghai', in Shanghai Statistics Yearbook, 2004 (Shanghai: Xuelin, 2004). Also, Xuefei Ren, 'Forward to the Past: Historical Preservation in Globalizing Shanghai', in Breslauer Graduate Student Symposium, 'The Right to the City and the Politics of Space', University of California, Berkeley, 14–15 April 2006.

22. Statistics cited in Urban Age 'Shaping Cities' conference presentation for Venice Biennale, 2016; https://urbanage.lsecities.net/conferences/shaping-cities-venice-2016.

23. Cf. Philip P. Pan, Out of Mao's Shadow: The Struggle for the Soul of a New China (New York: Simon & Schuster, 2008).

24. Xuefei Ren, Building Globalization: Transnational Architecture Production in Urban China (Chicago: University of Chicago Press, 2011), pp. 50–58.

25. Joseph Alois Schumpeter, Capitalism, Socialism and Democracy (1942) (London: Routledge, 2010), pp. 73, 77–9.

26. For Howard, see Richard T. LeGates and Frederic Stout, The City Reader (London: Routledge, 1996), p. 345. For Corbusier, each tower of twenty-eight storeys could hold 900 people; Corbusier began by thinking the plan would consist of fifty towers.

27. See Florian Urban, Tower and Slab (London: Routledge, 2012), pp. 148–64.

28. Campanella, The Concrete Dragon, pp. 144–71, especially pp. 163ff.

29. So, too, Marc Fried found that a level-and-rebuild urban renewal project in Boston in the mid-twentieth century prompted profound social disorientation; see Marc Fried, 'Grieving for a Lost Home: Psychological Costs of Relocation', in Urban Renewal: The Record and the

Controversy, ed. James Q. Wilson (Cambridge, Mass.: MIT Press, 1966), pp. 359-79.

30. Herbert J. Gans, *The Urban Villagers: Group and Class in the Life of Italian-Americans* (New York: Free Press, 1982).

31. Sharon Zukin, *Loft Living: Culture and Capital in Urban Change* (Baltimore: Johns Hopkins University Press, 1982).

32. Richard Florida, *The Rise of the Creative Class: And How It's Transforming Work, Leisure, Community and Everyday Life* (New York: Basic Books, 2002).

33. Patti Waldmeir, 'Shanghai Starts Search for Its Heritage', *Financial Times*, 22 February 2013, p. 8.

34. James Salter, *Light Years* (New York: Random House, 1975), p. 69.

35. See Marc Masurovsky, 'Angelus Novus, Angel of History, by Paul Klee', *Plundered Art*, Holocaust Art Restitution Project (HARP), 26 February 2013, http://plundered-art.blogspot.co.uk/2013/02/angelus-novus-angel-of-history-by-paul.html.

36. Walter Benjamin, *On the Concept of History*, Gesammelte Schriften I:2 (Frankfurt am Main: Suhrkamp Verlag, 1974). My translation.

37. Walter Benjamin, *Moscow Diary*, trans. Richard Sieburth (Cambridge, Mass.: Harvard University Press, 1986), p. 126.

38. Ibid., pp. 37, 61.

5 THE WEIGHT OF OTHERS

1. Foreign readers can find an excellent account of this event in 'Germans Take to the Streets to Oppose Rise of Far-Right "Pinstripe Nazi" Party', *The Guardian*, 5 January 2015; https://www.theguardian.com/world/2015/jan/05/germans-march-oppose-pegida-far-right-racism-tolerance.

2. See Charles Westin, 'Sweden: Restrictive Immigration Policy and Multiculturalism', Migration Policy Institute Profile, 1 June 2006, http://www.migrationpolicy.org/article/sweden-restrictive-immigration-policy-and-multiculturalism/.

3. For a general overview, cf. Michael R. Marrus, *The Unwanted: European Refugees in the Twentieth Century* (Oxford: Oxford University Press, 1985).

4. An irony: one of Wagner's sources was a story by Heinrich Heine, in which endless travel marked the lives of Jews (with whom Wagner notoriously had no sympathy).

5. Dennis Hirota, 'Okakura Tenshin's Conception of "Being in the World"', *Ryūkoku Daigaku Ronshū*, no. 478 (2011): 10-32.

6. Adam Sharr, *Heidegger's Hut* (Cambridge, Mass.: MIT Press, 2006), p. 63.
7. Paul Celan, 'Todtnauberg', in *Selected Poems* (London: Penguin, 1996).
8. Paul Celan, 'Hut Window' ('Hüttenfenster'), in *Selected Poems*.
9. Elfriede Jelinek, *Totenauberg: Ein Stück* (Hamburg: Rowohlt, 2004).
10. Susan Buck-Morss, *The Dialectics of Seeing: Walter Benjamin and the Arcades Project* (Cambridge, Mass.: MIT Press, 1991), pp. 34ff.
11. Martin Heidegger, 'Building Dwelling Thinking', trans. Albert Hofstadter, in *Poetry, Language, Thought* (New York: Harper and Row, 1971), p. 362.
12. Richard Sennett, *The Foreigner: Two Essays on Exile* (London: Notting Hill Editions, 2017), pp. 1–45.
13. Emmanuel Levinas, 'Martin Buber and the Theory of Knowledge', in Maurice Friedman and Paul Arthur Schilpp (eds), *The Philosophy of Martin Buber* (London: Cambridge University Press, 1967), pp. 133–50 (essay written in 1958; first published in German in 1963).
14. See Richard Sennett, *The Corrosion of Character: The Personal Consequences of Work in the New Capitalism* (New York: W. W. Norton, 1998).
15. Paul Willis, *Learning to Labour* (London: Routledge, rev. edn, 2000); Katherine S. Newman, *Falling from Grace: Downward Mobility in the Age of Affluence* (Berkeley and Los Angeles, Calif.: University of California Press, 1999).
16. Plus, for me, Richard Sennett and Jonathan Cobb, *The Hidden Injuries of Class* (New York: W. W. Norton, 1972); Sennett, *The Corrosion of Character*; Richard Sennett, *Respect: The Formation of Character in an Age of Inequality* (New York: W. W. Norton and London: Allen Lane, 2003); Richard Sennett, *The Culture of the New Capitalism* (New Haven: Yale University Press, 2006).
17. The classic study of gentrification is Sharon Zukin, *Loft Living: Culture and Capital in Urban Change* (Baltimore: Johns Hopkins University Press, 1982). 'Holdouts' are described by ShelterForce, a community organization. See shelterforce.org.
18. See Rachel Lichtenstein, *Diamond Street: The Hidden World of Hatton Garden* (London: Hamish Hamilton, 2012).
19. Robert D. Putnam, *Bowling Alone: The Collapse and Revival of American Community* (New York: Simon & Schuster, 2000).
20. For Robert Frost, see Thomas Oles, *Walls: Enclosure and Ethics in the Modern Landscape* (Chicago: University of Chicago Press, 2015), pp. 6–8.

21. Cf. John Demos, *A Little Commonwealth: Family Life in Plymouth Colony*, 2nd edn (Oxford: Oxford University Press, 1999), pp. 148–9.

22. See Russell Hardin, *Trust* (Cambridge: Polity Press, 2006), pp. 26, 90–91, particularly the discussion of 'weak trust'.

6 TOCQUEVILLE IN TECHNOPOLIS

1. Alexis de Tocqueville, *Democracy in America*, trans. Henry Reeve, vol. 2 (New York: The Modern Library, 1981).

2. Richard Sennett, *Together: The Rituals, Pleasures and Politics of Cooperation* (New Haven: Yale University Press/London: Allen Lane, 2012), pp. 24–9.

3. Nathan Heller, 'California Screaming', *The New Yorker*, 7 July 2014, pp. 46–53; the figure is quoted on p. 49.

4. Richard Sennett, *The Culture of the New Capitalism* (New Haven: Yale University Press, 2006), pp. 15–83. I was able to spend time in Silicon Valley thanks to the Center for Advanced Study in the Behavioral Sciences, in Palo Alto, where I was a Fellow in 1996–7.

5. Frank Duffy, *Work and the City* (London: Black Dog Publishing, 2008).

6. An excellent general study of office design is Nikil Saval, *Cubed: A Secret History of the Workplace* (New York: Doubleday, 2014).

7. John Meachem, 'Googleplex: A New Campus Community', 2004, http://www.clivewilkinson.com/case-studies-googleplex-a-new-campus-community/.

8. Radcliffe quoted in Paul Goldberger, 'Exclusive Preview: Google's New Built-from-Scratch Googleplex', *Vanity Fair*, 22 February 2013.

9. John Dewey, *Art as Experience* (New York: Perigee Books, 2005), p. 143.

10. Richard Sennett, *The Craftsman* (New Haven: Yale University Press, 2008).

11. George Packer, *The Unwinding: An Inner History of the New America* (New York: Farrar, Straus and Giroux, 2013) and Bill Gates, *The Road Ahead* (New York: Viking Press, 1995), pp. 180–82.

12. Paul Merholz, ' "Frictionless" as an Alternative to "Simplicity" in Design', *Adaptive Path* blog, 22 July 2010; http://adaptivepath.org/ideas/friction-as-an-alternative-to-simplicity-in-design/.

13. Evgeny Morozov, *To Save Everything, Click Here: Smart Machines, Dumb Humans, and the Myth of Technological Perfectionism* (New York: Perseus Books, 2013).

14. Nicholas Carr, *The Shallows: What the Internet Is Doing to Our Brains* (New York: W. W. Norton, 2011).

15. Sherry Turkle, *Alone Together: Why We Expect More from Technology and Less from Each Other* (New York: Basic Books, 2012).

16. Norman J. Slamecka and Peter Graf, 'The Generation Effect: Delineation of a Phenomenon', *Journal of Experimental Psychology: Human Learning and Memory* 4, no. 6 (1978): 592–604.

17. Christof van Nimwegen, 'The Paradox of the Guided User: Assistance Can Be Counter-Effective', SIKS Dissertation Series no. 2008–09, University of Utrecht, 2008.

18. For Peirce's relation to architecture, see Alexander Timmer, 'Abductive Architecture', MArch thesis, Harvard University Graduate School of Design, 2016.

19. Leon Festinger, *A Theory of Cognitive Dissonance* (Stanford: Stanford University Press, 1957), p. 3.

20. Leon Festinger and James M. Carlsmith, 'Cognitive Consequences of Forced Compliance', *Journal of Abnormal and Social Psychology* 58, no. 2 (1959): 203–10.

21. Two technical papers, among many: Jeffrey D. Holtzman, Harold A. Sedgwick and Leon Festinger, 'Interaction of Perceptually Monitored and Unmonitored Efferent Commands for Smooth Pursuit Eye Movements', *Vision Research* 18, no. 11 (1978): 1545–55; Joel Miller and Leon Festinger, 'Impact of Oculomotor Retraining on the Visual Perception of Curvature', *Journal of Experimental Psychology: Human Perception and Performance* 3, no. 2 (1977): 187–200.

22. Elijah Anderson, *Code of the Street: Decency, Violence, and the Moral Life of the Inner City* (New York: W. W. Norton, 2000).

23. Maarten Hajer and Ton Dassen, *Smart about Cities: Visualising the Challenge for 21st Century Urbanism* (Rotterdam: Nai010 Publishers, 2014), p. 11.

24. Adam Greenfield, *Against the Smart City: A Pamphlet* (New York: Do Projects, 2013).

25. Dave Eggers, *The Circle* (New York: Vintage Books, 2014).

26. Anthony M. Townsend, *Smart Cities: Big Data, Civic Hackers, and the Quest for a New Utopia* (New York: W. W. Norton, 2013), pp. 93–115.

27. See Greenfield, *Against the Smart City*.

28. See http://www.masdar.ae/en/masdar-city/the-built-environment.
29. Sam Nader, 'Paths to a Low-Carbon Economy – The Masdar Example', *Energy Procedia* 1, no. 1 (2009): 3591–58.
30. Suzanne Goldenberg, 'Climate Experts Urge Leading Scientists' Association: Reject Exxon Sponsorship', *The Guardian*, 22 February 2016.
31. Norbert Wiener, *Cybernetics*, revised edn (Cambridge, Mass: MIT Press, 1965), especially 'Preface to the Second Edition', pp. vii–xiii.
32. Gianpaolo Baiocchi and Ernesto Ganuza, 'Participatory Budgeting as if Emancipation Mattered', *Politics & Society* 42, no. 1 (2014): 29–50.
33. Carlo Ratti and Anthony Townsend, 'Harnessing Residents' Electronic Devices Will Yield Truly Smart Cities', *Scientific American*, September 2011.
34. Animesh Rathore, Deepti Bhatnagar, Magüi Moreno Torres and Parameeta Kanungo, 'Participatory Budgeting in Brazil' (Washington, DC: World Bank, 2003), http://siteresources.worldbank.org/INTEM POWERMENT/Resources/14657_Partic-Budg-Brazil-web.pdf.
35. 'Supporting decision making for long term planning', ForCity, http://www.forcity.com/en/.
36. Robert Musil, *The Man without Qualities*, Vol. 1: *A Sort of Introduction and Pseudoreality Prevails*, trans. Sophie Wilkins and Burton Pike (London: Picador, 1997), pp. 26, 27.

7 THE COMPETENT URBANITE

1. See Tom Feiling, *Short Walks from Bogotá: Journeys in the New Colombia* (London: Allen Lane, 2012), p 00.
2. William James, *The Principles of Psychology*, Vol. 1 (New York: Henry Holt, 1890), Chapter 9.
3. Sara Fregonese, 'Affective Atmospheres, Urban Geopolitics and Conflict (De)escalation in Beirut', *Political Geography* 61, (2017): 1–10.
4. James, *The Principles of Psychology*, Vol. 1, pp. 403–4.
5. Frank R. Wilson, *The Hand: How Its Use Shapes the Brain, Language, and Human Culture* (New York: Pantheon, 1998), p. 99.
6. Clifford Geertz, *Local Knowledge: Further Essays in Interpretive Anthropology* (New York: Basic Books, 1983), p. xi.
7. See Morris Bishop, *Petrarch and His World* (Bloomington: Indiana University Press, 1963), pp. 102–12.

8. Iain Sinclair, *London Orbital: A Walk around the M25* (London: Penguin Books, 2009).

9. Rebecca Solnit, *Wanderlust: A History of Walking* (London: Granta, 2014), pp. 173–80.

10. The foundational work here is David Marr, *Vision* (Cambridge, Mass.: MIT Press, 2010). I am describing 'stereopsis', particularly motion-in-depth perception.

11. Yi-Fu Tuan, *Space and Place: The Perspective of Experience* (Minneapolis: University of Minnesota Press, 2003), p. 71.

12. Michel Lussault, *L'Homme spatial* (Paris: Seuil, 2007), pp. 64ff.

13. Geoffrey Scott, *The Architecture of Humanism: A Study in the History of Taste* (1914) (New York: W. W. Norton, 1999), p. 159.

14. Allan B. Jacobs, *Great Streets* (Cambridge, Mass.: MIT Press, 1995), pp. 272–80.

15. Jan Gehl, *Cities for People* (Washington, DC: Island Press, 2010), pp. 34–5.

16. M. M. Bakhtin, *The Dialogic Imagination: Four Essays*, ed. Michael Holquist, trans. Caryl Emerson and Michael Holquist, University of Texas Press Slavic Series 1 (Austin: University of Texas Press, 1981), p. 291.

17. See Michael Holquist, *Dialogism: Bakhtin and His World* (London: Routledge, 1990).

18. Bakhtin, *The Dialogic Imagination*, p. 323.

19. Bernard Williams, *Truth and Truthfulness: An Essay in Genealogy* (Princeton: Princeton University Press, 2002), p. 107.

20. See, for example, Horace R. Cayton and St Clair Drake, *Black Metropolis* (London: Jonathan Cape, 1946).

21. Holquist, *Dialogism*, p. iv.

22. Bakhtin, *The Dialogic Imagination*, pp. 262–3.

23. Teju Cole, *Open City: A Novel* (New York: Random House, 2011), p. 155.

24. Richard Sennett, *The Foreigner: Two Essays on Exile* (London: Notting Hill Editions, 2017).

25. Gaston Bachelard, *The Poetics of Space*, trans. Maria Jolas (Boston: Beacon Press, 1969), pp. 27, 239.

26. Gaston Bachelard, *The New Scientific Spirit*, trans. Arthur Goldhammer (Boston: Beacon Press, 1985).

27. Louis Althusser, *Essays in Self-Criticism*, trans. Grahame Lock (London: New Left Books, 1976), pp. 107–17.

8 FIVE OPEN FORMS

1. John M. Camp, *The Athenian Agora: Excavations in the Heart of Classical Athens* (London: Thames and Hudson, 1986), p. 72.

2. Still the best account of this planning is Sigfried Giedion, 'Sixtus V and the Planning of Baroque Rome', *Architectural Review* 111 (April 1952): 217–26.

3. Manuel de Solà-Morales, 'Cities and Urban Corners', in *Cities, Corners* exhibition, *The B.MM Monographs* 4 (2004), pp. 131–4, http://www.publicacions.bcn.es/b_mm/abmm_forum/131-134ang.pdf.

4. Sunniva Harte, *Zen Gardening* (New York: Stewart, Tabori & Chang, 1999), p. 18.

5. A good, brief description of Nolli's project is online at Allan Ceen, 'The Nolli Map and Cartography', http://nolli.uoregon.edu/nuova Pianta.html.

6. See Spiro Kostof, *The City Assembled: The Elements of Urban Form through History* (Boston: Little, Brown, 1992), pp. 28–33.

7. R. Murray Schafer, *The Soundscape: Our Sonic Environment and the Tuning of the World* (New York: Knopf, 1994), p. 11.

8. Footfall measurement by Richard Sennett.

9. Schafer, *The Soundscape*, pp. 77–9.

10. Alexander Cohen et al., ' "Sociocusis"– Hearing Loss from Non-Occupational Noise Exposure', *Sound and Vibration* 4, no. 11 (1970), pp. 12–20.

11. Todd Longstaffe-Gowan, *The London Square: Gardens in the Midst of Town* (London and New Haven: Yale University Press, 2012), pp. 202–4, 209.

12. These calculations are taken from the landscape architect's bible, Robert Holden and Jamie Liversedge, *Construction for Landscape Architecture* (London: Laurence King Publishing, 2011), pp. 114–17.

13. Gaston Bachelard, *The Poetics of Space*, trans. Maria Jolas (Boston: Beacon Press, 1969), p. xv.

14. Roland Barthes, *A Lover's Discourse: Fragments*, trans. Richard Howard (New York: Hill and Wang, 2010), p. 31.

15. Richard Sennett, *The Craftsman* (New Haven: Yale University Press, 2008), pp. 125–6.

16. See Marta Bausells, 'Superblocks to the Rescue: Barcelona's Plan to Give Streets Back to Residents', *The Guardian*, 17 May 2016.

17. Kevin Lynch, *The Image of the City* (Cambridge, Mass.: MIT Press, 1960), pp. 9–10.

18. Kevin Lynch, *Good City Form* (Cambridge, Mass.: MIT Press, 1981), pp. 37–50.

19. See Colin Rowe and Fred Koetter, *Collage City* (Cambridge, Mass.: MIT Press, 1979), pp. 168ff.

20. Edward R. Tufte, *The Visual Display of Quantitative Information*, 2nd edn (Cheshire, Conn.: Graphics Press, 2001).

21. Larry A. Hickman (ed.), *The Correspondence of John Dewey, 1871–1952* (Carbondale: Southern Illinois University Press, 1999–2004), Vol. 3, 25 September 1949, Letter 11135, http://www.nlx.com/collections/132.

22. See Henri Focillon, *The Life of Forms in Art* (New York: Zone Books, 1992).

9 THE BOND OF MAKING

1. Michel Callon, Pierre Lascoumes and Yannick Barthe, *Acting in an Uncertain World: An Essay on Technical Democracy*, trans. Graham Burchell (Cambridge, Mass.: MIT Press, 2011).

2. See Richard Sennett, *The Craftsman* (New Haven: Yale University Press, 2008), pp. 39–45.

3. Samir Khalaf and Philip S. Khoury (eds), *Recovering Beirut: Urban Design and Post-War Reconstruction* (Leiden: E. J. Brill, 1993).

4. Sennett, *The Craftsman*, pp. 84–8.

5. Richard Sennett and Jonathan Cobb, *The Hidden Injuries of Class* (New York: W. W. Norton, 1972).

6. Richard Sennett, *The Corrosion of Character: The Personal Consequences of Work in the New Capitalism* (New York: W. W. Norton, 1998).

7. Richard Sennett, *Together: The Rituals, Pleasures and Politics of Cooperation* (New Haven: Yale University Press/London: Allen Lane, 2012), pp. 38–40.

8. See the description of this event at http://en.wikipedia.org/wiki/Grenfell_Tower_fire, with the caveat that I have contributed to this Wikipedia entry.

10 TIME'S SHADOWS

1. See Stephen Greenblatt, *The Swerve: How the World Became Modern* (New York: W. W. Norton, 2012).
2. Titus Lucretius Carus, *De rerum natura (On the Nature of Things)* (London: Macmillan, 1893, et seq. editions), 2.216–224, 2.256–567.
3. Horace Walpole to Sir Horace Mann, 28 January 1754, in *The Yale Edition of Horace Walpole's Correspondence*, ed. W. S. Lewis (New Haven: Yale University Press, 1937–83), vol. 20: *Horace Walpole's Correspondence with Sir Horace Mann IV* (1960), ed. W. S. Lewis, Warren Hunting Smith and George L. Lam, pp. 407–8.
4. See Sandra Banholzer, James Kossin and Simon Donner, 'The Impact of Climate Change on Natural Disasters', University of British Columbia, Vancouver, Canada; https://earthobservatory.nasa.gov/Features/RisingCost/rising_cost5.php.
5. Pei Li, Jinyuan Xin, Yuesi Wang, Guoxing Li, Xiaochuan Pan, Shigong Wang, Mengtian Cheng, Tianxue Wen, Guangcheng Wang and Zirui Liu, 'Association between Particulate Matter and Its Chemical Constituents of Urban Air Pollution and Daily Mortality or Morbidity in Beijing City', *Environmental Science and Pollution Research* 22, no. 1 (2015): 358–68.
6. A good general overview of this complex subject is François Gemenne, 'The Anthropocene and Its Victims', in Clive Hamilton, Christophe Bonneuil and François Gemenne (eds), *The Anthropocene and the Global Environmental Crisis: Rethinking Modernity in a New Epoch* (New York: Routledge 2015).
7. Philipp Rode and Ricky Burdett, 'Cities: Investing in Energy and Resource Efficiency', in *Towards a Green Economy: Pathways to Sustainable Development and Poverty Eradication* (United Nations Environment Programme, 2011), pp. 331–73.
8. Neil Johnson, *Simply Complexity: A Clear Guide to Complexity Theory* (London: Oneworld, 2009), pp. 39–40. Originally published as *Two's Company, Three is Complexity* in 2007.
9. Geert Mak, *Amsterdam: A Brief Life of the City*, trans. Philipp Blom (New York: Vintage, 1999), p. 5.
10. Quoted in Richard Sennett, 'The Public Realm', lecture delivered at the Quant Foundation, July colloquium, 2002.
11. See Michael Hough, *Cities and Natural Process: A Basis for Sustainability*, 2nd edn (London: Routledge, 2004), p. 31.

12. Rebuild by Design is one of hundreds of such efforts across the globe, but a model which is guiding many of these international initiatives. Its work can be found online at 'Rebuild by Design', http://www.rebuild bydesign.org/.

13. For a balanced account of this project, see Jessica Dailey, 'See the 10-Mile "Dryline" That Could Protect NYC's Waterfront', 10 March 2015, http://ny.curbed.com/2015/3/10/9982658/see-the-10-mile-dryline-that-could-protect-nycs-waterfront.

14. Marjorie Hope Nicolson, *Mountain Gloom and Mountain Glory: The Development of the Aesthetics of the Infinite* (1959) (Seattle: University of Washington Press, 1997), p. 16.

15. Lord Byron, *Childe Harold's Pilgrimage* (1812–16), Canto III, stanza LXII.

16. Marx translated and cited in William Leiss, *The Domination of Nature* (Montreal: McGill-Queen's University Press, 1994), p. 73.

17. Karl Marx, *Grundrisse der Kritik der politischen Ökonomie* (1857–8) (Moscow: Verlag für Fremdsprachige Literatur, 1939).

18. Émile Durkheim, *The Elementary Forms of Religious Life* (Oxford: Oxford University Press, 1912), p. 424.

19. See Richard Sennett, *Together: The Rituals, Pleasures and Politics of Cooperation* (New Haven: Yale University Press/London: Allen Lane, 2012), pp. 212–20.

CONCLUSION: ETHICS FOR THE CITY

1. Eric Klinenberg, *Going Solo: The Extraordinary Rise and Surprising Appeal of Living Alone* (New York: Penguin Books, 2012).

2. Christoph Martin Wieland, 'Das Geheimniss des Kosmopolitenordens' (1788), quotation translated in Kwame Anthony Appiah, *Cosmopolitanism: Ethics in a World of Strangers*, Issues of Our Time (New York: W. W. Norton, 2006), p. xv.

3. Immanuel Kant, *Idea for a Universal History from a Cosmopolitan Point of View* (1784). I use the standard English translation by Lewis White Beck, in which the German mouthful is reduced to the English title *On History* (New York: Bobbs-Merrill, 1963). 'Unsocial sociability' appears in Thesis 4.

4. Cf. Ash Amin, *Land of Strangers* (Cambridge: Polity Press, 2012), p. 00.

5. Kant, *On History*, Thesis 6.

6. Augustine of Hippo, *The City of God* (426), XIX, xvii.

7. G. W. F. Hegel, *Phenomenology of Spirit*, trans. A. V. Miller (Oxford: Oxford University Press, 1977), pp. 111ff.

8. Adam Smith, *The Theory of Moral Sentiments*, ed. D. D. Raphael and A. L. Macfie (Oxford: Oxford University Press (Glasgow Edition), 1976), Part I, Section I, Chapters 1–2.

9. Muḥammad ibn Yaʿqūb al-Kulaynī, *Al-Kāfī*, Vol. 2, p. 146.

10. Confucius, *The Analects*, trans. David Hinton (Washington, DC: Counterpoint, 1998), XV.24.

11. Georg Simmel, 'Der Fremde' ['The Stranger'], in *Soziologie* (Leipzig: Duncker and Humblot, 1908). My translation.

Index

Chicago – *cont.*
   lakefront 271
   Musil and Tocqueville and 166
   and natural terrain 76
   Park-Burgess map 68, 138
   Plan of 69, 271–2
   Polish ghetto 193–4
   primary school project 246
   Robert Taylor Homes 77
   street furniture 215
   streetscape 284–5
   University of 63
   see also Chicago School; Park,
      Robert E.
Chicago School 64–70, 78, 79, 81,
      88, 101, 182, 191, 193–4, 224,
      250
children,
   accessibility for 56
   behaviour 65
   and bridges 46
   and drugs 42
   in Medellín 179, 236
   play-spaces 26, 223–4, 282
   as refugees 122, 123, 200
   and school 3, 80, 223
China,
   architecture 217
   'Chinese mission' 115
   clothing industry 102
   Cultural Revolution 107, 110,
      112, 115
   living space per person 106
   move to cities in 106
   pollution index 269
   skyscrapers 39
   trade with Venice 130
   and urban explosion 11, 159
   see also Shanghai
Chipperfield, David 117

Christianity,
   beliefs about Jews 178
   and cosmopolitanism 296
   early 1, 39
   in Lebanon 251
   meaning of 'city' in 1
   monasteries 124–5
   Okakura and 124–5
   in Spain 130
   in Venice 131–2, 135
CIAM (Congrès internationaux
      d'architecture moderne) 74–6
Cisco Systems 149, 159
cité,
   hard to read 26–30
   as heteroglossia 196
cité, and *ville* 1–17, 22, 235
   and ambiguous complexity 25
   bringing together 171, 204, 230,
      240–41, 242
   Cerdà and 42
   Chicago School and 68, 70
   Delhi (Nehru Place) and 94
   divorce of 63
   Haussmann and 37
   Jacobs and Mumford and 79–80,
      84
   Kant and 299
   open *cité* 297, 301
   open *ville* 254, 301
   and rupture 285
   Weber and 61
citizenship 2, 60, 85
city, cities,
   closed and open 144, 158, 171,
      300–302
   global 101–3
   growth of 11
   infrastructure 86–7
   octopus city 104–5, 106, 220